international review of social history

Supplement 12

Popular Intellectuals and Social Movements: Framing Protest in Asia, Africa, and Latin America

Edited by Michiel Baud and Rosanne Rutten

T0384770

CAMBRIDGE UNIVERSITY PRESS
Cambridge, New York, Melbourne, Madrid, Cape Town, Singapore, São Paulo

Cambridge University Press
The Edinburgh Building, Cambridge CB2 2RU, UK

www.cambridge.org
Information on this title: www.cambridge.org/9780521613484

© Internationaal Instituut voor Sociale Geschiedenis 2004

First published 2004

A catalogue record for this publication is available from the British Library

ISBN-13 978-0-521-61348-4 paperback
ISBN-10 0-521-61348-5 paperback

Transferred to digital printing 2006

CONTENTS

Popular Intellectuals and Social Movements:
Framing Protest in Asia, Africa, and Latin America

Edited by
Michiel Baud and Rosanne Rutten

NOTES ON CONTRIBUTORS

Michiel Baud, Centre of Latin American Studies (CEDLA), University of Amsterdam, Keizersgracht 395-397, 1016 EK Amsterdam, The Netherlands; e-mail: baud@cedla.uva.nl

Marc Becker, Department of History, Division of Social Science, Truman State University, 100 E Normal St, Kirksville, MO 63501, USA; e-mail: marc@yachana.org

Pablo Shiladitya Bose, Centre for Refugee Studies and Faculty of Environmental Studies, York University, 309 York Lanes, 4700 Keele Street, Toronto, Ontario, M3J 1P3 Canada; e-mail: pbose@yorku.ca

Sean Chabot, Department of Sociology, Eastern Washington University, 526 5th Street, Cheney, WA 99004, USA; e-mail: sean.chabot@ewu.edu

Baz Lecocq, Zentrum Moderner Orient, Kirchweg 33, D-14129 Berlin, Germany; e-mail: baz@lecocq.nl

Joanne Rappaport, Department of Spanish and Portuguese, Georgetown University, Bunn Intercultural Center, Washington, DC 20057, USA; e-mail: rappapoj@georgetown.edu

Rosanne Rutten, Department of Sociology and Anthropology, University of Amsterdam, Oudezijÿds Achterburgwal 185, 1012 DK Amsterdam, The Netherlands; e-mail: R.A.Rutten@uva.nl

David Smilde, Department of Sociology, University of Georgia, Baldwin Hall, Athens, GA 30602-1611, USA; e-mail: dsmilde@arches.uga.edu

Oskar Verkaaik, Research Center Religion and Society, University of Amsterdam, Oudezijds Achterburgwal 185, 1012 DK Amsterdam, The Netherlands; e-mail: O.G.A.Verkaaik@pscw.uva.nl

Quintan Wiktorowicz, Department of International Studies, Rhodes College, 2000 North Parkway, Memphis, TN 38112-1690, USA; e-mail: wiktorowiczq@rhodes.edu

IRSH 49 (2004), Supplement, pp. 1–18 DOI: 10.1017/S0020859004001610

Introduction

MICHIEL BAUD AND ROSANNE RUTTEN

"Any political movement against oppression", wrote Barrington Moore, "has to develop a new diagnosis and remedy for existing forms of suffering, a diagnosis and remedy by which this suffering stands morally condemned".[1] Moore refers to the process of interpretation and reflection that takes places in all forms of protest and social mobilization. Social actors interpret specific situations as unjust, identify victims and perpetrators, translate local grievances into broader claims, and set out a course of action. Their perception of society and their specific claims and collective demands are shaped by interpretations through which they make sense of the world. They use these interpretations to convince potential supporters, fellow activists, and adversaries of the accuracy of their views and the legitimacy of their claims. In the process they also define collective identities, which demarcate the objectives and lines of contention. In short, participants in social protest and social movements are involved in "meaning work", that is, "the production of mobilizing and counter-mobilizing ideas and meanings".[2]

The concept of "framing" is particularly useful in exploring this articulation of protest. Framing refers to "the conscious strategic efforts by groups of people to fashion shared understandings of the world and of themselves that legitimate and motivate collective action".[3] Such shared understandings are an essential part of any social movement. David Snow and Robert Benford speak of "collective action frames", interpretive frames that "underscore and embellish the seriousness and injustice of a social condition or redefine as unjust and immoral what was previously seen as unfortunate but perhaps tolerable".[4] Created in the course of

---

1. Barrington Moore, Jr, *Injustice: The Social Bases of Obedience and Revolt* (London, 1978), p. 88.
2. Robert D. Benford and David A. Snow, "Framing Processes and Social Movements: An Overview and Assessment", *Annual Review of Sociology*, 26 (2000), pp. 611–639, 613.
3. Doug McAdam, John D. McCarthy, and Mayer N. Zald, "Introduction", in *idem* (eds), *Comparative Perspectives on Social Movements: Political Opportunities, Mobilizing Structures, and Cultural Framings* (Cambridge [etc.], 1996), pp. 1–20, 6.
4. David A. Snow and Robert D. Benford, "Master Frames and Cycles of Protest", in Aldon D. Morris and Carol McClurg Mueller (eds), *Frontiers in Social Movement Theory* (New Haven, CT, 1992), pp. 133–135, 137. This approach is inspired by Erving Goffman, *Frame Analysis: An Essay on the Organization of Experience* (New York, 1974). The term "frame" denotes a mental model, a framework of interpretation, that enables individuals to perceive, identify, and interpret events in their own local society and in the world at large. Benford and Snow, "Framing Processes and Social Movements", p. 614.

contention and proved successful, such frames may become "modular", available for adoption and adaptation by activists across the globe.

However, the point that framing is the work of individuals is often lost in the literature on contentious politics. Many studies tend to invest social movements with an agency of their own, and fail to take a closer look at the women and men who are instrumental in interpreting conditions and articulating demands: their backgrounds, the contexts in which they emerged, their role and position in social movements, and their sources of inspiration. Moreover, by focusing on framing activities, rather than on the individual persons who undertake this work, these studies tend to overlook the histories of interpersonal contacts and interactions that may be crucial in shaping contentious ideas and their reception. Such interactions also include the debates and conflicts that may occur between framing specialists themselves.

In this Supplement to the *International Review of Social History*, the people who create, use, and diffuse activist frames are centre stage. We have tentatively called these individuals "popular intellectuals". We refer here to persons who – formally educated or not – aim to understand society in order to change it, with the interests of popular classes in mind. They seek to define the problems of subaltern groups, articulate their grievances, and frame their social and political demands. To what extent they actually voice the concerns of popular classes, and represent their interests may differ from case to case. Focusing on popular intellectuals in specific societies and historical contexts, this volume explores the social dynamics of their ideological work. It deals in particular with the following questions. How did these individuals develop and disseminate their ideas in social interaction with others, in particular with (fellow) activists, other intellectuals, adversaries, and the people they claimed to represent? How were these processes shaped by the societies in which these intellectuals were embedded, as well as by their own backgrounds and the networks in which they were involved? And in what ways did their ideological work, in turn, affect the trajectory of social movements?

Here, we concentrate on popular intellectuals in Asia, Africa, and Latin America. The specific sociocultural and political developments on these continents warrant a regional focus, we believe, as does the relative lack of studies on popular intellectuals in the region compared to studies on the Western world. In his classic analysis of anticolonial intellectuals in British India, Partha Chatterjee has shown how the implantation of categories and frameworks of thought, produced in other cultural contexts, changed original domains of thought and created new political and ideological processes.[5] (Post)colonial conditions, social inequality, and economic

---

5. Partha Chatterjee, *Nationalist Thought and the Colonial World: A Derivative Discourse?* (London, 1986).

underdevelopment profoundly marked the societies in these regions which affected, in turn, the social movements and popular intellectuals that emerged. We do not wish to overstate, however, the differences with the Western world, nor the similarities between the societies on these three continents. Instead, we believe that the contributions to this volume will provide valuable insights on framing and contention worldwide.

INTELLECTUALS AND CONTENTIOUS ACTION: SOME LINES OF ENQUIRY

An obvious point of reference for reflections on the social and political role of popular intellectuals is the work of the Italian Marxist, Antonio Gramsci. "All men are intellectuals", he observed, "but not all men have in society the function of intellectuals".[6]

> Each man [...] outside his professional activity, carries on some form of intellectual activity, that is, he is a 'philosopher', [...] he participates in a particular conception of the world, has a conscious line of moral conduct, and therefore contributes to sustain a conception of the world or to modify it, that is, to bring into being new modes of thought.[7]

The *function* of intellectuals, however, is reserved for those who are specialized in intellectual work. These are, in particular, people who develop and express certain "conceptions of the world". In his analysis of Italian society, Gramsci distinguished in this sense between "traditional" and "organic" intellectuals. Traditional intellectuals, in their proverbial ivory towers, perceive themselves as politically independent and autonomous, but in historical reality they defend the interests of hegemonic social groups.[8] In contrast, organic intellectuals possess fundamental, structural ties to particular classes and demonstrate a genuine political and social engagement. As a class becomes a self-conscious entity it produces its own "organic" intellectuals, who articulate the perceptions and interests of that particular class. Gramsci's concern was with the intellectuals who could articulate the interests of the Italian working class. Many people, therefore, came to understand organic intellectuals as meaning working-class intellectuals. However, this was not Gramsci's original conceptual objective. The dominant classes and hegemonic power-holders also possess their own organic intellectuals.

For the purpose of this collection, Gramsci's analysis (and the discussion it has recently provoked) is particularly relevant for mapping out some clear lines of enquiry. First, it favours a historical, dynamic analysis of the

6. Antonio Gramsci, *Selections from the Prison Notebooks of Antonio Gramsci*, Quintin Hoare and Geoffrey Nowell Smith (tr. and eds) (New York, 1971), p. 9.
7. *Ibid.*
8. *Ibid.*, pp. 6–7.

position of intellectuals. Specific categories of intellectuals are "historically formed" in connection with other social groups, and the specific type of these connections shape the position and function of these intellectuals.[9] In this process new groups, as well as new intellectual roles, emerge. Ron Eyerman has further developed this historical analysis. In his book *Between Culture and Politics: Intellectuals in Modern Society*, he speaks of intellectuals "as an historically emergent category, continually being reinvented", and shows how social movements themselves became new "arenas [...] where 'intellectuals' can be made".[10]

Secondly, it invites us to analyse the diverse social and political positions of intellectuals in different societal settings. This allows us to apply Gramsci's ideas to societies that have developed differently from the western European model. In Africa and Asia, but also in Latin America with its long Western-influenced academic tradition, social movements often found their inspiration outside hegemonic (colonial) ideologies. Non-Christian religious influences, local patterns of political and social organization, and colonial structures all gave a specific edge to the emergence of contentious interpretations. Although Gramsci did not elaborate upon these societal differences, his interpretation of Italian society certainly stimulates their analysis.[11]

Thirdly, it asks pertinent questions about the relations between (popular) intellectuals and the social groups to which they belong, or for which they speak. Following Gramsci's analysis, popular intellectuals would primarily emerge from the popular classes: "Every social group [...] creates together with itself, organically, one or more strata of intellectuals which give it homogeneity and an awareness of its own function not only in the economic but also in the social and political fields".[12] In his view, intellectuals are not autonomous, but originate in the class-relations in a given society. History shows, however, that many popular intellectuals, who speak in the name of popular classes, do not originate from these classes themselves.[13] Gramsci did allow for the possibility that "traditional" intellectuals (who perceive themselves as autonomous) might be assimilated and "ideologically conquered" by social groups that develop towards dominance, including popular classes such as the working class.[14] However, tensions always exist between intellectual leaders and the rank-and-file concerning the former's legitimacy and representativity.

---

9. *Ibid.*, p. 10.
10. Ron Eyerman, *Between Culture and Politics: Intellectuals in Modern Society* (Cambridge, 1994), pp. 99, 11.
11. See also Kate Crehan, *Gramsci, Culture and Anthropology* (London [etc.], 2002).
12. Gramsci, *Prison Notebooks*, p. 5.
13. Crehan, *Gramsci, Culture and Anthropology*, p. 139.
14. Gramsci, *Prison Notebooks*, p. 10.

Recent research on social movements has drawn attention to additional lines of enquiry that are relevant here. One is the focus on the interactive dynamics of framing. Since activists develop interpretations of their world in constant dialogue with others, such interactions should be a point of attention. Doug McAdam, Sidney Tarrow, and Charles Tilly have stressed "the interactive construction of disputes among challengers, their opponents, elements of the state, third parties, and the media", and they consider this an essential part of framing.[15] One might say that framing concerns "ideas forged in dialogue".[16]

Contentious interactions are, after all, at the core of social movements: social movements concern sustained challenges against authorities and other powerful opponents, in which claims are made in the name of aggrieved populations.[17] This involves both a mobilization of support and alliances, and a confrontation with opponents. Ideological work figures prominently in these interactions. At the local level as well, such interpretive work is an ongoing process. It includes "the interactive processes of talk, persuasion, arguing, contestation, interpersonal influence, subtle rhetoric posturing, outright marketing that modify – indeed, continually modify – the contents of interpretative frames".[18] In this volume, we have recast this focus on the social dynamics of framing into a perspective that considers popular intellectuals as they operate within relevant networks of interaction. It includes the history of these interactions, and considers how these have shaped the ideas and actions of popular intellectuals, and their effects.

This leads to another point of interest: the relevance of the personal histories of intellectuals. Traditionally, there has been a clear conceptual separation between the history of ideas which focused on the individual lives of intellectuals, and the literature on social movements and contentious politics which tended to obscure personal histories in favour of the activities and development of collective actors. Where social movements are treated as collective actors, attention to individuals may be limited to specific leaders, often perceived as the embodiment of a collective history and the product of specific social and political (class) relations. However, by paying attention to the personal histories of popular intellectuals, the importance of individual agency in the ideological work within and outside of social movements is acknowledged. The individual accumulation of experiences, contacts, and ideas partly shapes

15. Doug McAdam, Sidney Tarrow, and Charles Tilly, *Dynamics of Contention* (Cambridge [etc.], 2001), p. 44.
16. Anthony Milner, *The Invention of Politics in Colonial Malaya: Contesting Nationalism and the Expansion of the Public Sphere* (Cambridge, 1994), p. 289.
17. Sidney Tarrow, *Power in Movement*, 2nd edn (Cambridge [etc.], 1998), p. 2.
18. Pamela E. Oliver and Hank Johnston, "What a Good Idea! Ideology and Frames in Social Movement Research", *Mobilization*, 5 (2000), pp. 37–54, 42.

the perceptions of those who become popular intellectuals, as well as their role in social movements.[19] Recent studies on democratic transitions, for instance, try to escape an excessive structuralism as well. They tend "to emphasize the role of leadership and crafting, thus signalling the importance of individuals, rather than collective actors".[20] This becomes clearest in moments of "high indeterminacy" when individual choices and perspectives become all the more relevant and, we may add, framing activity by popular intellectuals is most salient.[21]

This perspective should not be understood as advocating individualized interpretations, but rather as a recognition of the importance of individuals – of popular and dominant classes alike – in political change. One argument that may support this view is the importance attached, within movements themselves, to the personal characteristics and history of their political and intellectual leaders. They are widely and explicitly discussed, and taken into account in the political and strategic debates within social movements. The issue of representation and authority is closely linked to the personal history of leaders. The history of the *Zapatistas* or al-Qaeda would have been different without Sub-comandante Marcos or Osama bin Laden. Also, less well-known popular intellectuals are venerated and remembered in local contexts, long after they have lost their political or social importance. A second argument is that the personal history of popular leader-intellectuals has become an arena of struggle in itself. A dramatic case which reached the headlines of international newspapers concerned Rigoberta Menchú, the famous indigenous leader in Guatemala, and winner of the Nobel peace prize, who was openly criticized when some of the facts presented in her life story did not match historical reality.[22] Her position as indigenous leader, and consequently the position of the indigenous movement at large, also became compromised.

POPULAR INTELLECTUALS

Our focus on popular intellectuals builds, obviously, on earlier studies. Since Gramsci and, more notably, since the cultural turn in labour history and social-movement studies, the old conceptual dichotomy between "intellectuals" and "masses" (where "intellectuals" stood for educated, urban, and vanguard), is replaced by a much wider conception of intellectuals as articulate knowledge specialists who are found in all sectors of society. Of particular interest are those persons who function as

19. See, for example, Javier Auyero, *Contentious Lives: Two Argentine Women, Two Protests, and the Quest for Recognition* (Durham [etc.], 2003).
20. Ruth Berins Collier, *Paths Toward Democracy: The Working Class and Elites in Western Europe and South America* (Cambridge, 1999), p. 6.
21. *Ibid.*, pp. 3–5, 48–49.
22. David Stoll, *Rigoberta Menchú and the Story of All Poor Guatemalans* (Boulder, CO, 1999).

framing specialists: women and men who develop, borrow, adapt, and re-work interpretive frames that promote collective action and that define collective interests and identities, rights and claims.

Social historians and anthropologists have retrieved from obscurity a wide variety of such intellectuals. They include "artisan intellectuals", whose workshops functioned as informal debating clubs;[23] worker-poets in nineteenth-century France, who developed new images of workers as a proud, assertive class;[24] "labour intellectuals", who shaped the struggle of industrial workers in England and Australia;[25] "peasant intellectuals", who organized social movements in Tanzania and developed new critical discourses in the process;[26] provincial journalists in late-colonial Java, who translated Western liberal and socialist ideas into local models;[27] indigenous intellectuals in Latin America, who try to formulate alternatives to a homogeneous and hegemonic nation-state;[28] and Muslim teachers and missionaries in southeast Asian villages, who communicate new Islamic political identities.[29]

These are clearly very different types of people, who articulate their ideas in diverse historical, political, and cultural contexts. But they do share some significant traits. They are people who articulate reflexive knowledge on the society they live in and are able to convert this analysis in ideological work and ultimately in political activism. They are also people who hold an authoritative position within social movements, and whose reflexive knowledge is instrumental for militancy and political leadership. The differences between labour intellectuals in nineteenth-century England and present-day indigenous intellectuals in Latin

---

23. E.J. Hobsbawm and Joan Wallach Scott, "Political Shoemakers", *Past and Present*, 89 (1980), pp. 86–114. On cigarmakers, see Fernando Ortiz's classic study, *Cuban Counterpoint: Tobacco and Sugar* (Durham [etc.], 1995; Spanish orig. 1940); Jean Stubbs, *Tobacco on the Periphery: A Case Study in Cuban Labour History, 1860–1958* (Cambridge [etc.], 1985); Michiel Baud, "La huelga de los tabaqueros, Santiago, 1919. Un momento de la lucha obrera en la República Dominicana", *Estudios Sociales*, 23 (1990), pp. 3–19.
24. Jacques Rancière, *The Nights of Labor: The Workers' Dream in Nineteenth-Century France* (Philadelphia, PA, 1989).
25. Michael Vester, *Die Entstehung des Proletariats als Lernproces: Zur Soziologie der Arbeiterbewegung* (Frankfurt am Main, 1970); Terry Irving and Sean Scalmer, "Australian Labour Intellectuals: An Introduction", *Labour History*, 77 (1999), pp. 1–10.
26. Steven Feierman, *Peasant Intellectuals: Anthropology and History in Tanzania* (Madison, WI, 1990).
27. Takashi Shiraishi, *An Age in Motion: Popular Radicalism in Java, 1912–26* (Ithaca, NY [etc.], 1990).
28. Edward F. Fischer, *Cultural Logics and Global Economics: Maya Identity in Thought and Practice* (Austin, TX, 2001); Joanne Rappaport, *Cumbe Reborn: An Andean Ethnography of History* (Chicago, IL [etc.], 1994); Kay B. Warren, *Indigenous Movements and Their Critics: Pan-Maya Activism in Guatemala* (Princeton, NJ, 1998).
29. Robert W. Hefner and Patricia Horvatich (eds), *Islam in an Era of Nation-States: Politics and Religious Renewal in Muslim Southeast Asia* (Honolulu, HA, 1997).

America, for example, concern the historical circumstances and the socio economic and cultural context in which they emerged. Nevertheless, they are similar in that they are embedded in local constituencies while simultaneously addressing a larger, national political constituency.

To define the persons we call "popular intellectuals", we may come up with the following characteristics:

(1) They are acknowledged as producers of meaning and as representatives of collective interests by a popular group or local society. However, their legitimacy and authority is never uncontested and all the time new "intellectuals" and intellectual leaders emerge who may challenge their legitimacy, or who may express new or previously silenced interests of specific populations (for example women, peasants, younger generations, indigenous groups).

(2) They possess the explicit ambition to transform society and to put into practice their recipes for change. They are, in this sense, "engaged intellectuals" who combine reflexive activity with cultural and political activism.

(3) They include members of the popular classes and persons who gained their knowledge outside of the realm of formal education, as well as formally-educated members of the upper and middle classes who may have started out as "traditional intellectuals", but redefined their position and political mission.

This exploratory definition[30] draws attention to two important issues. First, it is clear that there is no sharp distinction between popular intellectuals on the one hand and popular leaders and movement activists on the other. Although some framing specialists succeed in maintaining their distance from the actual social or political struggle of social movements, most are actively involved in that struggle from the outset or become involved in it the moment their ideas start to appeal to followers and wider audiences. They become leaders or activists in the process. Moreover, many popular leaders acquire (part of) their authority on the basis of their framing capabilities.[31] In this volume, most authors do not

30. In our definition of popular intellectuals there is a slight overlap with "public intellectuals", i.e. engaged intellectuals with the credentials of a formal education, who speak out on matters of public concern and try to reach a popular audience, though these intellectuals may not connect to social movements. On the other side of the spectrum, there is an overlap with the category of "movement intellectuals", "those intellectuals who gain the status and the self-perception of being 'intellectuals' in the context of their participation in political movements rather than through the institutions of the established culture"; Eyerman, *Between Culture and Politics*, p. 15.

31. This category resembles the type of "people-oriented" leaders of social movements described by by Ron Aminzade *et al.* In contrast to "task-oriented" or "pragmatic" leaders specialized in organization, people-oriented leaders are concerned with evoking "a state of

rigidly distinguish between the two positions. Instead, they allow for the flexible interaction between political and intellectual work and focus on its (historical) consequences.

Secondly, *local* intellectuals are not necessarily *popular* intellectuals. Distinguished by their local knowledge within their communities, local intellectuals do not always intend to use this knowledge to change societal conditions to the advantage of popular classes. Their historical role may just as well be the maintenance and reproduction of the existing social order. In her comparative analysis of popular nationalism in nineteenth-century Mexico and Peru, Florencia Mallon writes: "local intellectuals were those who labored to reproduce and rearticulate local history and memory, to connect community discourses about local identity to constantly shifting patterns of power, solidarity, and consensus".[32] She shows how local intellectuals in Mexico sometimes reproduced hegemonic Eurocentric and racist ideas, and tended to disregard the indigenous population: "the use of authoritarian and racist discourses also tied local intellectuals to wider webs of complicity and social control emerging in Mexico after 1867".[33] This ambiguity is also noted by Claudio Lomnitz-Adler, who shows how local intellectuals in Mexico could be instrumental both in articulating protest and in consolidating the status quo.[34]

These examples draw attention to the ambiguous position of popular intellectuals which so haunted Gramsci. Their political position is never uncontested. To be able to act and function in a meaningful way, intellectuals need to be recognized and accepted as (ideological) leaders by the rank-and-file. They need to possess authority, and their knowledge and suggestions must elicit recognition and respect. At the same time, their specific position as intellectuals sets them apart from the rest of a political movement. James Scott has demonstrated how difficult this balancing act can be in situations where intellectual leaders share very little of the daily realities and world views which prevail among the rank-and-file of a movement.[35] Moreover, to gain respect and authority among followers and wider audiences is not an easy task, because the nature of their work

motivation and commitment, often identification, with the leader or with a movement or goal", and may be described as visionary or charismatic; Ron Aminzade *et al.*, "Leadership Dynamics and Dynamics of Contention", in *idem, Silence and Voice in the Study of Contentious Politics* (Cambridge [etc.], 2001), pp. 126–154, 130.

32. Florencia E. Mallon, *Peasant and Nation: The Making of Postcolonial Mexico and Peru* (Berkeley, CA, 1995), p. 12.

33. *Ibid.*, p. 294.

34. Claudio Lomnitz-Adler, *Exits from the Labyrinth: Culture and Ideology in the Mexican National Space* (Berkeley, CA [etc.], 1992), and *idem*, "Provincial Intellectuals and the Sociology of the so-called Deep Mexico", in *idem, Deep Mexico, Silent Mexico: An Anthropology of Nationalism* (Minneapolis, MN, 2001), pp. 263–286.

35. James C. Scott, "Revolution in the Revolution: Peasants and Commissars", *Theory and Society*, 7 (1979), pp. 97–134.

makes popular intellectuals vulnerable to accusations that they are unpractical dreamers, pedantic snobs, or simply unreliable activists.[36]

Trust between (intellectual) leaders and followers is, then, not self-evident, and it may not last long. Too many politicians and intellectuals pretend to defend the interests of "the people" without really caring for or even understanding these interests. Among intellectuals, and between intellectuals and their followers, there exists a constant struggle over the content and direction of contentious politics. Following Talal Asad, Steven Feierman asks the essential question: "Who succeeds in defining a set of issues or a course of action as the appropriate one, pre-empting the space of opposed utterances or alternative practice?"[37] Popular intellectuals are embedded in relations of power, not only between social movements and powerholders, but also within social movements.

These tensions have acquired new meaning with changes in the dissemination of ideas. From the late nineteenth century onwards, the means of communication have changed dramatically, adding new ways in which popular intellectuals can make themselves heard. Traditional means of articulating protest towards local publics or individual authorities never disappeared (such as the writing of petitions or the staging of demonstrations), but in the course of the twentieth century, mass media allowed social movements and activist intellectuals to address large national and international publics as well. As local activists were drawn into wider activist networks, the context of their struggle and the ideological work it implied also changed. Increasingly, they started to address different audiences at the same time, employing multiple frames in the process. Moreover, the intensified process of global intellectual exchange, which was initially limited to the world of traditional intellectuals, began to affect all domains of political and intellectual activity, including popular intellectuals in the remotest corners of the world. Political activism became embroidered in an international tapestry of ideas that historians have scarcely started to unravel.

POPULAR INTELLECTUALS IN NONWESTERN SOCIETIES

More than forty years ago, Edward Shils wrote a seminal article on the political significance of intellectuals in what he called the "new states", the newly independent countries of Asia and Africa.[38] Though his article shows clear signs of the dominant modernization paradigm of the period, and obviously lacks an analysis of more recent trends, it contains valuable

36. Terry Irving and Sean Scalmer, "Labour Intellectuals in Australia: Modes, Traditions, Generations, Transformations", *International Review of Social History*, forthcoming.
37. Feierman, *Peasant Intellectuals*, p. 31.
38. Edward Shils, "The Intellectuals in the Political Development of the New States", *World Politics*, 12 (1960), pp. 329–368.

insights into the specific position of intellectuals in (post)colonial societies and the historical dynamics of their activist role.

(Post)colonial societies and developing economies provide specific contexts that shape the political roles and types of intellectuals. In societies with limited formal education, small elites, and unstable political systems, Shils argues, Western-educated intellectuals acquired a relatively important political position. Given the relatively small size of the social and intellectual elite, they ascended quite easily into politically powerful positions, whereas alternative employment opportunities were scarce within weak national economies. "Persons who acquired intellectual qualifications had only a few markets for their skills."[39] Moreover, the agrarian, nonindustrialized settings of many of these countries influenced the form and intellectual leadership of social movements. It was not so much the labour intellectuals of industrial societies who took pride of place here, but leaders who emerged from within local, often agrarian, social and cultural networks. One of the interesting issues for historians is to analyse how these networks acquired new political meaning under rapidly changing political and economic circumstances from the late nineteenth century onwards.

Secondly, Shils discusses the emergence of activist intellectuals by referring to the specific history of colonial domination, cultural contact, and political confrontation. In this context, the "nation" and nationalism became a crucial factor in the intense politicization of (post)colonial intellectuals. The colonial experience also played an important role in the emergence of socialist and populist politics, influenced by intellectual models adopted from abroad. Shils writes: "The socialism of the intellectuals of underdeveloped countries [...] is a product of their pained awareness of the poverty of their own countries. The heightening of national sensibility led perforce to the discovery of the 'people'."[40] The first generations of Western-educated intellectuals, who were alienated from traditional indigenous authorities (chiefs, princes, landlords, priests) and from the foreign or Westernized rulers of their society, "had only the 'people', the 'African personality', the 'Indian peasant' etc., as supports in the search for the salvation of their own souls and their own society".[41] There is no doubt that attempts to analyse popular intellectuals in these societies constantly stumble upon vestiges of this postcolonial nationalism, which tends to speak "for" the people, instead of (re)presenting the popular voice.[42]

39. *Ibid.*, p. 334.
40. *Ibid.*, p. 347.
41. *Ibid.*, p. 349.
42. Chatterjee, *Nationalist Thought and the Colonial World*; Nicola Miller, *In the Shadow of the State: Intellectuals and the Quest for National Identity in Twentieth-Century Spanish America* (London, 1999); Michiel Baud, *Intelectuales y sus utopías. Indigenismo y la imaginación de América Latina* (Amsterdam, 2003).

Partha Chatterjee has argued that in the colonized world the ideological development of social movements was marked by the confrontation of radically different modes of social organization and cultural production. This confrontation was influenced by conditions of forced economic modernization and the imposition of new political relations in a new colonial – and thus global – setting.

The introduction of Western education in colonial settings is one crucial process that linked global and local cultural networks. According to Shils, it produced specific "generations" of activist intellectuals. Western education, at home or in universities in Europe, connected local men (and later women) to the worldwide flow of Western liberal and socialist ideas, which shaped their views of their society and themselves. Confronting these ideas with local colonial realities, they developed a sense of political mission as they defined their own societies as "backward" and in need of catching up with the Western world, and as they perceived colonialism as the main obstacle. Adding to their public role was the local status attached to an "educated" person.

The first generation of these "modern intellectuals" consisted mainly of lawyers and journalists who, from the nineteenth century onward, began to strive for reform within the colonial structure. Born of wealthy and influential families, and inspired by liberal ideas, they acted – at least initially – more as interest groups for indigenous elites and educated middle classes, than as spokesmen for the popular classes. Moreover, the journalists, who were instrumental in the emergence of an indigenous press, only reached a very limited literate audience at first.[43]

Students formed the backbone of the second generation of modern intellectuals, who had more traits of "popular intellectuals" in our sense of the term. Emerging in the early twentieth century, this second generation produced committed pro-independence activists. Influenced by Western socialism, by the Russian Revolution, and by the new type of popular politics developed by Mahatma Gandhi, they became populist activists. It was this category, in particular, that began to speak in the name of "the people".[44] Politics became a vocation for them. Though the leadership of nationalist movements was often still in the hands of lawyers and other professionals, it was among the students of universities, colleges, and high schools that many of the activists were found.[45]

After independence, many intellectuals joined the ruling political elite, and transformed into politicians and bureaucrats. Others turned to the opposition, in legal or extremist forms, depending on the form of

43. Shils, "The Intellectuals in the Political Development of the New States", pp. 354–357.
44. *Ibid.*, p. 360.
45. For a classic article on South Africa, see Colin Bundy, "Street Sociology and Pavement Politics: Aspects of Youth and Student Resistance in Cape Town, 1985", *Journal of Southern African Studies*, 13 (1987), pp. 303–330.

government. The role of critic and oppositionist was, for many modern intellectuals, part of their self-definition. Revolutionary intellectuals deserve special mention in this regard. Western-educated intellectuals have played a leading role in revolutionary movements across continents. As authorities in "scientific" Marxist knowledge, they could style themselves as the vanguard of more "ignorant" peasant populations, raising questions, however, about the popular content of their programmes.[46] In the last decades, the tremendous increase in public education in non-Western countries, and the rise of nongovernmental organizations staffed by educated persons who are well-versed in modern advocacy work, is witness to a new category of activist intellectuals.

Religious intellectuals, on their part, have a specific history of activism in (post)colonial societies as well. In challenging colonialism, and in shaping the post-colonial state, many religious leaders have been instrumental in defining "the nation" in religious terms, and in providing forceful collective-action frames to articulate and legitimize nationalist struggles. In colonial societies of Asia and Africa, for instance, movements for religious and moral self-renewal emerged, which were led, in many cases, by an "indigenous traditional intelligentsia made up of the custodians of sacred writings".[47] These "protagonists of the traditional cultures" sought to establish the worth of their culture and society, "in the face of the encroachment of Western culture and religion".[48] They helped to shape a national self-consciousness that resonated among large parts of the population, and many of these traditional (religious) intellectuals would link up with a new generation of nationalist Western-educated intellectuals. The modern religious-nationalist movements that developed in the process would be headed and staffed by religious intellectuals. The present-day Islamist and Hindu-nationalist movements are among the most well-known examples.[49]

The extensive Arabic-Islamic intellectual tradition has produced its own popular intellectuals in Asia and Africa. Ousmane Kane has argued that, at least for sub-Saharan Africa, the importance of a large Arabic-Islamic intellectual community, with its own media and centres of learning and debate, has been quite disregarded by Western historians, who rather focused on Westernized intellectuals in the former colonies (not least because of the accessibility of the European languages in which this latter

46. Alvin Gouldner, *The Future of Intellectuals and the Rise of the New Class* (New York, 1979); Michael Walzer, "Intellectuals, Social Classes, and Revolutions", in Theda Skocpol (ed.), *Democracy, Revolution, and History* (Ithaca, NY, 1998), pp. 127–142.
47. Shils, "The Intellectuals in the Political Development of the New States", p. 357.
48. *Ibid.*
49. Peter van der Veer, *Religious Nationalism: Hindus and Muslims in India* (Berkeley, CA [etc.], 1994); Quintan Wiktorowicz (ed.), *Islamic Activism: A Social Movement Theory Approach* (Bloomington, IN, 2003).

category of intellectuals communicated).[50] Besides the Western (colonial) ideologies introduced by colonial powers and educational institutions, Arabic-Islamic institutions produced their own "field of meaning", which gained political relevance. Islamic intellectuals, for instance, headed political movements for the "purification of Islam" in nineteenth-century African societies. In the postcolonial period, thousands of students from African countries studied at Islamic universities in the Maghreb and the Middle East (paid for by their host countries), and many returned with an Islamist vision on the politics of their own societies. Political Islam offered a new interpretation for the lack of development in African countries in the decades after independence.[51] A similar process has taken place among Islamic students in Asia.

In the margins of these arenas of "high culture" (i.e. established religious communities and Western educational enclaves) a third category of activist intellectuals operated in many non-Western societies: the practitioners of local and syncretic religions, who would become leaders of prophetic or millenarian movements. These movements were, to a varying extent, directed against the colonial order. Their leaders were often lower-class, provincial, self-styled religious intellectuals, who combined indigenous worldviews with imported religious ideologies (Christian, in many cases).[52] Initial studies stressed the point that these leaders – lacking a Western education – had no access to secular ideologies and models of political activism that were effective under the new conditions of a colonial state. More recent studies show, instead, a dynamic process of ideological syncretism that made sense in local society.[53]

The contributions presented in this volume form a rich set of case studies that further explore the relationship between popular intellectuals and social movements. Given the scope of the issues at hand, the volume's geographic reach and the size of the available literature, the volume's aim can only be modest. The strength of the collection lies, we think, in bringing together different perspectives and historical cases that illuminate a number of vital issues, and that provide possible directions for analysis and future research.

Sean Chabot sets out to reverse the stereotypical image of a one-way flow of ideas from the West to the "rest", by showing how African-American civil rights activists adopted and adapted the Gandhian

50. Ousmane Kane, "Intellectuels non europhones", Document de Travail, Conseil pour le développement de la recherche en sciences sociales en Afrique (CODESRIA), Dakar, Sénégal, 2003.
51. *Ibid.*
52. Michael Adas, *Prophets of Rebellion: Millenarian Protest Movements Against the European Colonial Order* (Chapel Hill, NC, 1979).
53. Reynaldo C. Ileto, *Pasyon and Revolution: Popular Movements in the Philippines, 1840–1910* (Quezon City, 1979); Jonathan Spence, *God's Chinese Son: The Taiping Heavenly Kingdom of Hong Xiuquan* (London, 1996).

repertoire of non-violent collective action. Tracing the history of inter-actions between activist intellectuals in India (including Mahatma Gandhi) and African-American theologians, college professors, and civil rights activists in the 1930s to 1950s, the author argues that the eventual application of the Gandhian action repertoire in the United States (epitomized by Martin Luther King, Jr) was neither automatic nor self-evident. It was the result of intensive efforts by successive "generations" of African-American activists to articulate the Gandhian repertoire in ways that made it acceptable to activists at home. The author shows how these "itinerant intellectuals", who made regular visits to India to meet with Gandhian activists, succeeded in the transnational diffusion of Gandhian ideas precisely because of their creative work of reinterpretation.

Marc Becker discusses cultural brokerage across ethnic and class divides in his essay on activist alliances between indigenous peasants and urban socialists in early twentieth-century Ecuador. The author challenges the view that urban socialists and Indian peasants hardly understood each other nor shared the same goals, and that such alliances were inherently unequal. By tracing the close cooperation, in the 1920s, between indigenous peasant leader Jesús Gualavisí and the urban, white, educated leader of the newly formed Ecuadorian Socialist Party, Ricardo Paredes, he argues that there was a "cross-pollination" of ideas and experiences. Both parties profited from the alliance. The cultural brokerage by the Indian leader Gualavisí was central to this relationship: he linked local experiences and analyses with an imported socialist frame and merged these in such a way that both class and ethnic interests were acknowledged. This went hand in hand with his role as a social broker. As he linked networks of indigenous peasant communities to the institutional networks of a socialist party, he was able to address both Indian peasants and urban socialists in ways that both audiences understood.

The two main ideologues of the Sindhi separatist movement in Pakistan, discussed in Oskar Verkaaik's essay, used a religious frame to bridge class divides and sharpen a sense of regional nationalism. The author shows how these two men emerged as popular intellectuals within the context of new intellectual milieus, created by the expansion of secular education and popular politics. One was the son of a peasant, who became a teacher, Marxist, and leading figure of a new intellectual vanguard, developed from within the new category of educated village youths. The other was the son of a landlord, who followed a career as an upper-class politician-intellectual, mystic, and *enfant terrible* of national politics. Connected, in the course of their careers, to religious networks, student milieus, and party-political spheres, they were inspired by discourses as diverse as Islamic revivalism, Marxism, nationalism, Gandhianism, and Sufi mysti-cism. When they began to cooperate in political activism in the 1960s, the Marxist and the mystic developed together a new, powerful, nationalist ideology, framed as a type of reformed Sufism, which inspired many Sindhi youths. Central to its initial success was the institutional setting of secular education: both popular intellectuals were inspired by new ideas and ideologies transmitted through secular education, and they, in turn, used schools to disseminate their own message of religious nationalism, create a new intelligentsia, and develop activist networks of students who would form the basis of their separatist movement.

The role of (formal) education runs like a thread through all contributions, but most explicitly so in the contribution by Verkaaik (discussed above) and by Baz Lecocq. Analysing the recent separatist Tuareg rebellions in Mali and Niger from the viewpoint of different types of Tuareg intellectuals, Lecocq shows how the experience of a formal education created a socio-political dividing line among local intellectuals. Young Tuareg educated in state schools along Western lines accentuated the need for social and economic change within Tuareg society, with less concern for political matters regarding state and nationality. Their autodidact age-mates, whose interpretation of their society's wrongs was shaped by their experiences as marginalized migrant labourers in neighbouring countries such as Libya and Algeria, and by the revolu-tionary discourses disseminated by the state within these countries, stressed the need for political autonomy. Both categories of young Tuareg intellectuals, in turn, disagreed with the older generation of local intellectuals: the Muslim religious specialists and tribal leaders who tended to legitimize the social and political status quo in which they thrived. The debates and disagreements between these groups partly shaped the form and outcome of the Tuareg rebellions of the 1990s.

Such debates and disagreements illuminate the heterogeneous composi-tion of the category of "popular intellectuals" who are somehow connected to a social movement. They also provide a welcome glimpse behind the scenes of the social dynamics of framing. Joanne Rappaport takes up this issue in her analysis of conflicts and negotiations among intellectuals in an indigenous organization in Colombia. She shows how the indigenous movement includes different types of popular intellectuals, whose worldviews and discourses differ significantly. Indigenous cultural activists, indigenous politicians, local shamans, urban leftwing intellectuals supportive of the cause of indigenous politics, and even foreign anthro-pologists play a part – each in their own way – in the social and political struggle for meaning. Graphically illustrated by a confrontation between cultural activists and an indigenous politician, the essay argues for a closer look at internal differences within the broad category of "organic intellectuals" that emerged from within the indigenous population. Such differences are related, among others, to the social position and interests of each type of intellectual within the movement and beyond, and the specific audiences they address.

The issue of multiple audiences is one of the topics discussed by Pablo Bose as well. In his essay on two major public figures of the anti-dam movement in the Narmada Valley, India, he shows how these two women became so prominent in the movement because (among other reasons) they were able to frame the issue convincingly for very different audiences, all of which were of strategic importance. College-educated and with a middle-class background, Medha Patkar and the writer Arundhati Roy were able to address, at levels that ranged from the local to the international, politicians, citizens, authorities, and development organizations, in a language and imagery that resonated with their audiences. By framing local problems as broad issues of ecology, development policy, and human rights, they connected to sympathizers and opponents beyond the level of the Narmada region, and thereby strengthened the case of the anti-dam movement considerably. At the same time, their success in national and international circles raised doubt about the nature of their links with the local aggrieved populations whose interests they claimed to represent – in particular, the villagers in the Narmada Valley whose communities would be submerged. Did they actually represent their views and aspirations? Bose analyses public discussions about the perceived legitimacy and credibility of these popular intellectuals as spokespersons in the anti-dam movement, and thereby sheds light on the broader questions of representation and strategy.

Quintan Wiktorowicz discusses the credibility of popular intellectuals from a particular angle: intramovement rivalry. The reputation of popular intellectuals is itself a contentious issue, in particular when rival groups within a movement seek to assert their claims to authority by presenting their own intellectuals as far superior to those of their rivals. At stake is the authority of a certain group within a movement to speak on behalf of a constituency or issue, and the persuasive force of its interpretive frame. Wiktorowicz explores the framing contest between al-Qaeda and non-violent Islamic fundamentalists over the use of violence, and identifies several framing strategies used by rival groups to discredit the intellectuals of the opponent and credit one's own. These contests and their outcome, the author argues, highlight a causal connection between the reputation of popular intellectuals and the extent to which their message resonates with a wider audience. After all, the authority of a message derives to a large extent from the perceived credibility of those who articulate it, but this credibility needs to be constantly asserted and guarded against attacks from rivals. Therefore, intellectuals themselves have become the object of framing. The intramovement group or faction that successfully deals with this has a good chance of reaching a position of power and authority within the movement. We may add that such credibility contests are equally salient when they take place between a movement and its opponents, for instance, concerning movement intellectuals and government experts.

In his essay on "popular publics", David Smilde proposes a shift in focus from the category of individual intellectuals to the relational context of intellectual activity. Among popular sectors in the developing world, Smilde argues, few people have the explicit function or occupation of an intellectual. A focus on these individuals would obscure much of the discussion and interaction regarding collective social life that takes place among ordinary people. To capture such intellectual activity and exchange, he uses the concept of "popular publics". This refers to relational contexts in which diverse networks and discourses come into contact. In other words, these are public spaces where people with diverse backgrounds and views come into contact in open-ended ways, debate understandings of their world, bridge social networks and fields of discourse, and create and disseminate new understandings in the process. Smilde illustrates his point with two cases of popular public participation in Caracas, Venezuela: protesting members of the informal economy, who frame their claims towards sympathetic bystanders as issues of public interest, and Pentecostal plaza preachers and their audience, who offer interpretations of Venezuela's problems in biblical terms. The concept of popular publics portrays public intellectual activity in terms of relational contexts rather than actors. Moreover, it draws attention to the "extended networks and expanded discourses" that may endure "beyond the shifting composition of the actors involved".

In closing, the editors discuss some salient insights emerging from the different contributions.

IRSH 49 (2004), Supplement, pp. 19–40 DOI: 10.1017/S0020859004001622
© 2004 Internationaal Instituut voor Sociale Geschiedenis

Framing, Transnational Diffusion, and African-American Intellectuals in the Land of Gandhi

Sean Chabot

SUMMARY: Most of the contentious-politics scholars who pioneered the study of framing in social movements now also recognize the importance of transnational diffusion between protest groups. Interestingly, though, they have not yet specified how these two processes intersect. This article, in contrast, explores the framing-transnational diffusion nexus by highlighting three historical moments of inter-action between African-American intellectuals and Gandhian activists *before* Martin Luther King, Jr traveled to India in 1959. After briefly reviewing the relevant literature, it illustrates how three different types of "itinerant" African-American intellectuals – *mentors* like Howard Thurman, *advisors* like Bayard Rustin, and *peers* like James Lawson – framed the Gandhian repertoire of nonviolent direct action in ways that made it applicable during the American civil rights movement. The final section considers possible implications for social movement theory and fertile areas for further research.

In February 1959, a few years after the Montgomery bus boycott had anointed him as a prophet of nonviolence, Martin Luther King, Jr arrived in India to talk with fellow disciples of Gandhi and witness the effects of the Indian independence movement. He and his wife, Coretta, toured the country, had dinner with Prime Minister Jawaharlal Nehru, visited Gandhi's *ashrama* (self-sufficient communes), participated in conferences, and attended numerous receptions in their honor. During their four-week stay in India, the Kings discussed Gandhian nonviolent action with native experts like Dr Radhakrishnan, India's Vice-President; Jayaprakash Narain, a contemporary protest leader; and G. Ramachandran and R.R. Diwakar of the Gandhi Smarak Nidhi (Gandhi Memorial Trust).[1] Upon return to the United States, Martin Luther King, Jr wrote an article for *Ebony*, the popular African-American magazine, describing the journey's personal impact:

It was wonderful to be in Gandhi's land, to talk with his son, his grandsons, his

---

1. Swami Vishwananda, "I Go Round With The Kings", in William R. Miller, *With the Kings in India: A Souvenir of Dr Martin Luther King's Visit to India, February–March 1959* (New Delhi, 1959), pp. 2–7.

cousins and other relatives; to share the reminiscences of his close comrades, to visit his *ashrama*, to see the countless memorials for him and finally to lay a wreath on his entombed ashes at Rajghat. I left India more convinced than ever before that nonviolent resistance is the most potent weapon available to oppressed people in their struggle for freedom.[2]

Following his pilgrimage to "the Land of Gandhi", all doubt about King's Gandhian credentials vanished and in the early 1960s he became the civil rights movement's most prominent intellectual and "framing specialist".[3] As their indisputable leader, he encouraged participants in the African-American freedom struggle to adopt and apply the Gandhian repertoire of nonviolent direct action in the United States.[4]

King's interaction with Gandhian scholars and activists in India was crucial for his legitimacy and effectiveness as the civil rights movement's leading representative.[5] It invested his interpretations of the social problem in need of change (racial segregation in the United States), his views on who or what was to blame for this situation (white supremacy), his ideas about means and ends for challenging the status quo (nonviolence and integration), and his calls for collective action campaigns with credibility and persuasive power. At the same time, King's journey also contributed to the dissemination of the Gandhian repertoire from the Indian independence movement to the American civil rights movement. Theoretically, therefore, his pilgrimage to India was a vivid example of how *framing* and *transnational diffusion* intersect – a subject that has not received sufficient scholarly attention.[6]

To explore the framing–transnational diffusion nexus, I start with a brief review of existing social movement theories. Then, I discuss three specific "moments" of interaction between African-American intellectuals and Gandhians in India, and their effects on African-American frames and applications of the Gandhian repertoire in the United States. This empirical section illustrates that King's trip was not an isolated event, but occurred after numerous other African-American intellectuals had preceded him. It also points to the importance of creative framing for constructing transnational linkages between social movements embedded

2. James M. Washington (ed.), *I Have a Dream: Martin Luther King, Jr, Writings and Speeches that Changed the World* (San Francisco, CA, 1986), p. 43.
3. Charles Kurzman and Lynn Owens, "The Sociology of Intellectuals", *Annual Review of Sociology*, 28 (2002), pp. 63–90; Ron Eyerman and Andrew Jamison, *Social Movements: A Cognitive Approach* (Cambridge, 1991); Robert D. Benford and David A. Snow, "Framing Processes and Social Movements: An Overview and Assessment", *Annual Review of Sociology*, 26 (2000), pp. 611–639.
4. Sean Chabot, "Crossing the Great Divide: The Gandhian Repertoire's Transnational Diffusion to the American Civil Rights Movement" (Ph.D., University of Amsterdam, 2003).
5. Of course none of this would have been possible (at least not at the same level of intimacy) if King and his Indian hosts had not spoken the same language, English.
6. Benford and Snow, "Framing Processes".

in different cultural and historical contexts. The final section considers the relevance of my empirical findings for the subjects discussed in this supplement and suggests several lines of future research.

FRAMING AND TRANSNATIONAL DIFFUSION IN SOCIAL MOVEMENT THEORY

Both framing and transnational diffusion are now popular subjects of investigation in the field of contentious politics, but so far scholars have not studied how these two processes overlap. Research on collective-action frames and framing dynamics took off in the mid-1980s, with the pioneering work of David Snow, Robert Benford, and their colleagues. They helped incorporate Erving Goffman's social psychological concept into social movement theory by focusing on movement actors as "signifying agents actively engaged in the production and maintenance of meaning for constituents, antagonists, and bystanders or observers".[7] Based on this perspective, they and others emphasize that "popular intellectuals" are responsible for three core interpretive tasks: diagnostic framing refers to the identification and attribution of a social problem; prognostic framing to the articulation of possible strategies for solving this social problem, given certain environmental opportunities and constraints; and motivational framing to the construction of compelling "vocabularies" for sustained social protest.[8] Snow and Benford have also sparked considerable interest in the strategic alignment of collective-action frames with potential constituents or resource providers. These alignment processes include: frame bridging, the linking of previously unconnected frames regarding a particular issue; frame amplification, the reinterpretation of existing values or beliefs; frame extension, the expansion of a social movement organization's frames beyond its initial interests; and frame transformation, the generation of new public understandings and cultural meanings.[9] Since the mid-1990s, leading theorists recognize that cultural framing is a central dynamic in the emergence and development of

7. *Ibid.* Erving Goffman, *Framing Analysis: An Essay on the Organization of Experience* (New York, 1974), p. 21 defines frames as "schemata of interpretation" that allow individuals (and groups) "to locate, perceive, identify, and label" events in their lives and the external world.

8. See e.g., Robert D. Benford, "'You Could Be the Hundredth Monkey': Collective Action Frames and Vocabularies of Motive within the Nuclear Disarmament Movement", *Sociological Quarterly*, 34 (1993), pp. 195–216; William A. Gamson, "The Sociological Psychology of Collective Action", in Aldon D. Morris and Carol M. Mueller (eds), *Frontiers in Social Movement Theory* (New Haven, CT, 1992), pp. 53–76; David A. Snow and Robert D. Benford, "Ideology, Frame Resonance, and Participant Mobilization", *International Social Movement Research*, 1 (1988), pp. 197–218; *idem*, "Master Frames and Cycles of Protest", in Morris and Mueller, *Frontiers*; James M. Jasper, *The Art of Moral Protest* (Chicago, IL, 1997).

9. David A. Snow *et al.*, "Frame Alignment Processes, Micromobilization, and Movement Participation", *American Sociological Review*, 51 (1986), pp. 464–481.

social movements, together with political opportunities and mobilizing structures.[10]

Research on transnational diffusion between social movements is a more recent development. In 1993, Doug McAdam and Dieter Rucht broke new ground by concentrating on how contentious ideas and practices spread across borders, between similar transmitting and receiving protest groups. Building on the classical diffusion theory of Everett Rogers, and the findings of "world society" scholars like John Meyer and David Strang, they propose several guidelines for analyzing the influence of American New-Left students on their German counterparts.[11] They suggest that receivers must define themselves as equivalent to transmitters and speak the same language; that the timing and pace of the receiving movement must lag behind those of the transmitting movement; that the two social movements must share common social contexts, ideologies, tactics, organizational forms, and cultural items; and that specific interpersonal and media-based channels of communication must link receivers to transmitters.[12]

In the past decade, the number of publications on this subject has grown rapidly. But most of them still rely on the approach of McAdam and Rucht, emphasizing that transnational diffusion tends to flow along established channels of interaction, involve similar groups of transmitters and receivers, link similar social settings, and consist of adaptive emulation within a given political system.[13] The majority of empirical studies, moreover, continue to focus almost exclusively on the dissemination of information and tactics among Western activists – that is, among or between American and European activists.[14]

10. Doug McAdam et al., Comparative Perspectives on Social Movements: Political Opportunities, Mobilizing Structures, and Cultural Framing (Cambridge, [etc.], 1996).

11. Everett M. Rogers, Diffusion of Innovations (New York, 1995, 4th edn); David Strang and John W. Meyer, "Institutional Conditions for Diffusion", Theory and Society, 22 (1993): pp. 487–511.

12. Doug McAdam and Dieter Rucht, "The Cross-National Diffusion of Movement Ideas", Annals of the American Academy of Political and Social Science, 528 (1993), pp. 56–74, 66, 71.

13. David Strang and Michael W. Macy, "In Search of Excellence: Fads, Success Stories, and Adaptive Emulation", American Journal of Sociology, 107 (2001), pp. 147–182.

14. See e.g., Marco G. Giugni, "The Cross-National Diffusion of Protest", in Hanspeter Kriesi et al. (eds), New Social Movements in Western Europe: A Comparative Analysis (Minneapolis, MN, 1995), pp. 181–206; Sarah A. Soule, "The Student Divestment Movement in the United States and Tactical Diffusion: The Shantytown Protest", Social Forces, 75 (1997), pp. 855–882; David Strang and Sarah A. Soule, "Diffusion in Organizations and Social Movements: From Hybrid Corn to Poison Pills", Annual Review of Sociology, 24 (1998), pp. 265–290; Sidney Tarrow, Power in Movement: Social Movements and Contentious Politics (Cambridge, [etc.], 1998, 2nd edn); Doug McAdam, "'Initiator' and 'Spinoff' Movements: Diffusion Processes in Protest Cycles", in Mark Traugott (ed.), Repertoires and Cycles of Collective Action (Durham, NC, 1995), pp. 217–239; Doug McAdam, Sidney Tarrow, and Charles Tilly, Dynamics of Contention (Cambridge, 2001). Cf. Sean Chabot and Jan Willem Duyvendak, "Globalization

The main exception is recent work by Snow and Benford, which criticizes the approach of McAdam, Rucht, and other influential scholars, arguing that transnational diffusion may also involve the construction of *new* channels of interaction, between *different* social movements and environments.[15] They stress that the spread of contentious ideas and practices often requires *creative* agency, by individual and collective receivers seeking fundamental change in the existing power structure, and discuss *Western as well as non-Western* cases.

Following the lead of Snow and Benford, my earlier work introduces an alternative theoretical framework for studying transnational diffusion between social movements.[16] It highlights the role of "critical communities" in overcoming mainstream stereotypes and the contribution of underlying relational mechanisms like brokerage and appropriation. Critical communities, according to Thomas Rochon, are networks of popular intellectuals who "have developed a sensitivity to some problem, an analysis of the sources of the problem, and a prescription for what should be done about the problem".[17] Their members make the adoption of foreign protest methods possible by employing them to develop new oppositional discourses or organize collective action campaigns. Brokerage, moreover, represents the formation of new or revitalization of old ties between transmitters and receivers, while appropriation reflects the ways that receivers mobilize traditional or new institutions to implement foreign protest methods in their own contexts.[18]

Recent scholarship on framing protest and transnational diffusion between social movements has produced useful insights. Yet none of these studies focuses explicitly on the interrelationships between these two processes. Even Snow and Benford, who have called for more attention to

and Transnational Diffusion between Social Movements: Reconceptualizing the Dissemination of the Gandhian Repertoire and the 'Coming Out' Routine", *Theory and Society*, 31 (2002), pp. 697–740; Sean Scalmer, "The Labor of Diffusion: The Peace Pledge Union and the Adaptation of the Gandhian Repertoire", *Mobilization*, 7 (2002), pp. 269–286.

15. David A. Snow and Robert D. Benford, "Alternative Types of Cross-national Diffusion in the Social Movement Arena", in Donatella della Porta *et al.* (eds.), *Social Movements in a Globalizing World* (London, 1999), pp. 23–39. As Snow and Benford, "Framing Processes", pp. 14–15 put it: "framing activity is most relevant to social movement diffusion processes when [...] the conditions of similarity or compatibility between transmitters and potential adopters are not given but are problematic and in need of construction".

16. Chabot, "Crossing the Great Divide"; Chabot and Duyvendak, "Globalization and Transnational Diffusion between Social Movements"; Sean Chabot, "Transnational Diffusion and the African-American Reinvention of the Gandhian Repertoire", in Jackie Smith and Hank Johnston (eds), *Globalization and Resistance: Transnational Dimensions of Social Movements* (Lanham, MD, 2002), pp. 97–114.

17. Thomas Rochon, *Culture Moves: Ideas, Activism, and Changing Values* (Princeton, NJ, 1998), p. 22.

18. McAdam, Tarrow, and Tilly, *Dynamics of Contention*, pp. 26, 45–48.

this important subject, have not done so themselves.[19] The following empirical section is an initial attempt to fill this gap in the literature. Continuing the narrative of the introduction, it discusses three historical moments of interaction between African-American intellectuals and Gandhians in India. By concentrating on how such moments enabled the spread of Gandhian protest methods between very *different* social movements and environments – from an Asian independence movement to a Western civil rights movement – it highlights a rare yet momentous case where successful transnational diffusion largely depended on innovative framing, and vice versa.

AFRICAN-AMERICAN JOURNEYS TO INDIA AND FRAMING AT HOME

As I noted in the introductory paragraphs, King's trip to India in 1959 illustrates the influence of transnational diffusion on domestic framing, on the one hand, and the significance of domestic framing for transnational diffusion, on the other. At the same time, though, it also tends to *overstate* the role of one individual actor and *underestimate* broader historical processes. It glosses over the fact that two contextual factors strongly affected King's decision to travel to India and meet with "authentic" Gandhians. First of all, members of his inner circle started urging him to visit the Gandhian repertoire's country of origin as early as 1956. Although King had read several of Gandhi's books as a university student, other African-American intellectuals knew much more about the techniques and implications of nonviolent direct action than he did. By taking the trip to the land of Gandhi, and writing about his experiences, he demonstrated – to himself, other civil rights activists, and the outside world – that he was a competent Gandhian in his own right. And secondly, King actually followed in the footsteps of several African-American predecessors, who first ventured on the long journey in 1935. Inspired by the Indian independence movement, and particularly the Salt March campaign in 1930, these pioneers set out to meet Gandhi and ask whether his methods were relevant for fighting racial discrimination in the United States. Whereas most observers and scholars stress King's personal debt to Gandhi, therefore, I emphasize that he built on the shoulders of earlier generations of African-American intellectuals and activists.

Howard Thurman, liberation theology, and nonviolent direct action

The first African-American leader to embark on a pilgrimage to India was Howard Thurman, professor in the School of Religion at Howard

19. Snow and Benford, "Framing Processes", pp. 14–15.

University (Washington DC), the premier black college in the United States and an important training ground for "race rebels".[20] In 1935, the International Committee of the YMCA and YWCA invited him to head an African-American delegation (which included his wife, Sue, as well as Reverend Carroll and his wife) to the Student Christian Movement in Burma, Ceylon, and India. Initially, Thurman wanted to turn down the invitation because he did not want to represent a religious institution – *American* Christianity – that condoned racial segregation. But after talking with Miriam Slade, an English member of Gandhi's *ashram*, he decided to take advantage of this unique opportunity to tour the Indian subcontinent and meet with the famous proponent of nonviolent direct action.[21]

Thurman was certainly not the only African-American intellectual interested in the Gandhian repertoire of contention. During the 1920s, prominent figures like W.E.B. Du Bois and Marcus Garvey had frequently referred to the Indian independence movement and its leader to support their respective views on international racial solidarity. And the dramatic Salt March in 1930, during which Gandhi and millions of Indians engaged in civil disobedience of British laws, had received a great deal of coverage in African-American journals and newspapers.[22]

Before 1935, however, many African-American intellectuals admired Gandhi's efforts in India without considering adoption of his ideas or practices in the United States. They generally felt that the moderate methods of the National Association for the Advancement of Colored People (NAACP) – such as lobbying for legal reform, publicity campaigns, and court action – were more practical and effective in the American context than Gandhian protest on a mass scale. Although he was not a radical or an activist, Thurman believed that existing methods for desegregating the Christian church and American society were inadequate. He looked to Gandhi and India for new insights on how to reinvent Christianity and achieve first-class citizenship for the African-American minority.[23]

---

20. See Robin D.G. Kelley, *Race Rebels: Culture, Politics, and the Black Working Class* (New York, 1994).
21. Howard Thurman, *With Head and Heart: The Autobiography of Howard Thurman* (San Diego, CA, 1979), pp. 103–107.
22. Sudarshan Kapur, *Raising Up a Prophet: The African-American Encounter with Gandhi* (Boston, MA, 1992).
23. In the early 1920s, Thurman was a youth leader of the YMCA and the Christian student movement, and toward the end of the decade he became the first African-American board member of the pacifist Fellowship of Reconciliation (FOR). As a follower of the Quaker mystic, Rufus Jones, Thurman focused on the spiritual affirmation of personal experiences without denying the relevance of religious, cultural, class, and racial barriers in the social world; Walter Earl Fluker and Catherine Tumber (eds), *A Strange Freedom: The Best of Howard Thurman on Religious Experience and Public Life* (Boston, MA, 1998), pp. 1–17.

During their visit, the four African-American Christians interacted with various Indian audiences and activists. After a public lecture at Law College in Ceylon, for example, the chairman asked Thurman why he had come to India as representative of a religion that had participated in the slave trade and continued to deny the African-Americans minority its civil rights. Thurman answered that he had not come to defend the Christian church or to proselytize:

> It is far from my purpose to symbolize anyone or anything. I think the religion of Jesus in its true genius offers me a promising way to work through the conflicts of a disordered world. I make a careful distinction between Christianity and the religion of Jesus [...]. From my investigation and study, the religion of Jesus projected a creative solution to the pressing problem of survival for the minority of which He was a part in the Greco-Roman world. When Christianity became an imperial and world religion, it marched under banners other than that of the teacher and prophet of Galilee. Finally, the minority in my country that is concerned about and dedicated to experiencing that spirit that was in Jesus Christ is on the side of freedom, liberty, and justice for all people, black, white, red, yellow, saint, sinner, rich, or poor. They, too, are a fact to be reckoned with in my country.[24]

In other parts of the Indian continent, people confronted the African-American delegation with this question about the relationship between Christianity and racial segregation as well. Besides participating in numerous public meetings, the members of Thurman's group also went to Shantiniketan, the international university of Rabindranath Tagore, the famous Indian poet and Nobel Prize winner. Here, they met with Dr Singh, the head of the division of Oriental studies, who shared their ideal of crossing religious, cultural, social, and political barriers. In Hyderabad, moreover, they talked about Gandhian nonviolence with Sarojini Naidu, the poetess who had played such an important role during the Salt March campaign.[25]

For the Thurmans and the Carrolls, the highlight of the trip was undoubtedly their encounter with Gandhi in Bardoli. As Thurman writes in his autobiography, after greeting them warmly, the Indian leader immediately began asking a series of profound questions about slavery, voting rights, public education, lynching, discrimination, and so forth, demonstrating a keen interest in African-American history.[26] When they discussed practical means for achieving fundamental social change, Gandhi told them that:

> The effectiveness of a creative ethical ideal such as nonviolence [...] depends upon

---

24. Thurman, *With Head and Heart*, p. 114.
25. *Ibid.*, pp. 128–129, 136. See also, Gene Sharp, *Gandhi Wields the Weapon of Moral Protest: Three Case Histories* (Ahmedabad, 1960).
26. Thurman, *With Head and Heart*, p. 132.

the degree to which the masses of the people are able to embrace such a notion and have it become a working part of their total experience. It cannot be the unique property or experience of the leaders; it has to be rooted in the mass assent and creative push.[27]

He added that, from what he had heard, the African-American minority was no less capable of sustained nonviolent direct action than the Indian population.[28] At the time, though, talk about a nonviolent social movement by African Americans seemed remote to Howard Thurman, who was particularly eager to hear Gandhi's views on religion. Before leaving the *ashram*, therefore, he inquired: "What do you think is the greatest handicap to Jesus Christ in India?". Gandhi responded: "Christianity as it is practised, as it has been identified with Western culture, with Western civilization and colonialism. This is the greatest enemy that Jesus Christ has in my country – not Hinduism, or Buddhism, or any of the indigenous religions – but Christianity itself."[29] Thurman could not have agreed more and, from that moment on, he set out to develop an alternative Christian discourse that *did* focus on removing the worldwide color line.

The interaction of Thurman and his group with leading intellectuals and activists in India affected the *framing* of the Gandhian repertoire in the United States in several significant ways. In the first place, after returning to Howard University, Thurman's own thinking and writings emphasized the need to create a form of religion that avoided the racist and imperialist foundations of Western Christianity and contributed to human community among diverse ethnic groups and cultures.[30] In his most important work, *Jesus and the Disinherited*, Thurman suggests that such an activist gospel should build on the ethics of Jesus Christ because:

> His message focused on the urgency of a radical change in the inner attitude of the people. He recognized fully that out of the heart are the issues of life, that no external force, however great and overwhelming, can at long last destroy a people if it does not first win the victory of the spirit against them.[31]

Inspired by his meeting with Gandhi in 1936, this "liberation theology frame" expresses basic insights of the Gandhian repertoire in familiar Christian language.[32]

Secondly, the positive experiences of the Thurmans and Carrolls stimulated other members of their critical community to embark on the same pilgrimage. At the end of 1936, Benjamin Mays, dean of Howard University's School of Religion, and Channing Tobias, secretary of the

27. *Ibid.*, p. 133.
28. *Collected Works of Mahatma Gandhi* (CWMG) (New Delhi, 1999), vol. 68, pp. 237–238.
29. Thurman, *With Head and Heart*, p. 135.
30. Fluker and Tumber, *A Strange Freedom*, pp. 200–210.
31. Howard Thurman, *Jesus and the Disinherited* (Nashville, TN, 1949), p. 21.
32. Fluker and Tumber, *A Strange Freedom*, pp. 211–219.

YMCA's Colored Men's Department, went to India to participate in the World Conference of the YMCA and talk with Gandhi at his *ashram*. The Indian leader told them that nonviolent direct action was an active rather than a passive force, that its effects were three-fourths invisible and only one-forth visible, and that African Americans should experiment with it in their own settings.[33] And in 1947, after becoming dean of Howard University's School of Religion in 1940, William Stuart Nelson also traveled to the Indian subcontinent and discussed protest strategies with Gandhi. Following their return to the United States, these African-American theologians further developed Thurman's frame in articles, books, and lectures, illustrating how the Gandhian repertoire contributed to a Christian approach to race relations.[34]

Finally, and most importantly, the African-American theologians' journeys to India set the stage for a new "nonviolent direct action frame". In 1942, one of Thurman's students, James Farmer, decided to translate his mentor's activist Christian discourse into practice. Soon after graduating from Howard University, Farmer drew on his knowledge of the Gandhian repertoire to formulate a detailed plan for challenging American racial segregation, and shared it with his colleagues at the Fellowship of Reconciliation (FOR). Like Thurman, he asserted that existing means of protest – such as those of the NAACP – were inadequate and called for the adaptation of Gandhian methods to conditions in the United States:

> Certain societal and cultural differences between the United States and India, and certain basic differences between the problems to be dealt with in the two countries, militate strongly against an uncritical duplication of the Gandhian steps in organization and execution. The American race problem is in many ways distinctive, and must to that extent be dealt with in a distinctive manner. Using Gandhism as a base, our approach must be creative in order to be effectual.[35]

Like Thurman (as well as Mays, Tobias, and Nelson), moreover, Farmer argued that the only way to reach the African-American masses was through the "The Negro Church".[36] Guided by classic works on Gandhi's methods like Richard Gregg's *The Power of Nonviolence* (Philadelphia,

33. CWMG, vol. 70, pp. 261–264, 269; Benjamin Mays, *Born to Rebel* (New York, 1971), pp. 155–157.
34. *Idem*, "The Color Line Around the World", *Journal of Negro Education*, 6 (1937), pp. 134–143; Lawrence Edward Carter, Sr (ed.), *Walking Integrity: Benjamin Mays, Mentor to Martin Luther King, Jr* (Macon, GA, 1998); William Stuart Nelson (ed.), *The Christian Way in Race Relations* (New York, 1948); William Stuart Nelson, "Satyagraha: Gandhian Principles of Non-Violent Non-Cooperation", *Journal of Religious Thought*, Autumn–Winter (1957–1958), pp. 15–24; Keith D. Miller, *Voice of Deliverance: The Language of Martin Luther King, Jr and Its Sources* (New York, 1992); Chabot, "Crossing the Great Divide", pp. 115, 132.
35. James Farmer, *Lay Bare the Heart: An Autobiography of the Civil Rights Movement* (Fort Worth, TX, 1985), p. 356.
36. *Ibid.*, p. 359.

PA, 1934) and Krishnalal Shridharani's *War Without Violence* (New York, 1939), he and his pacifist friends in Chicago then employed a nonviolent direct action frame to organize and mobilize the first Gandhian campaigns in the United States. These campaigns, co-sponsored by the FOR, subsequently inspired activists in other parts of the country to initiate their own Gandhian campaigns and led to the foundation of the Congress of Racial Equality (CORE) in 1942, with Farmer as president.[37] Thurman's interpretation of the Gandhian repertoire thus not only influenced other African-American theologians in his critical community, but eventually also prepared the soil for small-scale and experimental applications of Gandhian nonviolent direct action in American communities.

Bayard Rustin, nonviolent direct action, and the civil rights movement

Farmer was not the only African-American framing specialist involved in CORE. Bayard Rustin, a fellow organizer of the religious-pacifist FOR, was also a prominent strategist and participant of the first explicitly Gandhian protest organization in the United States. Like Farmer, he spent most of the 1940s leading workshops on nonviolence throughout the country and applying the Gandhian repertoire to fight racial segregation.[38] During World War II, he took part in CORE's "sit-ins" against the discriminatory practices of Northern restaurants and, in 1947, he helped initiate the Journey of Reconciliation to test federal laws on interstate public transportation in the American South.[39]

But as the Cold War began heating up at the end of the decade, the nonviolent direct-action frame developed and implemented by Farmer, Rustin, and other leaders could no longer motivate CORE groups into confrontational Gandhian campaigns. In a domestic climate averse to any type of radicalism, most supporters of African-American civil rights preferred to engage in more moderate forms of protest, like those promoted by the NAACP.[40] Faced with an inhospitable environment at home, and inspired by the experiences of Thurman, Mays, and Nelson, Rustin decided to continue his study of the Gandhian repertoire in India.

37. August Meier and Elliott Rudwick, *CORE: A Study in the Civil Rights Movement, 1942–1968* (New York, 1973).
38. Rustin's career as a peace activist started in 1937, when he joined the Emergency Peace Campaign to prevent a new world war. During the orientation sessions Rustin first met Muriel Lester, a fellow Quaker and the British ambassador for the International Fellowship of Reconciliation, and from then on he devoted himself to pacifism and racial justice. Unlike Farmer, Rustin was involved in a wide variety of protest groups and social causes, both American and international ones; Jervis Anderson, *Bayard Rustin: Troubles I've Seen* (New York, 1997), pp. 40–68.
39. *Ibid.*, pp. 113–124.
40. Meier and Rudwick, *CORE*.

When Rustin arrived in Delhi at the end of 1948, Gandhi was no longer alive. Yet many veterans of the Salt March and other Gandhian events were still around, eager to discuss the Indian leader's legacy. Accompanied by Muriel Lester, FOR's international ambassador and a long-time supporter of Indian independence, Rustin first met Devadas, the son of Gandhi. Then he attended the All-India Congress Party convention and talked with Prime Minister Jawaharlal Nehru and Deputy Prime Minister Sardar Patel, who shared their perspectives on Gandhi's contributions. And after leaving Delhi, he came in contact with various young Gandhian intellectuals, engaging in heated debates about nonviolent direct action principles and strategies. One of them, Devi Prasad, later noted that:

> He met us and gave us some idea of what was going on in the world of nonviolence in the United States. He sang spirituals that won everybody's heart. The Martin Luther King phenomenon had not yet started, but we got a very profound impression that Bayard was doing Gandhi's work in North America.[41]

Prasad and other native Gandhians also appreciated the fact that, during his tour of the country, Rustin adopted Indian customs and wore Gandhian clothing.[42]

Rustin's interactions with local intellectuals and activists were quite different from those of his predecessors. While Thurman, Mays, Tobias, and Nelson had visited India at the height of Gandhi's influence, Rustin came after the country had gained national independence and Gandhi had passed away. With Nehru and the Indian National Congress party in power, the Gandhian repertoire was no longer considered a practical means for achieving social or political change. Unlike the African-American theologians, therefore, Rustin was actually quite negative about the prospects for effective nonviolent direct action in India, although he admired the commitment of Gandhian youth groups. Ironically, Indian intellectuals and activists like Devi Prasad now felt that the American environment for sustained Gandhian campaigns was more favorable than their own.[43]

After coming back, Rustin became widely known as one of the foremost experts on the Gandhian repertoire in the United States. Some pacifist friends even started calling him "Rustiji", just as Indian activists had referred to their leader as "Gandhiji". During the early 1950s, he applied the nonviolent direct-action frame to various domestic and international causes. He joined the Peacemakers, a group opposing the American development of nuclear weapons and preparations for war. He traveled to Africa to express his support of African independence movements. And in 1953, after leaving the FOR, he became executive secretary of the War

41. Anderson, *Bayard Rustin*, p. 131.
42. *Ibid.*, p. 132.
43. *Ibid.*, p. 134.

Resisters' League (WRL).[44] But by far his most significant contribution to the interpretation and application of the Gandhian repertoire began in 1956, as the strategic advisor of King and the Montgomery bus boycott.

Impressed by the nonviolent spirit of the African-American community in Montgomery, Rustin introduced himself to King and started working for the Montgomery Improvement Association (MIA) in February 1956.[45] MIA leaders, in turn, recognized the expertise of Rustin and began taking the strategic implications of the Gandhian repertoire more seriously. They learned how to use familiar Christian language to communicate fundamental Gandhian principles to their constituency. They agreed to use positive terms like "bus protest" instead of "bus boycott," which implied an illegal restraint of the local economy. And King himself relied on Rustin to write many of the texts that helped establish his reputation as a proponent of Gandhian methods and a prophet of nonviolence. Rustin drafted "Our Struggle" for the April 1956 issue of the journal *Liberation* and helped revise *Stride Toward Freedom*, King's autobiographical account of the Montgomery bus boycott.[46]

One of the main lessons Rustin had learned in India was that the impact of sporadic symbolic nonviolent protest tended to be limited. Following the Montgomery bus boycott, therefore, Rustin thought of ways to expand a single Gandhian campaign into a sustained *social movement* for ending the system of racial segregation in the South. In 1957, he helped create the Southern Christian Leadership Council (SCLC), persuaded King to become its leader, and developed a suitable frame for guiding the civil rights movement in the South. Drafted by Rustin, the SLCL's statement of purpose outlines the main elements of the Gandhian "civil rights movement frame":

> SCLC activity revolves around two main focal points: the use of nonviolent philosophy as a means of creative protest; and securing the rights of the ballot for every citizen [...]. The basic tenets of Hebraic-Christian tradition coupled with the Gandhian concept of *satyagraha* – truth force – is at the heart of SCLC's philosophy [...]. SCLC believes that the American dilemma in race relations can best and most quickly be resolved through the action of thousands of people, committed to the philosophy of nonviolence, who will physically identify themselves in a just and moral struggle [...]. SCLC sees civil disobedience as a natural consequence of nonviolence when the resister is confronted by unjust and immoral laws.[47]

Besides identifying the appropriate means, it also highlighted the main end

44. *Ibid.*, chs 8, 9, and 11.
45. Miller, *Voice of Deliverance*, pp. 95–96.
46. Anderson, *Bayard Rustin*, pp. 194, 209.
47. Francis L. Broderick and August Meier (eds), *Negro Protest Thought in the Twentieth Century* (Indianapolis, IN, 1965), pp. 269–273.

of the African-American freedom struggle: "The ultimate aim of SCLC is to foster and create the "beloved community" in America where brotherhood is a reality [...]. Our ultimate goal is genuine intergroup and interpersonal living – *integration*. Only through nonviolence can reconciliation and the creation of the beloved community be effected."[48] Although King would receive most of the credit, Rustin's role in formulating the original civil rights movement frame – and translating it into organized collective action – was no less crucial.

James Lawson, student activists, and the civil rights movement

Among the many students Rustin encountered in his nonviolent workshops during the 1940s was James Lawson, a radical African-American pacifist.[49] Lawson first learned about the Indian independence movement from reports in African-American newspapers like the *Pittsburgh Courier*, from sermons and essays by African-American theologians like Thurman and Mays, and from books by and about Gandhi.[50] Yet it was Rustin who taught him how to translate these inspiring ideas into action. During the Korean War, Lawson served a year in federal prison as a conscientious objector and, in 1953, he opted to complete his term as a fraternal worker in India.[51]

During his three years on the Indian subcontinent, Lawson worked for the Methodist Church as a teacher at Hislop College in Nagpur. In his free time, though, he tried to learn as much as possible about the Gandhian repertoire and its implications. Besides discussing the independence movement with local students, he talked and interacted with prominent Gandhians such as Vinoba Bhave, now the country's primary symbol of nonviolence; J.C. Kumarappa, the famous Gandhian economist; and Asha Devi, one of the more militant Gandhian activists since 1947. He also participated in various conferences, workshops, and seminars held by Serva Seva Sangh, the nationwide organization devoted to continuing Gandhi's efforts.[52]

---

48. Broderick and Meier, *Negro Protest Thought*, pp. 272–273.
49. Lawson, son of an African-American Methodist minister, became a radical pacifist during his college years, after an encounter with FOR leader, A.J. Muste. As a university student, moreover, he read Gandhi's autobiography and became convinced that a Gandhian-Christian form of nonviolence was the best way of applying the New Testament in everyday life; Kapur, *Raising Up a Prophet*, p. 155.
50. James Lawson, videotaped interview by Steve York for the documentary *A Force More Powerful*, Los Angeles, 26 October 1998.
51. Kapur, *Raising Up a Prophet*, p. 155; Taylor Branch, *Parting the Waters: America in the King Years 1954–63* (New York, 1988), p. 143; David Halberstam, *The Children* (New York, 1998), pp. 12, 47–49.
52. Kapur, *Raising Up a Prophet*, p. 155.

Lawson derived two important insights from his experiences in postcolonial India. First of all, he realized that young students (like those at Hislop College) were more likely to engage in the kind of radical action required for achieving significant social change than well-known symbolic leaders (like Vinoba Bhave). And secondly, he observed that decentralized and "group-oriented" organizations encouraged the repressed community *to help itself*, while centralized and "leader-oriented" organizations tended to act *in name of* the subordinated population. So when Lawson read about the Montgomery bus boycott in the *Nagpur Times*, he was impressed by the eloquence and influence of Martin Luther King, Jr, but also eager to expand the involvement of African-American students and other Southern communities.[53]

In 1957, after returning to the United States, Lawson met King at Oberlin College in Ohio and, inspired by their conversation, decided to work as the FOR's secretary of race relations in the South.[54] He settled in Nashville, Tennessee and became Chairperson of Direct Action of the Nashville Christian Leadership Council (NCLC), the SCLC's local branch. In 1958, he began organizing a series of community workshops on local forms of racial segregation and the power of nonviolent direct action. Most of the participants in these gatherings were students at African-American universities and members of African-American churches in Nashville. Initially, they just discussed the history of nonviolence, the responsibility of Christians, and the implications of Gandhian methods. After several months, however, they decided to test their knowledge in practice by experimenting with ways to desegregate the restaurants in downtown Nashville. Eventually, these talking sessions and preliminary efforts set the stage for Nashville's sit-in movement.[55]

In February 1960, when students in Nashville joined the wave of sit-ins spreading across the South, they used Lawson's framing of the Gandhian

53. Lawson was not the only one to read about the Montgomery bus boycott in the Indian press. The mainstream newspaper *Hindustan Times*, for example, regularly published articles on what it called "Mass 'Gandhi-Type' Protest in Alabama" (Saturday, 3 March 1956, p. 5; see also *Hindustan Times*, Sunday, 23 December 1956, p. 7). Indian activists who continued to organize nonviolent direct action campaigns after Gandhi's death in 1948, moreover, were inspired by the successful application of Gandhian methods during the African-American civil rights movement. Ram Manohar Lohia, for instance, came to the United States in 1964 to meet with SNCC students involved in the Freedom Summer campaign in Mississippi. Although his main purpose was to teach Gandhian strategy to young civil rights activists, Lohia also sought motivation for further activism at home; Edwin King, "Lohia and the American Civil Rights Movement", *Gandhi Marg*, 59 (1971), pp. 270–277. I leave the theoretical implications of such "cross-fertilization" for future work.
54. Lawson, York interview; Halberstam, *The Children*, pp. 16–17.
55. *Ibid.*, pp. 90–92; John Lewis (with Michael D'Orso), *Walking with the Wind: A Memoir of the Movement* (New York, 1998), p. 86.

repertoire to guide their campaign.[56] Leading student activists like John Lewis, Diane Nash, James Bevel, and Bernard Lafayette faithfully implemented the rules of nonviolent direct action they had learned during his workshops. As Lewis describes in his autobiography, the night before the first sit-ins he and Lafayette drafted a code of behavior, based on the Gandhian principles emphasized by Lawson:

DO NOT:
    1. Strike back nor curse if abused.
    2. Laugh out.
    3. Hold conversations with floor walker.
    4. Leave your seat until your leader has given you permission to do so.
    5. Block entrances to stores outside nor the aisles inside.

DO:
    1. Show yourself friendly and courteous at all times.
    2. Sit straight; always face the counter.
    3. Report all serious incidents to your leader.
    4. Refer information seekers to your leader in a polite manner.
    5. Remember the teachings of Jesus Christ, Mahatma Gandhi, and Martin Luther King. Love and nonviolence is the way.[57]

And in their interactions with the authorities, student activists employed the same Christian-Gandhian language as Lawson. When the local judge offered all those arrested the choice of paying a $50 fine or serving thirty days in jail, Nash answered: "We feel that if we pay these fines, we would be contributing to and supporting the injustice and immoral practices that have been performed in the arrest and conviction of the defendants."[58]

Instead of relying on the decisions of one dominant leader, moreover, they tried to reach consensus collectively and appointed different leaders for each event. And rather than merely representing the repressed minority in Nashville, they initiated an economic boycott of all downtown stores that directly involved the entire African-American community.[59] In short, the student activists adopted each of Lawson's fundamental ideas about how to engage in Gandhian protest: express love in word and deed, "group-oriented" leadership, decentralized organizational style, and inclusion of the aggrieved population as a whole.

The influence of Lawson's civil-rights-movement frame was not limited to Nashville. In April 1960, delegates of sit-in groups throughout the South held a conference in Raleigh, North Carolina, and founded the

56. Aldon D. Morris, "Black Southern Sit-in Movement: An Analysis of Internal Organization", *American Sociological Review*, 38 (1981), pp. 744–767; Clayborne Carson, *In Struggle: SNCC and the Black Awakening of the 1960s* (Cambridge, 1981); Lewis, *Walking with the Wind*.
57. Lewis, *Walking with the Wind*, p. 98.
58. *Ibid.*, p. 103.
59. *Ibid.*, pp. 105–106.

Student Nonviolent Coordinating Committee (SNCC). As a keynote speaker at the meeting, Lawson criticized traditional civil rights leaders (particularly those belonging to the NAACP) for concentrating on "fundraising and court action rather than developing our greatest resource, a people no longer the victims of racial evil who can act in a disciplined manner to implement the constitution".[60] In the same speech, he identified the main goals of the sit-in movement: first of all, to make clear that racial segregation and prejudice is morally reprehensible; secondly, to assert that the current pace of social change and civil rights protest was too slow.[61] He also drafted the SNCC's statement of purpose, highlighting the need for nonviolent means of collective action and expressing Gandhian principles in familiar Christian terms.[62] And finally, Lawson encouraged the SNCC to adopt a policy of rotating leadership, to make collective decisions by consensus, and to focus as much on community development in the rural South as on symbolic protest and national exposure.[63] By stimulating student activists to develop their own style of Gandhian protest and organization (which differed considerably from the "leader-oriented" style promoted by Rustin, King, and the SCLC), he helped the SNCC to become the most radical and innovative wing of the civil rights movement during the early 1960s.

THEORETICAL IMPLICATIONS AND SUGGESTIONS FOR FUTURE RESEARCH

The preceding discussion of African-American itinerants and their influence at home does not tell the whole story. It does not account for the role of Indian intellectuals in the United States, for example, or for the contribution of Euro-American intellectuals. It neither considers crossfertilization of ideas and practices, nor relationships with sympathetic American groups, although both processes helped shape how the framing and transnational diffusion of the Gandhian repertoire evolved.[64] And it does not pay much attention to the fact that both transmitters and receivers spoke the same language (which was, of course, the language of their respective oppressors). A comprehensive analysis would certainly have to incorporate such complex dynamics and relate specific empirical findings to social mechanisms like brokerage and appropriation.[65] This article is

---

60. Broderick and Meier, *Negro Protest Thought*, p. 280.
61. *Ibid.*, pp. 278–279.
62. *Ibid.*, pp. 273–274.
63. Carson, In Struggle; Charles M. Payne, *I've Got the Light of Freedom: The Organizing Tradition and the Mississippi Freedom Struggle* (Berkeley, CA, 1995).
64. For more on these subjects, see Chabot, *Crossing the Great Divide.*
65. McAdam, Tarrow, and Tilly, *Dynamics of Contention.*

merely a first step toward a more general explanation of framing protest and transnational diffusion between social movements.

But while they provide just a glimpse of the underlying processes, the three moments of interaction between African-American intellectuals and Gandhians in India were clearly crucial for the framing and transnational diffusion of the Gandhian repertoire. These encounters contributed directly to the interpretive tasks, alignment processes, and conditions for dissemination emphasized in the social movement literature.

The initial journeys of Thurman, Mays, and Tobias at the end of the 1930s (and of Nelson in 1947) enabled the development of a Christian liberation theology frame, which offered a new diagnosis of American racial relations and a new prognosis for improving them. This frame not only transformed religious discourse, but also motivated Farmer and other young activists to engage in small-scale nonviolent direct action and, in 1942, found CORE on the basis of the Gandhian repertoire.

In 1949, CORE's Rustin decided to embark on the same pilgrimage as the African-American theologians. During his stay in India, he learned that Gandhi's ideas and practices were most effective in the context of a social movement. When the opportunity arose, therefore, he helped King and other Southern ministers create a Gandhian frame for guiding the American civil rights movement – with its own diagnoses, prognoses, and motivations for transforming the racial status quo. The successful application of this new frame in Montgomery symbolized the completion of the Gandhian repertoire's diffusion from India to the United States.

Meanwhile, Lawson lived in India, serving his sentence for conscientious objection during the Korean War. After coming back in 1956, he began preparing inexperienced students in Nashville for militant sit-in campaigns, thereby extending the civil rights movement frame formulated by Rustin and popularized by King. In the early 1960s, the diagnoses, prognoses, and motivations characterizing Lawson's frame underpinned the SNCC and allowed the civil rights movement to expand its application of the Gandhian repertoire.

The significance of these three moments grew as the African-American intellectuals who traveled to India, and the activists they influenced, forged close ties with each other. Farmer was a student of Thurman and Mays; Rustin was a colleague of Farmer; and Lawson, who had participated in Rustin's workshops, shared his knowledge and experience with Lewis, Nash, Bevel, Lafayette, and other students involved in the sit-ins.[66] These African-American intellectuals and activists established their own linkages with King and the civil rights movement. Mays and Thurman (and, to a

66. These interpersonal ties were only the tip of the iceberg. Rustin and Farmer, for instance, shared the stage with Nelson and Tobias at a conference on the role of nonviolence for African-American protest in 1943. See John H. Bracey, Jr and August Meier (eds), *The Papers of A. Philip Randolph* (Bethesda, MD, 1990); Miller, *Voice of Deliverance*.

lesser extent, Nelson and Tobias) became King's mentors. Rustin served as strategic advisor of King and the SCLC, while Farmer was an important role model. Lawson was both an admirer of King and his peer. Like Thurman, Mays, Tobias, Nelson, and Rustin, he encouraged the civil rights movement's leader to continue the African-American tradition of traveling to the land of Gandhi and meeting "real" Gandhians. And finally, the African-American students in Nashville, and later of the SNCC, represented the radical wing of the civil rights movement; they tried to persuade King to support militant rather than moderate forms of nonviolent protest.

The historical evidence demonstrates that pilgrimages to India *before* 1959, and *before* King's rise to prominence, played an essential role in the African-American adoption of the Gandhian repertoire. Neither King's journey nor his interpretations and applications of Gandhi's protest methods would have been possible without the insights and efforts of his predecessors.

But what is the relevance of this single case study for social movement theory on the intersection between framing and transnational diffusion? Or, in other words, how does it help us understand the formulation of "ideas that inspire collective action" *as well as* the "flows of meaning" between local, national, and global fields of contention?

Following the lead of Snow and Benford, the majority of social movement scholars now take framing processes seriously. And inspired by the work of McAdam and Tarrow, among others, cutting-edge students of organized protest have recently started recognizing the relevance of transnational diffusion between activist groups. In this article, I have tried to move the field forward by focusing on several generations of "itinerant intellectuals", and by illustrating how the framing of foreign contentious methods is related to their transnational diffusion. Theoretically, my case study highlights at least four points with broader relevance.

First, social movement scholars usually assume that foreign ideas and practices enter the receiving country through diffusion, after which activists incorporate them into local discourses and strategies through framing. My case study indicates that these two processes are intricately related and, therefore, should not be analyzed separately. On the one hand, adopting the Gandhian repertoire from abroad increased the persuasive power of African-American frames for civil rights protest in the United States. On the other hand, transnational diffusion of the Gandhian repertoire succeeded because of interpretive constructs that stimulated the organization of nonviolent direct action – and eventually a Gandhian social movement – at home.

Second, my case study exemplifies the problematic implications of distinguishing sharply between the "West" and "non-West". It focuses on members of an African-American minority who traveled to India to learn about how to fight for civil rights in the United States. Categorizing such cases as primarily Western *or* non-Western does not make sense, because actors and processes in the core of the world system were inextricably related to actors and processes in the periphery, and vice versa. This does not mean that we should avoid analyzing cultural, political, economic, and social differences among groups, countries, or regions. I do suggest, however, that we should particularly stress the importance of framing for transnational diffusion when the differences between transmitters and receivers are apparent (as they were between Indian and African-American intellectuals). Historically, such cases are exceptional yet highly significant: although ideas and practices are *more likely* to spread between similar social movements and contexts, *truly innovative* ideas and practices often come from divergent social movements and contexts.

Third, this case study specifies who plays an important role in framing and transnational diffusion. It highlights three types of itinerant intellectuals that visited the country of origin, each with a unique relationship to the receiving social movement. The initial group of African-American travelers to India consisted of established theologians, who subsequently became *mentors* to movement leaders. Thurman, Mays, Tobias, and Nelson influenced King and other prominent figures in the civil rights movement, without participating in the protest campaigns themselves. Rustin was another type of itinerant intellectual: after returning to the United States, he served as an *advisor* to King and other leaders from within the civil rights movement (although from behind the scenes). And following his three years in India, Lawson evolved into an important *peer* of visible movement leaders like King. He helped found the SNCC, a movement organization that promoted and applied more radical forms of Gandhian action than dominant individuals or groups within the civil rights movement. My case study suggests that these three types of itinerant intellectuals – mentors, advisors, and peers – are crucial for translating intellectual insights from foreign expeditions into collective action with strong domestic roots. They are the "rooted cosmopolitans" that allow repressed groups to think globally and act locally.[67]

My case study's fourth theoretical point is that each type of itinerant intellectual has a distinct effect on the interpretation of foreign protest methods at home. African-American theologians (who served as King's mentors during the 1950s and 1960s) emphasized the relevance of the Gandhian repertoire for Christian *discourse* in the United States, while Farmer and fellow CORE activists used the Gandhian repertoire to engage in nonviolent direct *action*. Rustin, moreover, invoked Gandhi's ideas and

---

67. Sidney Tarrow, "Rooted Cosmopolitans: Transnational Activists in a World of States", paper presented at Amsterdam School for Social Science Research seminar, University of Amsterdam, 6 May 2003.

practices to develop a *leader-oriented* civil rights movement frame that suited his role as advisor to King. And, as a peer of King, Lawson employed similar ideas and practices to formulate an alternative, *group-oriented* civil rights movement frame. The relationship between these frames was always tense and fluid. Religious discourse sometimes encouraged and other times discouraged radical action. "Leader-oriented" activists sometimes cooperated and other times disagreed with "group-oriented" activists. Thus, African-American intellectuals interpreted and applied the Gandhian repertoire in diverse ways; they did not adopt it to develop a uniform "master frame".[68]

Thought provoking as these theoretical arguments may be, they remain hypothetical. The question remains, for example, whether my approach applies only to transnational diffusion between *different* transmitters and receivers, or also to transnational diffusion between *similar* ones. To evaluate the validity and scope of my conceptual framework, social movement scholars need to apply it to numerous other empirical situations. In closing, therefore, let me just point to one historical and one contemporary case in which itinerant intellectuals figured (and continue to figure) prominently. I hope that fellow *IRSH* authors and students of contentious politics will join me in analyzing these and other cases in greater depth, and help me set the stage for a more general theory of framing protest and transnational diffusion between social movements.

The international women's movement of the late nineteenth and early twentieth century is an obvious historical example of activism beyond borders.[69] Leila Rupp, for instance, describes how female activists from Europe and North America traveled across continents to attend meetings and conferences.[70] These interpersonal encounters shaped the construction of an international collective identity and persuaded increasing numbers of women to fight for civil rights, world peace, and economic justice. At the time, though, these transnational networks consisted almost exclusively of Western women with similar, middle-class backgrounds. My approach could add new insights into this form of "traveling feminism" by focusing directly on the framing-diffusion nexus, highlighting linkages between different transmitters and receivers (from within as well as outside the West), distinguishing among various types of itinerant intellectuals, and specifying the latter's influence on the production of meaning at home.[71]

68. David A. Snow and Robert D. Benford, "Master Frames and Cycles of Protest", in Aldon M. Morris and Carol M. Mueller (eds), *Frontiers in Social Movement Theory* (New Haven, CT, 1992), pp. 133–155.
69. Margaret Keck and Kathryn Sikkink, *Activists beyond Borders: Transnational Activists in International Politics* (Ithaca, NY, 1998).
70. Leila J. Rupp, "Constructing Internationalism: The Case of Transnational Women's Organizations, 1888–1945", *The American Historical Review*, 99 (1994), pp. 1571–1600.
71. For more on the international women's movement of this era, see e.g., Richard J. Evans, *The Feminists: Women's Emancipation Movements in Europe, America and Australasia 1840–1920*

My theoretical framework should also apply to contemporary movements in which itinerant intellectuals clearly play a prominent role, such as the so-called Global Justice Movements (GJMs). Most researchers assume that the main framing specialists and activist networks in the GJMs – the struggles against corporate globalization that first reached a wide audience during the Battle of Seattle in 1999 and continue to challenge international capitalist institutions today – are located in the United States and Europe.[72] Like the editors of this *IRSH* supplement, I seek to develop a more balanced perspective by paying particular attention to the influence of contentious ideas and practices originating in Asia, Africa, or South America. To what extent, for example, have American activists in the GJMs witnessed and learned from the innovative protest methods of their colleagues in the Brazilian landless movement (known as the MST)?[73] By exploring the specific contributions of various itinerant intellectuals, social movement scholars should learn more about whether (and how) transnational flows of meaning involve *cross-fertilization* between non-Western and Western groups. As African-American intellectuals before and during the civil rights movement realized, creative framing can overcome the obstacles involved in transnational diffusion between social movements – even if the political, social, economic, and cultural gaps between transmitters and receivers are vast.

(London, 1977), pp. 247–248; Bob Reinalda and Natascha Verhaaren, *Vrouwenbeweging en Internationale Organisaties 1868–1986* (Nijmegen, 1989); and Edith F. Hurwitz, "The International Sisterhood," in Renate Bridenthal and Claudia Koonz (eds), *Becoming Visible: Women in European History* (Boston, MA, 1977). For research on transnational advocacy networks among contemporary feminists outside of the West, see Millie Thayer, "Traveling Feminisms: From Embodied Women to Gendered Citizenship", in Michael Burawoy *et al.* (eds), *Global Ethnography: Forces, Connections, and Imaginations in a Postmodern World* (Berkeley, CA, 2000), pp. 203–233.

72. See e.g. Jackie Smith, "Globalizing Resistance: The Battle of Seattle and the Future of Social Movements", in Jackie Smith and Hank Johnston (eds), *Globalization and Resistance: Transnational Dimensions of Social Movements* (Lanham, MD, 2002), pp. 207–228; Tarrow, "Rooted Cosmopolitans"; Nick Crossley, "Global Anti-Corporate Struggle: A Preliminary Analysis", *British Journal of Sociology*, 53 (2002), pp. 667–691.

73. Sue Branford and Jan Rocha, *Cutting the Wire: The Struggle of the Landless Movement in Brazil* (London, 2002).

IRSH 49 (2004), Supplement, pp. 41–64 DOI: 10.1017/S0020859004001634
© 2004 Internationaal Instituut voor Sociale Geschiedenis

Indigenous Communists and Urban Intellectuals in Cayambe, Ecuador (1926–1944)*

MARC BECKER

SUMMARY: This case study provides an example of how people from two fundamentally different cultures (one rural, indigenous, Kichua-speaking and peasant, and the other urban, white, Spanish-speaking and professional) overcame their differences to struggle together to fight social injustices. Rather than relating to each other on a seemingly unequal basis, the activists recognized their common interests in fighting against the imposition of an international capitalist system on Ecuador's agrarian economy. Emerging out of that context, activists framed collective interests, identities, ideas, and demands as they worked together to realize common goals. Their actions challenge commonly held assumptions that leftist activists did not understand indigenous struggles, or that indigenous peoples remained distant from the goals of leftist political parties. Rather, it points to how the two struggles became intimately intertwined. In the process, it complicates traditional understandings of the role of "popular intellectuals", and how they interact with other activists, the dominant culture, and the state.

In May 1926, Jesús Gualavisí, an indigenous leader representing the Sindicato de Trabajadores Campesinos de Cayambe (Peasant Workers' Syndicate of Cayambe), traveled to the Ecuadorian highland capital city of Quito to participate as a delegate in the founding of the Partido Socialista Ecuatoriano (PSE, Ecuadorian Socialist Party). At the first session of the congress, Gualavisí proposed "that the assembly salute all peasants in the Republic, indicating to them that the Party would work intensely on their behalf".[1] When the assembly drafted its final resolutions, Ricardo Paredes, the General Secretary of the new party, proposed that they should include

* This essay is based primarily on research in the Fondo Junta Central de Asistencia Pública (JCAP) of the Archivo Nacional de Medicina del Museo Nacional de Medicina "Dr Eduardo Estrella", in Quito, Ecuador. Special thanks go to Antonio Crespo for facilitating access to that collection of government documents. Sandra Fernández Muñoz and Jorge Canizares lent access to the private collection of Leonardo J. Muñoz, an early leftist leader, which provides a counterpart to the JCAP documents. Additional primary-source documentation of this history is from Quito's main daily newspaper, *El Comercio*, and the Biblioteca Ecuatoriana Aurelio Espinosa Pólit [hereafter BEAEP] in Cotocollao, Ecuador.
1. Partido Socialista Ecuatoriano (PSE), *Labores de la Asamblea Nacional Socialista y Manifiesto del Consejo Central del Partido (16–23 May), Quito, 1926* (Guayaquil, 1926), p. 33.

Figure 1. Ecuador.

a statement of support for Gualavisí's struggle in Cayambe against
landlord abuses. Paredes, a white medical doctor from Quito, justified
this resolution, stating that a fundamental demand of the new party was to
work for "the redemption of the Indian".[2]

These two resolutions, both of which the delegates accepted, represented the beginning of a decades-long collaboration between Gualavisí
and Paredes that reached a climax in 1944 when together they helped

2. *Ibid.*, p. 74.

found Ecuador's first indigenous-rights organization, the Federación Ecuatoriana de Indios (FEI, Ecuadorian Federation of Indians). Notably, the PSE was the first party in Ecuador to organize indigenous peoples as a political force. This was a radical departure from the actions of other parties which, as Marxist historian, Oswaldo Albornoz, noted, "never took Indians into account for anything, much less made them leaders, because they were considered to be inferior beings".[3] It was not until after illiterate people in Ecuador gained the right to vote in 1979, enfranchizing most indigenous peoples for the first time, that bourgeois parties began to court rural communities in their electoral strategies. Gualavisí's role as the first indigenous person to participate in a political party's congress in Ecuador helped set the stage for subsequent relations between rural communities and urban leftist activists. He helped merge indigenous social movements into a broader struggle for liberation, articulating dissent and building collaborative efforts with leftist urban intellectuals.

Gualavisí was what Steven Feierman justifiably would term a peasant intellectual. Feierman argues that such intellectuals gained the prestige and legitimacy necessary to shape discourse, define political language, and construct a peasant class-consciousness.[4] He was careful to note that in his definition a "peasant intellectual" is a social construct, referring to a person who gains legitimacy and a leadership role within a specific culture rather than through the importation of ideologies and initiatives from the outside. Feierman rejected the notion that peasants need to rely on a revolutionary vanguard to break out of a dominant culture's hegemonic influence. He challenged the interpretations of Marxists, including Gramsci, who viewed peasants as inert and requiring leadership from other classes to be effective actors. Speaking about the Italian peasantry in the first half of the twentieth century, Antonio Gramsci believed the peasantry was incapable of producing its own leaders and would remain dependent upon the urban working class organized into a communist party to articulate its dissent. As Kate Crehan notes, however, one must be careful in applying those views to other areas and situations "with possibly very different configurations of power".[5] Feierman observed that the peasantry in colonial Tanzania "did not need the leadership of the working class or of a Communist Party to create a dissenting discourse. It was the energy of the peasantry, which emerged locally but then merged with a nationalist party, which made

3. Oswaldo Albornoz Peralta, "Jesús Gualavisí y las luchas indígenas en el Ecuador", in Domingo Paredes (ed.), *Los comunistas en la historia nacional* (Guayaquil, 1987), pp. 155–188, 185.

4. Steven Feierman, *Peasant Intellectuals: Anthropology and History in Tanzania* (Madison, WI, 1990), p. 4.

5. Antonio Gramsci, *Selections from the Prison Notebooks*, tr. and ed. by Quintin Hoare and Geoffrey Nowell Smith (New York, 1971), p. 6; Kate A.F. Crehan, *Gramsci, Culture and Anthropology* (Berkeley, CA, 2002), pp. 124 and 143–145.

possible the end of colonial rule." He found peasant intellectuals who "were capable of creating their own counter-discourse". He called for a shift in the analytic approach in order to place "peasant intellectuals at the nexus between domination and public discourse".[6]

Ecuador provides a contrasting case study of how popular intellectuals can interact with outside forces. Active in organizing local community organizations, while at the same time participating in the formation of a national political party, Gualavisí provided a bridge between two dramatically different worlds. Dating back to the colonial period in Latin America, a profound cultural and racial divide excluded Indians from positions of power in their own lands. Urban areas, such as Ecuador's capital city of Quito, became poles of economic and political power for a white upper class that grew wealthy off the labor of indigenous peons on landed estates (called haciendas) in rural areas. To be Indian was to be rural and engaged in agricultural labor. This rural/urban, Indian/white divide replicated itself through language (Kichua/Spanish), education (only for white children), dress, food, religion, and other factors that traditional ethnographies have used to mark Indians as the "other".

Notably, however, influences did not flow across this bridge in only one direction. Rather than merely importing outside ideologies or merging a local organization with a national movement, Gualavisí facilitated cross-pollination, as the local and national emerged simultaneously in a struggle for liberation. The seemingly insurmountable class, ethnic, and geographic barriers make any collaboration between these two very different worlds truly remarkable. It is a reflection of the political concerns of popular intellectuals that they were able to frame their protests in such a manner that it would unify their social movements around common interests and concerns.

Although indigenous peoples had long utilized the legal mechanisms of state structures to present their demands to the government, their petitions lacked a direct voice. Mostly illiterate, they depended on local white or *mestizo* scribes (usually called *tinterillos*) who offered their Spanish-language skills and educational training to draft legal petitions and provide related services. Michiel Baud described *tinterillos* as "a group which was frequently vilified both by politicians and landowners, because they were supposed to stir up the credulous Indian peasants".[7] *Tinterillos* had a long history of negotiating relationships between indigenous peoples and the government, leading the Minister of Social Welfare to complain about the

6. Feierman, *Peasant Intellectuals*, pp. 19–20, 5.

7. Beate R. Salz, "The Human Element in Industrialization: A Hypothetical Case Study of Ecuadorean Indians", *American Anthropologist*, 57:6, pt 2, Memoir no. 85 (December 1955), p. 133; Michiel Baud, "Liberal Ideology, Indigenismo and Social Mobilization in Late Nineteenth-Century Ecuador", in A. Kim Clark and Marc Becker (eds), *Highland Indians and the State in Modern Ecuador* (forthcoming).

"tendency to litigation so characteristic of our rural folk".[8] Indigenous peoples contracted their services to record their demands in the proper format and on the legal paper which the government required, but these scribes were rarely involved in the political project of the petitioners. Rather, subalterns relied, as Andrés Guerrero noted, on others to construct "a 'ventriloquist's' political representation which became a channel for Indian resistance".[9]

The *tinterillos'* petitions probably do not represent a verbatim transcription of an illiterate worker's words. In highland Ecuador, the Indians' first language was Kichua; the *tinterillos* undoubtedly saw it as part of their mandate to polish the "uneducated" peasant's wording so it would be more presentable to an educated, urban audience. In the process, it would be hard for the *tinterillos'* own stereotypes and assumptions not to emerge in these petitions. In the Andean world, where identity is overwhelmingly local, and in a political situation where the Indians were not citizens, it is questionable whether hacienda workers would use language such as *infelices ecuatorianos* (miserable Ecuadorians) that commonly emerged in the petitions. Surrounded with family and rooted in a proud cultural tradition, would they see themselves as miserable, or as Ecuadorians for that matter, or was this just a ploy to gain the sympathy of governmental officials who articulated a theoretically inclusive liberal ideology? The resulting documents lacked a penetrating critique of indigenous exclusion and exploitation.

The absence of a direct voice encouraged Indians to search out new allies who could help them articulate a shared vision of the world. Popular intellectuals subsequently assumed a key role in formulating alliances that would place indigenous peoples and their interests at the center of debates on the shaping of Ecuador's future.

FRAMING RURAL SOCIALISMS

Jesús Gualavisí, born in 1867 on the Changalá hacienda in Cayambe in northern Ecuador, organized the Sindicato de Trabajadores Campesinos de Juan Montalvo (Peasant Workers' Syndicate of Juan Montalvo) in January 1926, as one of Ecuador's first rural syndicates. Unfortunately, very little biographical information remains on his family history. He was one of few literate Indians and was able to bridge the rural and urban worlds, which would seem to indicate that his family enjoyed a certain

8. Carlos Andrade Marín, *Informe que el Ministro de Previsión Social y Trabajo presenta a la nación, 1941* (Quito, 1941).
9. Andrés Guerrero, "The Construction of a Ventriloquist's Image: Liberal Discourse and the 'Miserable Indian Race' in Late 19th-Century Ecuador", *Journal of Latin American Studies*, 29 (1997), pp. 555–590, 555.

Figure 2. Jesús Gualavisí (1867–1962). Gualavisí was born on the Changalá hacienda in the parish of Juan Montalvo, where in 1926 he organized the first peasant syndicate in Cayambe. He was the only Indian representative at the founding of the Ecuadorian Socialist Party in 1926, and later was actively involved in communist politics. He helped found the FEI and served as its first president. In 1992, the municipal council of Cayambe commissioned statues of twelve "illustrious personalities" from the canton. Gualavisí was one of those twelve, and his statue stands at the entrance to the city from his home parish of Juan Montalvo.
Photograph by the author, 8 July 2003

amount of prestige and perhaps had traditionally provided leadership to the community. During the nineteenth century, Kichua Indians (now known locally as Kayambis) from surrounding haciendas "who managed to acquire land and a measure of independence" had founded the community of Juan Montalvo on the southern edge of the cantonal capital city of Cayambe. Juan Montalvo (1832–1889) was a famous liberal writer who repeatedly attacked conservative governments, and reportedly claimed to have killed the dictator, Gabriel García Moreno, with his pen.[10] Naming the community after such a personality would foreshadow

10. Elsie Clews Parsons, *Peguche, Canton of Otavalo, Province of Imbabura, Ecuador: A Study of Andean Indians*, University of Chicago Publications in Anthropology, Ethnological Series (Chicago, IL, 1945), p. 183; Frank MacDonald Spindler, *Nineteenth-Century Ecuador: A Historical Introduction* (Fairfax, VA, 1987), p. 89. Organized largely by an illiterate peasantry and in a context of severe repression by surrounding economic and political elites, no organizational archives and little historical documentation of the Juan Montalvo and other rural syndicates from the 1920s and 1930s have survived, if such material ever existed in the first place. Most of what we know about these early indigenous organizations is from governmental or media reports, or statements of sympathetic leftist activists.

the type of political activity in which its inhabitants would subsequently engage.

The immediate context of the formation of the peasant syndicate at Juan Montalvo was a petition from the Kayambis who claimed that the Changalá hacienda had taken over their lands. This hacienda, as with most of the landed estates in the heavily agrarian canton of Cayambe, was in the hands of absentee white landholders and produced a variety of crops (especially barley, wheat, and potatoes) for a local market. These estates often expanded until they covered vast geographic areas. They supplanted many of the ritual and civil functions of the church and state, including providing a space for weddings and baptisms and punishment of crimes. Exploiting poverty and misfortune in surrounding free communities, the haciendas slowly began to bind the Kayambis to the estate through a system of debt peonage known in Ecuador as the *huasipungo* system. In exchange for working on the hacienda, *huasipungueros* received a small wage, access to resources such as water, firewood, and pasture land on the hacienda, and the use of a small garden plot on which they could practice subsistence agriculture. The *huasipungo* system coincided with an erosion of a traditional land base as indigenous peoples were forced out of a peasant and into a wage economy.

When Changalá's owner (Gabriel García Alcázar, son of the nineteenth-century conservative leader, Gabriel García Moreno, who Juan Montalvo had claimed to have killed with his pen) ignored their demands, the Kayambis occupied the disputed land. García Alcázar called on the government to protect what he claimed as his property from "communist and bolshevik attacks". The struggle exploded into a violent conflict in February 1926, when the Pichincha and Carchi battalions from Quito and Ibarra arrived to suppress these land demands. The repression did not end the Kayambis' willingness to fight, and the following November the newspaper reported that a group attacked the police at Changalá shouting "Long Live Socialism".[11]

This call for socialism reflects the emergence of leaders with a knowledge of, and identification with, socialist ideologies. These new ideologies translated into demands that soon extended beyond a defense of traditional land claims and into the economic realm of agitating for better salaries, easier workloads, an end to nonpaid work, and gentler treatment from hacienda owners and their overlords.[12] These demands also reflect the growth of an agrarian capitalism, as modernizing land owners broke with traditional feudal-style reciprocal relations on the haciendas to focus

11. "El dueño de Changalá acude a la junta de gobierno", *El Comercio*, 25 February 1926, p. 1; "La razón y la fuerza", *El Comercio*, 8 March 1926, p. 1; "Se atacó a la policía de Cayambe", *El Comercio*, 6 November 1926, p. 1.
12. Lucía Salamea, "Transformación de la hacienda y los cambios en la condición campesina" (PUCE/CLACSO, Master en Sociología Rural, 1978), p. 52.

on maximizing their profits through the increased exploitation of the labor force. Broader political events, including a 1922 general strike in Guayaquil, a progressive military government that took power in July 1925, and a nascent socialist party, all influenced the development of new ideologies to counter the imposition of an agrarian capitalism.

Looking to expand and solidify support for their new political party, Ricardo Paredes, Luis F. Chávez, and other socialists from Quito came to the defense of the Kayambi struggle against the Changalá hacienda and helped present their demands to the national government. In an open letter to the government, Paredes, as secretary of the Núcleo Central Socialista (Central Socialist Nucleus), a forerunner of the PSE in Quito, called for the nationalization of the lands in question so that they could be returned to their rightful owners. Socialists pointed to the 1926 uprising at Juan Montalvo as the type of struggle against large landlords that peasants and workers should support.[13] "The movement in Cayambe", Paredes wrote in a report to the Communist International on the status of the worker movement in Ecuador, "demonstrated the important revolutionary role of the Indians in Ecuador against the capitalist yoke". For his vocal opposition to governmental policies, the military junta warned him to stay off the Changalá hacienda.[14] Although Gualavisí had participated in local protests before, this was the first time that Kayambis at Juan Montalvo received support from urban leftists or even had any contact with potential allies outside of their home community.

Although Paredes placed himself in a leadership position of rural struggles, these protest movements did not emerge as a paternalistic creation of urban leftist organizing efforts. Rather, both rural and urban activists found themselves confronting a similar economic situation, which led them to exchange ideological perspectives and organizational strategies. In fact, there is a certain amount of evidence that Indian uprisings in Cayambe may have strengthened the resolve of urban leftists to push forward with the creation of the PSE.[15] If this is the case, it reverses the standard stereotype of urban activists awakening a revolutionary consciousness in a pre-political peasant population, with instead subalterns gaining their own political consciousness and then helping to awaken that of their urban allies.

---

13. "Abusos de Gamonalismo", *La Vanguardia* 1:9–10 (1 March 1928), p. 13.
14. Ricardo A. Paredes, "El pueblo de Cayambe", *Germinal* (Quito), 26 February 1926, p. 1; idem, "El movimiento obrero en el Ecuador", *La Internacional Sindical Roja*, 1 (August 1928), pp. 76–81, 80; "El asunto de Changalá", *El Comercio*, 6 March 1926, p. 6; César Endara, "La fundación del partido: una experiencia testimonial", in Paredes, *Los comunistas en la historia nacional*, p. 55.
15. "El partido comunista organizador y defensor de los indios", *El Pueblo*, 2 June 1951, p. 6; René Maugé, "Las tareas actuales de nuestro movimiento", in Paredes, *Los comunistas en la historia nacional*, pp. 219–255, 223.

Unlike Gramsci, who believed that a historic subjugation of the Italian peasantry rendered them incapable of interpreting their reality in order to develop a counter-hegemonic discourse, the Kayambis' increasing encounters with capitalism forged a type of class-consciousness that led them to construct a broader view of the world. Gualavisí, and other Kayambi leaders, understood that in order to end the oppression and discrimination that they faced, they needed to demand radical changes in society. Local intellectuals molded these ideologies into the formulation of congenial relationships with urban leftists. Socialists and their rural indigenous allies together envisioned a different world and engaged in mutually beneficial relationships. When an administrator evicted Gualavisí from the neighboring Pisambilla hacienda, Gualavisí solicited assistance from Paredes to defend his right to organize on the hacienda under the stipulations of Ecuador's labor code. Together, they confronted government attempts to use repression and intimidation to end rural organizing efforts.[16]

Intergroup alliances are by no means unique to Cayambe in the 1930s, nor to the actions of leftist activists. In his study of peasant movements in Latin America, Henry Landsberger observes "the not infrequent situation in which non-peasants support peasants partly because the peasant movement is congruent with their own aims". He identifies the presence of these middle-class and intellectual allies as key to a movement's success.[17] In Ecuador, elites persisted in portraying Indians as ignorant of broader political and social issues, and accused urban communists of manipulating local complaints into opportunities to spread revolutionary propaganda. Reflecting the profound gap that divided rural and urban worlds, conservative white elites claimed they could not understand what good might come out of communist agitation, or even how it might benefit the communist movement. Engaging Indians who were not citizens (due to literacy restrictions) in political actions threatened to trigger dangerously uncontrollable mob action. Paredes, Chávez, and other activists, however, dismissed racist assumptions that Indians were incapable of understanding the nature of their oppression or participating in the political process. They called on the "indigenous race" (*raza indígena*) to claim their rightful place in Ecuador and to demand social justice.[18] Through these contacts between rural and urban worlds, Cayambe gained

16. Letter from J.A. Jalevalel, Personero Auxiliar to Director, Junta Central de Asistencia Pública, in Archivo Nacional de Medicina del Museo Nacional de Medicina "Dr Eduardo Estrella", Fondo Junta Central de Asistencia Pública in Quito, Ecuador [hereafter JCAP], Correspondencia Recibida [hereafter CR], segundo semestre, segundo parte (1946), p. 1554. On Gramsci, see Crehan, *Gramsci, Culture and Anthropology*, p. 104.
17. Henry A. Landsberger, "The Role of Peasant Movements and Revolts in Development", in *idem* (ed.), *Latin American Peasant Movements*, (Ithaca, NY, 1969), pp. 1–61, 46.
18. Pilo de la Peña, "Los indios aspiran socialimente", *La Antorcha* (Quito), 1:3 (29 November 1924), p. 3.

a reputation as an area where communism had "taken a strong hold on the Indian".[19]

Gualavisí served as the secretary-general of the Juan Montalvo agricultural syndicate from its founding until his death in 1962. He dedicated his entire life to the struggle for indigenous rights, becoming known as a *caudillo* (leader) of the Kayambis. In response, the government denounced him "for his activities of being a social agitator among the Indian class", and feared his ability to convoke local leaders who would follow his orders.[20] The weight and authority that Gualavisí's words carried in his own community meshes with one of Gramsci's criteria for being an "organic intellectual".[21] In addition to being one of the earliest and most important indigenous leaders in Ecuador, Gualavisí was also an important communist leader and organizer, beginning by representing the Kayambis at the Ecuadorian Socialist Party's founding congress in 1926. His participation in this congress symbolically represents the beginnings of a structural analysis of Ecuadorian society from an indigenous perspective. Perhaps as importantly, he was largely responsible for drawing indigenous communities into the orbit of Communist Party organizing efforts. While demonstrating that indigenous peoples did not need working-class leadership to develop a counter-hegemonic discourse, as Gramsci perceived as necessary for the Italian peasantry, Gualavisí still believed that communists could give organizational expression on a national level to the indigenous peoples' demands. Linking to social movements that extended beyond the local level would help develop strategies for overcoming their subaltern status. Oswaldo Albornoz argued that Gualavisí understood the exploitation of indigenous masses because of his communist orientation, which he saw as a way to combat those injustices. "This new form of organization, until then unknown by the Indians", Albornoz claimed, "gave strength and cohesion to their struggles".[22] Although not acknowledged by Albornoz, at the same time indigenous discontent provided urban activists with a base on which to build a movement toward socialism. The leaders of the two groups found the relative advantages brought by both parties to be mutually reinforcing.

Ricardo Paredes, an urban Marxist intellectual, was no stranger to radical politics, nor to agrarian struggles in Ecuador. He was born in 1898 in the Central Highland provincial town of Riobamba in the midst of the

19. Charles A. Page, "Memorandum with Regard to Communism in Ecuador", attached to letter from William Dawson to Secretary of State, Washington, no. 150, 29 January 1931, National Archives Records Administration [hereafter NARA] Record Group [hereafter RG] 59, 822.00B/ 24, pp. 16–17.
20. Letter from Juan Francisco Sumárraga to Director, JCAP, 21 March 1946, in JCAP, CR, segundo semestre, segundo parte (1946), p. 1555.
21. Gramsci, *Selections from the Prison Notebooks*, p. 8.
22. Albornoz, "Jesús Gualavisí", pp. 155–188, 166, 167, 182.

social transformations resulting from Eloy Alfaro's 1895 Liberal Revolution. Paredes received training as a doctor of medicine, and subsequently taught at the School of Medicine in Quito's Universidad Central. Known as the "Apostle of Ecuadoran Communism", friends indicated that he "was led to communism by seeing so much misery among the poor" which he observed from his medical work.[23] He converted the Ecuadorian Socialist Party into a communist party, became deeply involved in the Communist International, and was "known in Quito as one of the most fervent socialists of Ecuador with Bolchevistic tendencies".[24] Neptalí Ulcuango, a pioneer Kayambi educator who led the formation of rural schools in the 1950s, later remembered that it was Paredes who "began to mobilize people in the city to help organize in the countryside"; that he "was a good person"; and that he "was the first and best comrade" who defended Indian interests.[25] His activism brought him to the attention of the US State Department which appeared to fear Paredes, labeling him as a "fanatic".[26] The police monitored his movements, and arrested him numerous times, including an arrest in 1927 (along with ten associates) for criticizing the government at a meeting of the Socialist Party in Guayaquil.[27] Despite coming out of two separate movements for social justice and liberation, Gualaviší and Paredes merged their efforts to create the basis for an indigenous movement that by the end of the twentieth century would become one of the strongest social movements in Latin America.

In addition to Paredes, other urban socialist leaders played significant roles in framing protests in Cayambe. Luis F. Chávez was the son of a socialist lawyer (also named Luis F. Chávez) who supported Indian struggles, and provided the Kayambis with housing when they traveled to

23. Letter from William Dawson to Secretary of State, Washington, no. 921, 10 March 1933, NARA RG 59, 822.00B/43, p. 5; Letter from Gerhard Gade, Chargé d'Affairs *ad interim*, to Secretary of State, Washington, no. 1064, 10 March 1938, NARA RG 59, 822.00B/54, p. 3. Little biographical data has been recorded on Paredes, with authors preferring to focus on his political activity rather than his family background. See Clodoveo Astudillo, "Síntesis biográfica de Ricardo Paredes", *Revista Ecuatoriana de Pensamiento Marxista*, 14 (III Epoca) (1989), pp. 9–15; and Elias Muñoz Vicuña, *Temas obreros*, Biblioteca de autores ecuatorianos, 62 (Guayaquil, 1986), pp. 257–259.
24. W. Allen Rhode, American vice-consul in Guayaquil, to Secretary of State, no. 286, 10 January 1929, NARA RG 59, 822.00/B9.
25. Neptalí Ulcuango, interviewed by Mercedes Prieto, 7–8 July 1977, private collection of Mercedes Prieto, Quito; Manuel Catucuamba in José Yánez del Pozo, *Yo declaro con franqueza (Cashnami causashcanchic): memoria oral de Pesillo, Cayambe*, 2nd rev. edn (Quito, 1988), p. 183; Miguel Lechón in *ibid.*, p. 185.
26. Charles A. Page, "Memorandum with Regard to Communism in Ecuador", attached to letter from William Dawson to Secretary of State, Washington, no. 150, 29 January 1931, NARA RG 59, 822.00B/24, p. 5.
27. G.A. Bading, "General Conditions Prevailing in Ecuador, January 1–15, 1927", Quito, 15 January 1927, NARA RG 59, 822.00/695, p. 9.

Quito to press demands directly with governmental officials. The younger
Chávez became particularly active in rural communities, giving up his
studies in Quito to organize full-time in Cayambe. Paredes and Chávez
collaborated with local white activists, such as Rubén Rodríguez, a teacher
and a communist whom the government repeatedly imprisoned for his
political activism. Rodríguez's willingness to use his position to attract
attention to indigenous demands and to suffer for the struggle gained him
renown in rural communities. His activities also irritated local landlords,
since his participation lent legitimacy to the Kayambis' actions, drew in
other urban activists such as Chávez and Paredes from Quito, and caused
peons to press their wrong-headed demands. Pedro Núñez, Functional
Senator for the Indian Race, noted that the urban leftist activities on the
haciendas contributed to the emergence of a class-consciousness that
tended "to substitute collective protest for individual complaints".[28]
Recognizing that "racial oppression (prejudice for being an 'inferior race')
and economic oppression" led to a growing "consciousness of their
[Indian] distinct class interests", socialist leaders intensified their organizational efforts.[29] Together they created, similarly to Feierman's findings
in Tanzania, a counter-hegemonic discourse grounded in the needs and
concerns of both rural and urban masses.

A STRUGGLE FOR SOCIAL JUSTICE ON THE MOYURCO HACIENDA

In order to understand how popular intellectuals framed protest in rural
Ecuador, it is worth considering a specific case study on the Moyurco
hacienda in northern Cayambe. In 1904, as part of its anticlerical reforms, a
liberal government had expropriated the hacienda from the Catholic
Church. Kayambi workers on the hacienda expected to gain rights to the
land, but instead the government rented it out to wealthy landowners to
generate revenue for social welfare projects. Rather than accept a loss of
control over the land, the Kayambis fought for their rights. As popular
intellectuals engaged in disputes with elites over the role that subalterns
should play in Ecuadorian society, they acquired new skills and cultivated
alliances with sympathetic allies. These interactions led to new ideas about
the type of political economy that they wished to see developed in
Ecuador, and influenced their struggle for a more just and equitable
society.[30]

28. J.R. Sáenz to Director General de la Junta Central de Asistencia Pública, Quito, 25 April
1932, JCAP, CR, Enero–Junio 1932, p. 741; letter from William Dawson to Secretary of State,
Washington, no. 193, 26 March 1931, NARA RG 59, 822.00B/29, p. 2.
29. Paredes, "El movimiento obrero en el Ecuador", p. 77.
30. As the *zapatista* rebels in Chiapas, Mexico, claimed some sixty years later, "our struggle is
not against the future, but about who shapes that future and who benefits from it". Quoted in "In

On 31 March 1932, Julio Miguel Páez, the wealthy white landowner who rented the Moyurco hacienda, informed the Ministry of Government in Quito that four days earlier Antonio Lechón, an indigenous worker who had left the hacienda more than a year before, had returned and attempted to claim a piece of land as his personal *huasipungo*.[31] Páez's employees on the hacienda refused to let Lechón work, and as a result "the rest of the peons have abandoned their work and are in insurrection". Without acknowledging that they might have any legitimate complaints, Páez asked the government to send in a military squadron to put down the uprising and re-establish order on the hacienda.[32] The government agreed to this request, and quickly dispatched troops to suppress the strike. The government accused four peons (Marcelo Tarabata, Carlos Churuchumbi, Antonio Lechón, and José Quishpe) of leading the revolt and decided to expel them from the hacienda. The employees on the hacienda, along with soldiers, rounded up the four workers' animals and placed them in a corral, and confiscated everything from their houses (grain, clothes, and the few utensils that they owned) and dumped it into a pile on the patio of the hacienda. The soldiers padlocked their houses and took the four protestors to jail in Quito.

This uprising at Moyurco was part of a larger movement in the turbulent decade of the 1930s, as agricultural workers fought against an agrarian capitalism that undermined both their traditional land base as well as their standard of living. Following the lead of Gualavisí in Juan Montalvo, activists on the Moyurco hacienda had formed the rural syndicate "Tierra Libre" (Free Land) in 1930. This political mobilization occurred in the context of a global economic downturn that left many *hacendados* complaining that they could not meet their financial obligations. Whereas peasants in Juan Montalvo fought off the encroachment of a hacienda, the Moyurco syndicate primarily grouped agricultural workers who were going through a process of proletarianization through wage labor on the hacienda. Nevertheless, both shared similar objectives of gaining land rights, winning access to water and pasture, improving wages, constructing schools, and ending abuses from hacienda overlords. Furthermore, elites feared a repeat of a more prolonged strike that had spread throughout

Pursuit of Profit: A Primer on the New Transnational Investment", *NACLA: Report on the Americas*, 29, no.4 (1996), p. 10.

31. Their *huasipungos* were critical to indigenous survival strategies, but were also part of the service–tenancy relations that bound workers to the hacienda, which is why peons did not want to let go of these small garden plots.

32. Letter from Augusto Egas, Director, Junta Central de Asistencia Pública, to Sr Ministro de Gobierno y Asistencia Pública, Quito, 31 March 1932, Oficio no. 269, JCAP, Libro de Comunicaciones Dirigidas [hereafter CD] por la Junta Central de Asistencia Pública durante el año de 1932, p. 107.

haciendas in northern Cayambe the previous year.[33] As a result the *hacendados*, in alliance with the government and military, put this strike down much more quickly.

With the assistance of sympathetic outsiders, members of Tierra Libre drafted a petition to the Minister of Interior and Government in which they presented a counter-discourse, challenging elite statements. Lechón had been sick for the past year, they noted, and was therefore unable to work on the hacienda. When his brother died, he was forced to return to work and took the *huasipungo* plot of his recently departed brother. Lechón yoked up a pair of oxen to plow his brother's plot, but a *majordomo* (overseer) stopped him and cut the halter straps on the oxen. Other peons, who observed this, intervened and demanded that the *majordomo* allow Lechón to carry on with his work. If the *majordomo* would not permit Lechón to proceed, the peons threatened to stop working because the landlord had not paid them for three months. Páez had evicted Lechón because "el daba la gana" (he just wanted to), the Kayambis stated, and he declared he would also evict anyone who protested this action. Framing their protest around an existing legal tradition, they implored the minister to help defend the laws. "Our current plea of you", the syndicate declared, "is that you ensure that the renter leaves us alone in our *huasipungos*, with the houses we constructed, and of which Mr Páez should not rob us by whim or by his arbitrary will". They appealed to the Minister's humanitarian sentiments, and ended with a plea that the official should attend to the needs of a "few miserable and defenseless Ecuadorian Indians". Finally, they placed their faith in his favorable response to their petition.[34]

J. Rafael Sáenz, the hacienda's trustee, quickly responded to these charges against Páez, maintaining that accusations of confiscated goods and killed animals were lies.[35] Furthermore, Augusto Egas, the director of the *Asistencia Pública* (Public Assistance) program that administered the haciendas, resented the implication that the government only served the interests of the wealthy landowners. He minimized the significance of the complaints as merely a result of economic difficulties due to the global economic depression, leaving scarce resources for landlords to pay salaries to the peons. These Indians were continual thorns in the government's

---

33. On the 1931 strike, see Marc Becker, "Una Revolución Comunista Indígena: Rural Protest Movements in Cayambe, Ecuador", *Rethinking Marxism*, 10:4 (1998), pp. 34–51; and Mercedes Prieto, "Haciendas estatales: un caso de ofensiva campesina: 1926–1948", in Miguel Murmis *et al.* (eds), *Ecuador: cambios en el agro serrano* (Quito, 1980), pp. 101–130.
34. Petition quoted in letter from V.M. Cruz Caamaño, Subsecretario, Ministerio de Gobierno y Prevision Social to Director General de la Junta Central de Asistencia Pública, Quito, 5 May 1932, Oficio no. 290, JCAP, CR Enero–Junio 1932, p. 639.
35. J.R. Sáenz to Director General de la Junta Central de Asistencia Pública, Quito, 14 June 1932, JCAP, CR, Enero–Junio 1932, p. 742.

flesh, he noted, and accused them of not working on the hacienda and being engaged in no activity other than leading indigenous uprisings.[36]

This exchange of letters and petitions indicates the nature of the difficulties that indigenous workers on the haciendas faced in their struggle for social justice. Given the racist situation in Ecuador in the 1930s, who was the government more likely to believe: illiterate Indians long held in a subjugated position, who under Ecuadorian law did not enjoy the privileges and protections of citizenship, or educated white elites who came from the same social class and ethnic group as the government officials? Under these conditions, it became increasingly critical for the Indians to search out allies who could lend them legitimacy and help present their demands to the government.

URBAN MARXIST INTELLECTUALS

Militant rural movements in Ecuador emerged in the 1920s in the context of growing urban labor movements and the establishment of the Ecuadorian Socialist Party. These leftists gave critical strength and cohesion to the nascent indigenous organizations and brought rural syndicates that were spread throughout Ecuador into contact with one other. For example, urban leftists helped distribute a call for agricultural workers, peasants, and Indians to gather in Cayambe in February of 1931 to form a federation to "defend the interests of rural laborers".[37] They made the public aware of indigenous realities on the haciendas and helped the Indians present their demands to the government. When strikers from Cayambe arrived on foot in Quito in March of 1931 to present their demands directly to the government, these same leftists provided them with logistical support.

Somewhat paternalistically, Oswaldo Albornoz claimed that Marxists helped introduce a new form of organization to the Indians, including use of the strike which proved to be "a powerful battle arm which will never be abandoned and from the beginning demonstrated its great effectiveness".[38] As a popular intellectual, Gualavisí played an important role in shaping the application of these new strategies to the local context in Cayambe, both through his authority as a local leader as well as his position as a militant in the Communist Party. He secured provisions and economic assistance for the strikers, mobilized support for the strike among other Indians, and conveyed information to solidarity activists in Quito.[39] Urban leftists

---

36. Letter from Augusto Egas, Director, Junta Central de Asistencia Pública, to Sr Ministro de Gobierno y Asistencia Pública, Quito, 15 June 1932, Oficio no. 501, JCAP, CD, 1932, p. 193.
37. Letter from William Dawson to Secretary of State, Washington, no. 170, 27 February 1931. Indian congress, following up on despatch no. 158 of 7 February 1931, NARA RG 59, 822.00B/27.
38. Albornoz, "Jesús Gualavisí", p. 166.
39. *Ibid.*, p. 172.

provided significant assistance in sustaining these acts of resistance and the consolidation of indigenous movements in Ecuador.

Literacy, knowledge of governmental apparatuses, and access to public officials seemingly would give urban leftists an upper-hand in this relationship, which scholars have stereotypically derided as unequal, paternalistic, and manipulative.[40] Occasionally urban Marxists, including Albornoz, could fall back on the condescending language common of their environs with statements claiming that they led "the task of organizing our Indians", and "showed them the path that leads to victory".[41] For example, Paredes noted that in 1926 the nascent socialist party sent him to Cayambe to lead the movement at Changalá, seemingly exaggerating his role in organizing "the first peasant union among the Indians".[42]

Rather than framing protest on the haciendas for their rural allies, however, urban activists engaged in exchanges that facilitated the flourishing of new ideologies. Indigenous communities in the South American Andes were structured around patterns of reciprocity in which exchanges of resources provided a key component of survival strategies. For indigenous intellectuals, incorporating urban socialists into these patterns of reciprocity was a logical move that proved to strengthen both the urban and rural wings of the movement. Urban intellectuals had access to skills and tools that indigenous peoples typically did not enjoy, but these resources proved to benefit indigenous struggles. In turn, rural subalterns created, on the basis of their lived experiences, a penetrating analysis of exploitation that urban intellectuals often lacked. They did not need formal educational training to observe how the hacienda system's insertion into a global economy resulted in the erosion of working conditions and living standards.

In a presentation on the "indigenous question" to a 1929 gathering of South American communist parties in Buenos Aires, the Peruvian Marxist thinker, José Carlos Mariátegui, argued that "Indian peasants will only truly understand people from their midst, who speak their own language". He proposed training indigenous leaders who would then return to work for "the emancipation of their race", thereby giving an organizational cohesion to their demands. Pointing to a long history of insurrections, Mariátegui rejected the notion that Indians were incapable of a revolutionary struggle. The Indians already had "demonstrated a quite astounding level of resistance and persistence" in pursuit of their demands. Once indigenous peoples were introduced to a revolutionary consciousness,

40. Melina H. Selverston, "The Politics of Culture: Indigenous Peoples and the State in Ecuador", in Donna Lee Van Cott (ed.), *Indigenous Peoples and Democracy in Latin America* (New York, 1994), pp. 131–152; Amalia Pallares, *From Peasant Struggles to Indian Resistance: The Ecuadorian Andes in the Late Twentieth Century* (Norman, OK, 2002), p. 15.
41. Albornoz, "Jesús Gualavisí", p. 167.
42. Paredes, "El movimiento obrero en el Ecuador", p. 80.

they would be unequaled in their struggle for socialism.[43] Similarly, urban activists in Ecuador claimed that "it is no coincidence that today the Communist Party of Ecuador finds in its ranks numerous indigenous leaders, and that the party enjoys massive support from Indians who find that it is the only one that can carry them through to their liberation".[44] Socialists held out great expectations for rural indigenous activists swelling their ranks, which they hoped would give them the necessary momentum to carry their party to victory.

While urban leftists celebrated any indigenous support for their cause, conservative forces feared the spread of communist propaganda in rural areas. A confidential US State Department report noted that "communist agitators are devoting a great deal of attention to the Indians", making it the chief focus of their efforts. Currently, Paredes and Chávez were "practically the only agitators who have been willing to go out among them to stir up trouble", but if the communists were able to establish a permanent presence it would lead to a dangerous ideological shift in rural areas.[45] "The great mass of the population in the interior consists of illiterate indians, who probably have communistic traditions from the time of the Incas." The US Consul Harold Clum continued:

> As few of them can read, this mimeographed and printed propaganda can not reach them directly, but they can be reached in other ways, and their uprisings which occur from time to time at different places in the interior, and their seizure of lands belonging to neighboring estate owners, indicate that they are being reached by communistic agitators. If they ever become thoroughly imbued with communism and realize their power, the comparatively small number of white people of Spanish descent who, with those of mixed race, form the land owning and ruling element will not be able to withstand them.[46]

The US Consul urged Quito to take control of the situation to prevent such an alliance from shifting the balance of power in the country, even if it would mean violating constitutional guarantees.

The Ecuadorian Minister of the Interior concurred with this analysis, reporting "that propaganda is being translated into Indian dialects and read to the Indians at nocturnal gatherings", which contributed to growing

43. José Carlos Mariátegui, "The Indigenous Question in Latin America", in Michael Löwy (ed.), *Marxism in Latin America from 1909 to the Present: An Anthology* (Atlantic Highlands, NJ, 1992), pp. 33–37, 37, 34.

44. Milton Jijón, "La ideología de J.C. Mariátegui y su influencia en el Ecuador", in *Seminario internacional sobre la vida y obra de José Carlos Mariátegui* (Guayaquil, 1971), pp. 53–73, 65.

45. Charles A. Page, "Memorandum with Regard to Communism in Ecuador", attached to letter from William Dawson to Secretary of State, Washington, no. 150, 29 January 1931, NARA RG 59, 822.00B/24, pp. 15–17.

46. Letter from Harold D. Clum, American Consul, Guayaquil, to Secretary of State, Washington, no. 463, 12 February 1930, NARA RG 59, 822.00B/11, p. 2.

leftist strength in the country.[47] These simple peasants were easily and "shamefully deceived and exploited by false defenders of the destitute". Communists, the minister complained, were inflaming rebellion "in all forms and all the time" through the distribution of newspapers and fly sheets with "imprudent and exaggerated language" that were being distributed broadly in rural communities. Nevertheless, the minister claimed that:

> [...] the government has been able to maintain the public order despite the serious difficulties that communist agitations have caused and are still causing by some individuals and erroneously misty groupings in transplanting to the bosom of our healthy, peaceful, and moral people, certain violent procedures that lead to disruptive and dangerous doctrines.[48]

Privately, the minister declared that he had assumed control of the Interior Ministry in order "to combat communism in Ecuador".[49] By extension, this would also mean combating the growing strength and authority of popular intellectuals in rural communities.

The government feared the willingness of leftist activists to organize in rural areas, and believed that it was precisely these rural–urban alliances that represented the greatest threat to the elites' hegemonic control over the country. J. Rafael Sáenz, the trustee of the Moyurco hacienda, maintained that the 1932 uprising at Moyurco was a result of the support and instigation that Indians received from urban socialist leaders such as Ricardo Paredes, Luis F. Chávez, and Rubén Rodríguez. All of these activists had gained prestige and legitimacy in indigenous communities because of their willingness to leave the city and mingle with common people on the haciendas. The actions of the socialists, Sáenz maintained, resulted in slanderous accusations against Páez and "a misplaced compassion for the revolters".[50] Major Ernesto Robalino, who led military troops from Ibarra to put down these recurrent uprisings, also complained about the role of outsiders in supporting the organization of agrarian syndicates in Pesillo and Juan Montalvo. Socialist agitation, Robalino reported, has "resulted in an awakening of the consciousness of the Indians".[51]

47. Letter from William Dawson to Secretary of State, Washington, no. 96, 30 December 1930, NARA RG 59, 822.00B/17, p. 4.
48. M.A. Albornoz, Ministerio de Gobierno y Previsión Social, *Informe del Ministerio de Gobierno y Previsión Social a la nación, 1930–1931* (Quito, 1931), pp. 3–7.
49. Page, "Memorandum with Regard to Communism in Ecuador", p. 20.
50. J.R. Sáenz to Director General de la Junta Central de Asistencia Pública, Quito, 25 April 1932, JCAP, CR, Enero–Junio 1932, p. 741.
51. Letter from William Dawson to Secretary of State, Washington, no. 176, 9 March 1931, NARA RG 59, 822.00B/28. The United States was interested in uncovering foreign, particularly Soviet, support for these movements, but was never able to do so.

RURAL INDIGENOUS COMMUNISTS

The role of urban political allies was unquestionably important to the success of rural movements. John Uggen notes in his study of peasant mobilizations on the Ecuadorian coast in the 1920s that "the impulse for the formation of rural–urban coalitions usually arises in the cities, where an aspiring urban political group is challenging traditional elites for power". In these political power struggles, Uggen argues, peasants are paternalistically recruited as a junior ally "to broaden their base of support".[52] Such a conceptualization, however, is a bit too simplistic to explain the merging of urban and rural movements in northern Ecuador. Whereas the Indians previously had been forced to rely on outsiders to present their complaints to the government, increasingly they were able to turn to themselves for these resources. Utilizing tools and skills which they had learned from urban Marxists, the rural Indians gained confidence in their ability to present their own defenses and to create an alternative discourse that advocated the creation of an Ecuador that responded to their interests and concerns.

In a June 1932 petition, José M. Amaguaña, one of the few literate Kayambis, wrote to the Minister of Government and Social Welfare, asking him to provide more background and explanation for the events on the Moyurco hacienda. Framing the petition around legal issues, he proclaimed that "the constitution of the Republic guarantees the right of workers to organize unions". On that basis, the Kayambis had launched a peaceful strike for better pay and working conditions "which, in our humble understanding, could be attended to perfectly". Amaguaña maintained that their demands were not the result of outside agitators and a small handful of discontented people. Rather, officials only presented this as a convenient excuse to remove rural activists from the hacienda.[53] In the petition, Amaguaña does not assume the voice of the expelled workers, but attempts to explain the situation from the point of view of an indigenous worker on the hacienda.

Having a Kayambi hacienda worker author a petition led to a notable change in language. Gone are the references to the workers as the most miserable Ecuadorians. In its place, Amaguaña uses the ethnic marker, *indígena*, and furthermore uses it as a term of identification and pride rather than something that should be hidden or suppressed. Amaguaña's letter also served another function. Unlike a 1931 strike on the neighboring

52. John Uggen, "Peasant Mobilization in Ecuador: A Case Study in Guayas Province" (unpubl. Ph.D. thesis, University of Miami, 1975), pp. 14–15.

53. Petition quoted in letter from V.M. Cruz Caamaño, Subsecretario, Ministerio de Gobierno y Prevision Social to Director General de la Junta Central de Asistencia Pública, Quito, 10 June 1932, Oficio no. 395, JCAP, CR, Enero–Junio 1932, p. 657; Letter from Larrea Jijón, Ministerio de Gobierno y Asistencia Pública to Director General de la Junta Central de Asistencia Pública, Quito, 7 October 1932, JCAP, CR, Julio–Diciembre 1932, p. 422.

Pesillo hacienda that had been splashed across the front pages of the newspapers, up to this point the events at Moyurco had been largely hidden from the public eye. Now *El Comercio*, the main daily newspaper in Quito, noted that representatives of Tarabata, Churuchumbi, Lechón, and Quishpe had petitioned their case to the Ministry of Social Welfare. The brief story simply noted that the hacienda had fired the four for leading a strike on the hacienda.[54] Although the newspaper story presents no details, analysis, or explanation for these events, it did make it more difficult for the government to discount these events as isolated, insignificant occurrences. Their strikes and petitions drew ever increasing outside attention to the plight of the Kayambis, and in doing so threatened elite interests. Indigenous peoples, using skills they acquired from their urban allies, were inserting themselves into public debates.

Although Kayambis increasingly claimed the initiative in pressing demands with the government (as Amaguaña's letter illustrates), they still appreciated the assistance of their urban *compañeros* who made it more difficult for the government to ignore their demands. For example, in June 1935, landlords in Cayambe reported that "five known instigators who have made a profession out of these matters" were planning a massive strike for 1 July. "They should be confined or isolated in any place of the Republic", a landlord advocated, "and the problem would be solved".[55] Among these communist leaders who "corrupt the workers' spirit" were the noted local white activist, Rubén Rodríguez, and the Kayambi leader, Jesús Gualavisí. Indigenous leaders continued to value the solidarity of outsiders as they confronted this repression. Together, they pledged to wage a class struggle across Ecuador.

Expanding from a focus on local issues, activists soon began to organize strategically on a national level. In November 1935, Jesús Gualavisí and Ricardo Paredes organized a Conferencia de Cabecillas Indígenas (Conference of Indigenous Leaders) at the Casa del Obrero in Quito with the goal of creating a regional or national organization to defend indigenous interests. A flyer announcing the closing session of the conference stated that the indigenous leaders had discussed their common problems and had assembled a list of demands that they would present to the government. Indicating that the nascent Indian movement was not isolated from broader protests, they identified the conference as a "key moment in the movement for the emancipation of the working, peasant, and indigenous masses of the country". Indians, the statement declared, "have demonstrated yet again that organized they are perfectly conscious of their rights

54. "Queja presentada por indígenas de una hacienda", *El Comercio*, 12 June 1932, p. 8.
55. Letter from Augusto Egas, Director, Junta Central de Asistencia Pública, to Heriberto Maldonado, Quito, 25 June 1935, Oficio no. 555, JCAP, CD 1934–1935, p. 355; letter from Heriberto Maldonado to Augusto Egas, Director, Junta Central de Asistencia Pública, Quito, 27 June 1935, JCAP, CR Enero–Junio 1935, p. 862.

and are not criminals as they are sometimes described". Defending the legitimacy of subalterns organizing a national movement for social justice, the flyer noted that "all of their petitions are just, because the Indians only want bread, land, work, and freedom". In summary, participants at the Conference declared that indigenous peoples desired access to the rights and responsibilities that would allow them to become fully functioning and engaged members of society.[56]

Out of this meeting, Gualavisí emerged as the secretary-general of an organization called the Consejo General de Cabecillas Indios (General Council of Indigenous Leaders). He requested that syndicates, *comunas*, and indigenous leaders contact him to receive information about and help from the new organization.[57] Although this organization engaged in a minimal amount of activities, it created the groundwork for future national indigenous organizations. This led Oswaldo Albornoz to declare the conference to be a "success", providing the bases for realizing the objectives of the indigenous movement and building future organizations.[58] While not as tightly or centrally organized as later organizations, the group which emerged out of the 1935 meeting supported local organizing efforts, attempted to organize several strikes on haciendas (efforts which largely met with failure), and published an occasional bilingual (Spanish-Kichua) newspaper called *Ñucanchic Allpa* (Kichua for "Our Land") dedicated to the defense of indigenous concerns. In 1936, a local correspondent for the Quiteño conservative daily newspaper, *El Comercio*, lamented that known agitators were broadly distributing *Ñucanchic Allpa* in Cayambe, and that it was creating openings for leftist organizing efforts in the region.[59]

As a popular intellectual, Gualavisí continued to shape the discourse that drove local protest actions even as he engaged issues beyond the confines of rural estates. In 1942 Mexican labor leader, Vicente Lombardo Toledano, founder and president of the communist-dominated Confederación de Trabajadores de América Latina (CTAL, Confederation of Latin American Workers), met with the Kayambis and was duly impressed with their organizational capabilities.[60] In 1943, in the midst of the fight

56. Presídium de la Conferencia de Cabecillas Indígenas, "Hoy se Clasura la Conferencia de Cabecillas Indígenas" (Quito: Editorial de *El Correo*, 7 November 1935), BEAEP, Hojas Volantes, 1933–1938, p. 298.

57. "Organización y Peticiones de Indios", *Ñucanchic Allpa*, 1:8 (17 March 1936), p. 1.

58. Albornoz, "Jesús Gualavisí", p. 175; "El partido comunista organizador y defensor de los indios", *El Pueblo*, 2 June 1951, p. 6.

59. "De Cayambe", *El Comercio*, 6 April 1936, p. 7.

60. "Ecuador Runacunapa Lombardo Toledano campañerota saludai", *Antinazi* (Quito) 1:11 (9 October 1942), p. 2, facsimile edition in in Raymond Mériguet Cousségal, *Antinazismo en Ecuador, años 1941–1944: autobiografía del Movimiento Antinazi de Ecuador (MPAE–MAE)* (Quito, 1988), p. 130; "En Cayambe el Párroco Dr Caicedo, encabeza la manifestación a Vicente Lombardo Toledano", *Antinazi* (Quito) 1:12 (7 November 1942), p. 6, facsimile edn in Mériguet Cousségal, *Antinazismo en Ecuador*, p. 142; Muñoz Vicuña, *Masas, luchas, solidaridad*, p. 65.

against Nazism in Germany, Gualavisí organized a rural antifascist committee in his home community of Juan Montalvo. He was inspired to make this move because of the work of his urban allies who, in the context of the German invasion of the Soviet Union and the collapse of the Hitler–Stalin pact, had formed an antifascist committee in November 1941 to condemn Nazi attacks and to build solidarity with the people of the United States and the Soviet Union. Gualavisí observed that indigenous peoples should not be indifferent to the Nazi and fascist struggle against democracy; it was an issue which affected all of them. Author Nela Martínez later observed that in Kichua the Kayambis "condemned the fascism which they already had experienced".[61] Gualavisí utilized his position as a popular intellectual to borrow discourse from the antifascist movement, both to mobilize local followers as well as to gain more attention from urban allies for local concerns.

Collaborative efforts culminated in August 1944, when indigenous leaders, together with labor leaders and members of the socialist and communist parties, gathered in Quito to form the Federación Ecuatoriana de Indios (FEI, Ecuadorian Federation of Indians). Emerging out of the political party organizing efforts of rural peasants and urban leftists, the FEI was the first successful attempt in Ecuador to establish a national organization for and by indigenous peoples. Most of the activists at the founding of the FEI and those who subsequently provided leadership in the organization were from the Communist Party. This has led to a perception that "urban *mestizo* intellectuals and a few indigenous activists" led the federation.[62] This grows out of a mistaken assumption that the Communist Party, like other political parties of that era, was uniquely a phenomenon of urban elites. Indians, however, had a small but growing presence in the party, including on its Central Committee. These militants provided key leadership to the FEI, including Gualavisí who served as the indigenous organization's first President, and Dolores Cacuango, another

61. "Manifiesto del Movimiento Popular Antitotalitario del Ecuador" (11 December 1941), in in Mériguet Cousségal, *Antinazismo en Ecuador*, pp. 16–17; "Indígenas de Cayambe forman el primer Comité Antifascista del campo en Yanahuaico", *Antinazi* (Quito) 2:24 (17 August 1943), p. 2, facsimile edn in Mériguet Cousségal, *Antinazismo en Ecuador*, p. 253; "Comité indígena antifascista se organizó en Juan Montalvo", *Antinazi* (Quito) 2:25 (5 September 1943), p. 2, facsimile edn in Mériguet Cousségal, *Antinazismo en Ecuador*, p. 261; Movimiento Antifascista del Ecuador (M.A.E.), "Informes y resoluciones: Conferencia Provincial Antifascista de Pichincha, Septiembre 20–27 de 1943", pp. 28, 32, facsimile edn in Mériguet Cousségal, *Antinazismo en Ecuador*, pp. 283, 284; letter from Jesús Gualavisí to Raymond Mériguet, 24 December 1943, in Mériguet Cousségal, *Antinazismo en Ecuador*, p. 309; letter from Jesús Gualavisí, Comité Antifascista de Juan Montalvo, to Señor Ministro de Gobierno, 5 December 1943, published in *Antinazi* (Quito) 2:28 (20 January 1944): pp. 4–5, in Mériguet Cousségal, *Antinazismo en Ecuador*, pp. 324–325; letter from Luis Catucuamba to Raymond Mériguet, 26 January 1944, in Mériguet Cousségal, *Antinazismo en Ecuador*, p. 328; and Nela Martínez, "Prologo", in *ibid*.
62. Pallares, *From Peasant Struggles to Indian Resistance*, p. 13.

Kayambi leader, as the secretary-general. The FEI also designated Paredes as the functional representative for indigenous organizations to the 1944–1945 National Constituent Assembly. In this position, Paredes worked for constitutional reforms and other laws to benefit the Indians.[63] Reflecting a close alliance between rural and urban activists as together they framed a political agenda, the FEI denounced attacks against Paredes, referring to him as "our dignified functional representative".[64] Surveying the participation of activists in the founding of the FEI reveals that, far from white domination and the exclusion of indigenous activists, it suggests a shared space where indigenous and white activists worked together to struggle for social, political, and economic rights. Both rural and urban activists helped shape discourse and frame protest strategies for Ecuador's indigenous popular movements.

CONCLUSION

On an ideological level and in terms of logistical support, encounters between rural and urban popular intellectuals first emerged in the formation of peasant syndicates in the 1920s, solidified with organizing around common concerns in the 1930s, and flourished with the formation of the Ecuadorian Federation of Indians (FEI) in the 1940s. These events underscore the importance of popular intellectuals in shaping a counter-hegemonic discourse that has come to characterize indigenous movements in Ecuador. Kayambi leaders sought out interethnic alliances in order to realize their movements' objectives, embracing issues that extended far beyond immediate local community concerns. Despite entrenched racism and elite fears that communists were stirring up race hatred among the Indians to the point of urging the massacre of whites, indigenous struggles never took that direction. Rather, popular intellectuals borrowed anti-fascist ideologies from leftist discourse that rejected race hatreds, and instead focused on building coalitions across ethnic and cultural divides.[65]

Kayambi activists successfully framed their protest as part of a communist movement that linked their struggles with national and even

63. Ricardo Paredes, Archivo Palacio Legislativo, Quito, Ecuador, "Actas de la Asamblea Constituyente de 1944", t. 3, pp. 325–330 (21 September 1944).
64. "La Federación Indígena del Ecuador", 31 August 1944, Muñoz Collection, Hoja Volante.
65. Charles A. Page, "Memorandum with Regard to Communism in Ecuador", attached to letter from William Dawson to Secretary of State, Washington, no. 150, 29 January 1931, NARA RG 59, 822.00B/24, p. 16. Sixty years later, Subcomandante Marcos described why the *zapatista* struggle in Mexico had not converted itself into a race war of Indians against *ladinos*: "When community members meet with other white, red, black or yellow people and realize that they could be companions or siblings, and not enemies [...] but rather recognize another person with which one could speak and who could help, then that has an effect". See "Diálogo con el gobierno, si asume a plenitud la vía pacífica: *Marcos*", *La Jornada*, 18 November 1998; http://serpiente.dgsca.unam.mx/jornada/1998/nov98/981118/dialogo.html.

international networks. Together, rural and urban activists engaged in a popular struggle against exploitation and capitalism that concentrated the wealth of the country in the hands of a small elite. Urban leftists provided the rural Kayambis with inspiration, encouragement, and advice on how to pursue their struggles with the government, influencing how they articulated their demands and concerns. This fostered the emergence of a local variation on Feierman's peasant intellectuals, with activists such as Gualavisí providing a bridge that energized both the rural and urban wings of a popular movement. A legacy of this history for Ecuador's popular struggles for social justice is the emergence of indigenous movements that were neither the creation of paternalistic urban *indigenistas* nor racially directed against white and *mestizo* sectors of the population. Rather, indigenous communists and urban intellectuals were able to imagine together a more just social order, and this lent direction and meaning to a common struggle for social justice.

IRSH 49 (2004), Supplement, pp. 65–86 DOI: 10.1017/S0020859004001646
© 2004 Internationaal Instituut voor Sociale Geschiedenis

Reforming Mysticism: Sindhi Separatist Intellectuals in Pakistan

Oskar Verkaaik

SUMMARY: This article examines the revival of Sufism and mysticism by the Sindhi separatist movement in South Pakistan. It explores the emergence of a network of young intellectuals from rural and mostly peasant background, and focuses on two pioneers of Sindhi nationalism and Sufi revivalism: G.M. Syed and Ibrahim Joyo. Influenced by Gandhian as well as Marxist ideas on social reform and national identity, these two leaders transformed the annual *urs* celebration at local shrines into commemorations of the martyrs of Sindh. The article traces their relationship as well as their pioneering role as political leaders, education reformers, and teachers. Analysing their ideas as a particular form of Islamic reform, the article discusses the way they adapted and innovated existing cultural ideas on Islamic nationalism, ethnicity, and social justice.

In the late 1960s and early 1970s a rebellious movement emerged in Sindh, the southern province of Pakistan, which protested against the military regime, and later, after the first democratic elections in the history of Pakistan, called for the independence of Sindh. Although Pakistan is now widely associated with radical Islamist movements and authoritarian military regimes, this Sindhi movement does not fit in this picture at all. Its two main ideologues were a neo-Gandhian, wearing white clothes while writing treatises on the meaning of mysticism, and a Marxist struggling for the moral and social elevation of the local peasant population. The name of the former was G.M. Syed, the latter was called Ibrahim Joyo. The former was a well-known politician during the times of independence and a member of an aristocratic landlord family. The latter was the son of a peasant and one of the very few of his generation who had got the opportunity to pursue higher education. They had several things in common, for instance their physical appearance, which resembled the humble, homespun fashion of a disciplined vegetarian cultivated by Mahatma Gandhi. Both of them were concerned with the place of Sindh within Pakistan, and together they located the basis of the province's unique position in Pakistan in a reformed Sufism for which they were themselves responsible. Their reformulation of Sufism was a radical break with traditional Sufism, just as most forms of Islamic reform radically

Figure 1. Pakistan, with the region of Sindh.

differ from tradition. This contribution focuses on these two intellectuals, the peculiar form of Islamic reform they developed, as well as the context in which they operated.

I take Islamic reform as a response to a globalizing trend that starts with European colonialism and imperialism and continues after de-colonialization.[1] Part of this globalizing trend is the distribution of ideas, often in modern educational institutions. Islamic reformists have made use

1. See François Burgat, *Face to Face with Political Islam* (London, 2003), which analyses today's political Islam as a phase in a continuing process of decolonialization. See John Gray, *Al Qaeda and What It Means to be Modern* (London, 2003) for a provocative analysis of political Islam and today's globalization.

of these ideas while rejecting or criticizing them and they continue to do so.[2] While there is increasing academic consensus on these general views, less work has been done on the emergence of intellectual networks or milieus,[3] which critically engage with the influx of new ideas and ideologies. In this paper, I am especially interested in the emergence of new networks of political activists and Islamic reformists in relation to the introduction and spread of secular education.

This article is structured as follows: after some introductory remarks about the relationship between secular education and new forms of contentious politics framed in the language of Islam, I briefly discuss the setting of my case study, which is the province of Sindh in Pakistan. I introduce the various forms of Islamic reform in Pakistan and how these are related to the discourses of nation and ethnicity in Pakistan and particularly in Sindh. Next, I look at the secularization of education during the colonial period. The next sections focus on the main leaders of the Sindhi separatist movement, namely G.M. Syed and Ibrahim Joyo. By way of short life stories, based on written sources and interviews I had with Joyo, relatives of G.M. Syed, and followers of both men, I illustrate how these men formulated a reformed notion of Sufism, which radically differed from the folk Sufism of the rural areas, and which became the basis of a Sindhi separatist movement that gained much influence among the Sindhi population in the 1960s and 1970s. Throughout these life stories I will pay specific attention to how these two men used and reformed education as part of their political struggle.

ISLAMIC REFORM IN PAKISTAN

Of crucial importance for the rise of Sindhi separatism[4] was the introduction and spread of secular education. In that respect, it resembled

2. See Partha Chatterjee, *Nationalist Thought and the Colonial World: A Derivative Discourse?* (London, 1986); and *idem, The Nation and its Fragments* (Princeton, NJ, 1993) for an analysis of how Indian nationalism criticized colonial rule while using and reshaping liberal and Orientalist traditions. Chatterjee's work is especially relevant in my case as Indian nationalism and Islamic reform mutually influenced each other, leading to Muslim nationalism and the demand for an independent Pakistan. Olivier Roy, *The Failure of Political Islam* (Cambridge, MA, 2001); Gilles Kepel, *Jihad: The Trail of Political Islam* (London, 2002); Seyyed Vali Reza Nasr, *The Vanguard of the Islamic Revolution: the Jama'at-i Islami of Pakistan* (London, 1994), and others have emphasized the influence of Marxism and Leninism on today's Islamism, as well as how these influences has been turned into a critique of Marxism.
3. I prefer the terms network and milieu to community here because the connotation of the term community as a boundaried social unit is not entirely adequate. Although the term community may be useful in the case of militant political organizations – see David Apter, *The Legitimization of Violence* (London, 1997) – the intellectual circles connected to these organizations are networks or milieus rather than communities or organizations.
4. The Sindhi movement emerged as one of the most vocal parties in the popular uprising against

the development of other forms of Islamic reform. Indeed, secular education, as a major vehicle for modernization, has had many unexpected consequences, including the rise of political Islam. As Oliver Roy has argued for recent trends in Islamic reform, the "the cadres of the Islamist parties are young intellectuals, educated in government schools following a Western curriculum".[5]

The link between Islamic reform and secular education is not new. The success of Islamism in universities and other institutions of higher education in countries like Egypt, Algeria, Pakistan, and Turkey is rather the most recent manifestation. In fact, this is not surprising, since one of the main aspects of Islamic reform is the democratization of religious authority. Throughout the Muslim world, Islamic reform since the nineteenth century has been initiated by intellectuals not belonging to the milieu of the traditional *ulama*, that is, the body of lettered men who dominated education and intellectual production in theological schools and universities known as *madrassahs*. Whereas these *ulama* adhered to one of the four established legal schools (Shafii, Malik, Hanafi, and Hanbali), Islamic reformists in the nineteenth century called for the right to individual interpretation (*ijtehad*) of the founding texts of Islam (Quran and the Sunna) without regard to the tradition of these four legal schools. Reformists were equally critical of the Sufi brotherhoods (*silsilah*), which to them also constituted traditional authoritative bodies responsible for the decline of Muslim power and culture. Islamic reform, then, generally took place only outside the *madrassahs* and the brotherhoods. Its main protagonists were intellectuals educated in modern educational institutions.

The study of Islamic reform in Pakistan primarily focuses on two such traditions. First, the interpretation of Islam as an essentially progressive religion, which, in its truest form, promotes Muslim nationalism, social equality, and scientific inquiry, has become highly influential in the Pakistani intellectual, political, and military elite. This tradition harks back to the Muhammadan Anglo-Oriental College, later University, of Aligarh

the military regime at the end of the 1960s. It consisted of several organizations, including political parties, student organizations, and labour unions. It took part in demonstrations and strikes against the government. In the late 1960s and early 1970s, and again in the late 1980s, several Sindhi groups regularly clashed violently with so-called Muhajirs, migrants from India who constitute the second-largest ethnic group in Sindh since the time of the Partition. For a fuller discussion of this polarization between Muhajirs and Sindhis, see Oskar Verkaaik, *Migrants and Militants: "Fun" and Urban Violence in Pakistan* (Princeton, NJ, 2004). After the 1971 national elections, the Sindhi movement grew more radical, calling for an independent Sindhi homeland under the name of Sindhudesh in 1973. Although most Sindhi ethnic and/or separatist organizations have refrained from political violence, other groups have occasionally opposed the central government with violence, especially during the 1983 uprising of the Movement for Restoration of Democracy (MDR).

5. Roy, *The Failure of Political Islam*, p. 49.

in north India, established in 1875, and also to the works of Muhammad Iqbal, the intellectual founder of Pakistan. Second, the interpretation of Islam as essentially opposed to nationalism and secularism has informed anti-elitist, Islamist groups and parties, calling for the sovereignty of the *shariat* and for Islam as a total way of life. Although intellectual developments are never unilinear, this tradition is influenced by the theological academy (*dar-ul-ulum*) of Deoband, north India, established in 1867, and by the writings of Abul Ala Mawdudi, the founder of the Jamiat-i Islami.[6]

However, it is often overlooked that Pakistan has produced a third variety of Islamic reform, which is the reform of mystical traditions, or Sufism. Although Sufism is notoriously difficult to describe – it has been labelled as the "esoteric" dimension of Islam and the "folk" tradition of Islam – Sufism in South Asia mostly relates to brotherhoods (*tariqa*) connected to the shrines of holy men, which have been, and still are, important centers for popular piety.[7] As such, Sufism is widely seen as juxtaposed to the reform and modernization of Islam. Yet, precisely in the process of defining Sufism as the quintessential tradition of south Asian Islam, Sufism ceased to be merely a religious practice and became an object of intellectual activity. This intellectual trend, then, rejects the two other forms of Islamic reform as foreign, and looks instead for an indigenous, folk, sometimes ethnic, form of Islam. Downplaying the transnational character of Sufi brotherhoods, such an indigenous Islam is found in reformed Sufism.[8]

In the 1960s and 1970s, this reformed Sufism was a powerful ideological force behind left-wing and ethnic movements that protested the modernizing and centralizing policies and ideologies of the state, including the independence movement in East Pakistan that led to the founding of Bangladesh in 1971.[9] In order to prevent the fragmentation of Pakistan in various ethnic groups, the central government, during the early decades of Pakistan's existence, deemed it necessary actively to promote a modernized form of Islam as the basis for a national identity. Hence, the infamous *one-unit scheme*, which brought the provinces directly under the rule of the central government, went hand in hand with efforts to purify Islam from what was condescendingly seen as regional folk traditions,

6. See David Lelyveld, *Aligarh's First Generation: Muslim Solidarity in British India* (Princeton, NJ, 1978) and Barbara Dale Metcalf, *Islamic Revival in British India: Deoband, 1860–1900* (Princeton, NJ, 1982) for the various nineteenth-century educational centers in Muslim South Asia.
7. Katherine P. Ewing, *Arguing Sainthood: Modernity, Psychoanalysis, and Islam* (Durham, 1997), and Pnina Werbner and Helene Basu, *Embodying Charisma: Modernity, Locality and the Performance of Emotion in Sufi Cults* (London, 1998).
8. See Burgat, *Face to Face with Political Islam*, for a related argument on the Maghreb.
9. Asim Roy, *The Islamic Syncretistic Tradition in Bengal* (Princeton, NJ, 1983).

superstition, and non-Islamic elements. Particularly the well-known institution of the *pir* – that is, the descendents of the founders of Sufi brotherhoods, who embody the mystical powers attributed to these founders – was seen as a hindrance to the spread of a modern Islamic mentality. These *pirs*, often claiming to be descended from the Prophet Muhammad, often held powerful positions as spiritual leaders as well as landlords. In order to undermine their authority, the modernizing elites condemned the spiritual and healing practices of the *pirs* as backward and impure forms of Islam. The Sindhi turn to folk Islam, then, was partly a matter of reversing the stigma of backwardness. In the process, however, folk Islam was no longer seen as primarily connected to the power of the *pirs*, but reformed and refashioned into a deep-running inclination towards mysticism and Sufism.[10]

In the late 1960s, the combination of ethnic identity and Sufism proved to be attractive to student activists and others critical of the military regime. The flirtations with the folk, the traditional, and the mystical formed a powerful critique of the modernism and authoritarianism of the central government. The Sindhi movement was one of the main contributors to the popular protest that led Pakistan into a major crisis, resulting in the first democratic elections in 1970 and the foundation of Bangladesh in 1971. Following the model of the Bengalis, the Sindhi movement led by G.M. Syed called for the independence of Sindh in 1973. Confronted with similar ethnic movements in other parts of the country, the winner of the 1970 elections, the Pakistan People's Party, headed by Zulfiqar Ali Bhutto, acknowledged ethnic identity as a legitimate form of loyalty within the context of Pakistan, partly giving in to the demands of the ethnic movements. This was a break with earlier state discourse in which ethnicity and Islam were seen as incompatible.[11] In this respect, the Sindhi movement has remarkably influenced state ideology, even though the separatist parties have never managed to win real power.

The Sindhi separatist movement represents a particular form of Islamic reform because its main proponents were popular intellectuals. That is to say that they neither belonged to the ranks of traditional religious leaders nor to the mainly city-based middle-class intellectuals who had been engaged in earlier forms of Islamic reform. Furthermore, the Sindhi separatist intellectuals emerged on the scene after independence, when Islamic reform, itself developed in reaction to European colonialism and orientalism,[12] had left its mark on the dominant ideology of Pakistani

---

10. Verkaaik, *Migrants and Militants: "Fun" and Urban Violence in Pakistan*, ch. 1.

11. Oskar Verkaaik, "Ethnicizing Islam: 'Sindhi Sufis', 'Muhajir Modernists' and 'Tribal Islamists' in Pakistan", (paper presented at Columbia University, New York, 2003).

12. See Peter van der Veer, *Religious Nationalism: Hindus and Muslims in India* (Berkeley, CA, 1994) and Carol A. Breckenridge and Peter van der Veer, *Orientalism and the Postcolonial Predicament: Perspectives on South Asia* (Philadelphia, PA, 1993).

Muslim nationalism. Sindhi separatists intellectuals therefore had to frame their protest within the limits set by Muslim nationalism. Even in rejecting Pakistani Muslim nationalism, the Sindhi separatist intellectuals adhered to the notion that Islam constitutes the basis for national identity. Within these restrictions, however, they designed their own version of Islam, which allowed them to argue for a separate Sindhi national identity based on Sindh's unique experience with Sufism.

In terms of the themes central in this volume, this paper looks at how Sindhi separatist intellectuals appropriated certain aspects of official state discourse in order to pursue their own antistate activities. Whereas dominant Muslim nationalism left no room for ethnic identity within the Pakistani nation, the Sindhi intellectuals challenged this view, not by rejecting the importance of Islam in political discourse as such, but by interpreting Islam in terms of mystical traditions, subsequently linking this mysticism with loyalties of homeland and kinship. Besides appropriating state discourse, they also used and transformed various other discourses present in South Asia, notably Gandhian or theosophical notions on the shared core of all religions, as well as vaguely Marxist notions on feudalism and class struggle. In doing so, they also became cultural innovators producing a new language of ethnic politics eventually adopted by the Pakistani state. As most of these popular intellectuals were educated at institutions of secular education, I will now look at the modernization of the educational system in Sindh.

THE SECULARIZATION OF EDUCATION

When the British conquered Sindh in 1843, they found that the *syeds* played a crucial role in education as men of learning and education.[13] The *syeds*[14] claim to descend from the Prophet's grandsons, Hasan or Hussain. *Syeds* had an extraordinary powerful position as religious specialists and men of learning in Sindh. The status of the *syed* community had been enormously enhanced in the eighteenth century when the Moghul influence in Sindh was on the decline and Baluchi kings took over power. These kings relied heavily on the support of the *syeds* and *pirs* and granted them various privileges in return.[15] For this reason, the *syeds* and *pirs* enjoyed a much higher status as religious specialists than the *ulama* did. The latter are associated with theological seminaries, of which there were only few in Sindh prior to the British rule.

13. E.H. Aitken, *Gazetteer of the Province of Pakistan* (Karachi, 1986), p. 472, and H.T. Sorley, *Shah Abdul Latif of Bhit: His Poetry, Life and Times* (Karachi, 1968), p. 675.
14. Note that there are various ways of transliteration. *Syed* can also be spelled as *sayad, sayyad, sayyid, seyyid*, etc.
15. Sorley, *Shah Abdul Latif of Bhit*, pp. 154–162.

Before the colonial conquest, the *syed* community ran the *madrassahs* where Arabic and Persian – the latter being the language of administration – were taught. In total, there were six of these *madrassahs*, which were the apex of the Sindhi educational system. Apart from these *madrassahs*, there were Muslim primary schools, teaching the Quran, as well as Hindu primary schools, where Khudawadi, the language of commerce, was taught. In addition, many landlords employed private tutors for their children, of which some of the village children could also benefit. Private tutorage and primary education were often funded privately by local landlords and notables and they generally survived the British takeover of power. However, the *madrassahs* were state-funded, and these funds stopped soon after the British conquest. After five years of British rule, Sir Richard Burton, who then worked as an official interpreter for the British colonial government, remarked that "it is a matter of regret to me that under our enlightened rule, we should have suffered the native places of education to become all but deserted for want of means to carry on the system".[16]

By the time Sindh was conquered, the controversy about the language and education policy in British India had already been decided in favour of those who preferred English, rather than an oriental classical language, as the language of administration and higher education. A new education system was introduced based on the Bombay tradition, meaning that primary education was in the vernacular, while higher education was in English. As a result, Persian lost its status as the language of administration and learning. However, the British did little to promote higher education in Sindh. It was left to the missionaries to establish English schools, which it reluctantly did, particularly in Karachi, which, however, was primarily a colonial city and hardly accessible for most Sindhis. As a result, students who wanted to pursue higher education were forced to travel to Bombay.

Thanks to local initiatives, this situation gradually improved. In 1885, a Sindh Islamic *madrassah* was founded in Karachi on the model of the Muhammadan Anglo-Oriental College in Aligarh. Although the school was for Muslim students only, and its name may suggest a traditional Muslim curriculum, in practice it was meant to promote modern secondary education in English. Many of the teachers were in fact Hindus, from Sindh as well as from Gujerat and Bombay. Nonetheless, Sindhi students still had to travel beyond the borders of Sindh for higher education. Till independence, it was common practice for Sindhi students to finish their education in Bombay, the Muslim princely state of Junagadh in neighboring Gujerat, or in Aligarh.

As the highest place of education in Sindh, the Sindh *madrassah* played

---

16. Quoted in Hamida Khuhro, *The Making of Modern Sind: British Policy and Social Change in the Nineteenth Century* (Karachi, 1978), p. 260.

an important role in the creation of a new group of intellectuals who would form the core of the left-wing Sindhi separatist movement in the 1960s and 1970s. They were the first generation of students from non-elite village backgrounds who acquired modern education. These students came from Muslim families who had benefited from social transformations during the colonial period. Some had fathers or uncles who had been hired as village government servants (*tapedars*) by the colonial government. Others were from families who had recently managed to purchase some land, often from Hindu traders and moneylenders. Thirdly, the sons of village headmen (*wadero*), who acted as intermediaries between the landlords and the peasants, also got access to modern education. All these village boys started their education at village level, sometimes receiving private education from a local Hindu schoolteacher or at a village mullah school (*makhtab*). If they were lucky, there was a primary school in the vicinity to which they could go, where they received education in Sindhi for up to seven years. To be able to go on to the Sindh *madrassah* in Karachi, it was essential to have good contacts with traditional patrons such as landlords and *syeds*. As a result, only a few students who were not from high-caste (*ashraf*) family backgrounds managed to make it to the Sindh *madrassah* prior to independence, but of those who did several would join the Sindhi movement that emerged after 1958.

After the British conquest, Sindh had been ruled from Bombay, but in 1936 Sindh gained provincial autonomy, with the result that the education system and opportunities in Sindh improved. This continued after independence, despite the fact that many Hindu teachers left for India. Primary education was made compulsory in 1940. More primary and secondary schools were opened throughout the province. In 1947, a few months before independence, a university was opened. Originally located in Karachi, the Sindh University was moved to Hyderabad in 1951.

The establishment of the Sindh University was the major step in the secularization of education, a process that had started with the British conquest that destroyed the local education system in which the *syed* community played a crucial role. As the West Pakistan Gazetteer of 1968 remarked, "throughout [the colonial period] the [local] mullah schools or makhtabs were treated very much as the Cinderellahs [sic] of the educational world".[17] The *syed*-run *madrassahs* or places of secondary education also suffered from lack of funds. Instead a secular system based on the British model was established, a task for which the British colonial government showed little interest, leaving it to the Sindhi cultural elite to set up new schools and colleges. For this reason, the reconstruction of the educational system along secular lines was only seriously taken in hand between 1936 and 1947, when Sindh was no longer ruled from Bombay.

17. Sorley, *Shah Abdul Latif*, p. 680.

The secularization of the education system continued after independence, when the British system became the model for the new education system introduced throughout Pakistan.

As the following sections show, the institutions of secular education would become meeting places of new intellectuals, relatively independent of the traditional political and religious elite. They would adopt and reinterpret ideas about freedom, social equality, and social reform, which prevailed throughout south Asia, turning these ideas into a new and powerful frame of contentious politics, which consisted of a combination of Sindhi nationalism, Sufi reform, and Marxism.

G.M. SYED

Let me now turn to the main figure in this paper, who is Ghulam Murtaza Syed – generally known by his initials in Sindh and Pakistan. He was in many ways a remarkably productive, original, and largely autodidact intellectual, creating his own personal interpretation of Islam out of a range of intellectual influences such as nineteenth-century Islamic reform, Darwinian evolution theory, theosophy, eighteenth-century Sindhi poetry, Marxism, classical Sufism, German idealism, and probably more. He successfully managed to present this eclectic mix of ideas as the authentic and age-old Sindhi tradition of Islam. At the same time he was an experienced politician, at some point the main protagonist of the Muslim League in Sindh, while later becoming the most vocal and radical critic of Pakistan nationalism. But he became the intellectual leader of a rather small group of intellectuals from village backgrounds – an avant-garde or vanguard to some of its members – who, often thanks to G.M. Syed's patronage, were the first of their generation to pursue higher education outside their village or district, and who became his most loyal supporters.

When he died in 1995 at the age of ninety-one, Syed had become Pakistan's most controversial political figure. He had published books and interviews in which he had called Pakistan a mistake. He had argued that Islam acknowledged no borders between Muslims; therefore Islam could never be the basis of a modern state. However, he continued, it is a natural fact that Muslims are divided in historically and geographically determined cultures, but the advocates of Pakistan have not accepted this natural fact. He had criticized the founding fathers of Pakistan – Muhammad Iqbal and Muhammad Ali Jinnah in particular – for their un-Islamic behaviour. He had condemned animal sacrifice, circumcision, and the circumbulation of the Kaaba, that is part of the annual pilgrimage to Mecca, as pagan practices that had perverted the original message of the Prophet. He had called Islam a stage in the evolution of human spirituality rather than the final word of God. He had accepted Buddha, Christ, Gandhi, Jalalludin

Figure 2. Portrait of G.M. Syed (Sayed) in a photo gallery of Sindhi heroes in the Sindh Museum in Hyderabad.
Photograph by the author

Rumi, and the eighteenth-century Sindhi poet, Shah Abdul Latif, as prophets of mysticism (*tasawwuf*), which he considered the final stage of this spiritual evolution. Passages from the Quran, the *Bhagavad Gita*, the Bible, the Torah, and the *Shah-jo-risalo* (the collection of verses of Shah Abdul Latif) were read at his funeral. He had been arrested many times and had spent twenty-eight years under house arrest without trial, including twenty-two years between 1973 and his death in 1995. In the Sindh Museum, located on the campus of the Sindh University near Hyderabad, he is remembered as one of the most important figures in the history of Sindh.

According to Hamida Khuhro, a leading historian of Sindh and at some point a political ally of G.M. Syed, 'Syedism' was his first and most constant ideology. G.M. Syed was born in 1904 as the son of a *syed* landowner in a village known as Sann on the west bank of the Indus. After his father had died when he was two years old, he was brought up with the idea that a *syed* is a spiritual leader to his people, that is, the peasants (*haris*) working for him. Rather than the people of flesh and blood working on his fields, however, he soon took the *hari* as an abstract or imagined category including all landless Muslim peasants in Sindh. He saw the *haris* as an exploited and backward people, who needed to be freed and uplifted. To him, this was the main task of the *syed*. The organic bond that he felt existed between the *syed* and the *hari* was grounded in a shared spirituality rooted in the soil. This reinterpretation of the *syed*'s task from a local patron to a social reformer was enhanced further when he met Gandhi in 1921, who had come to Sindh to campaign for the Khilafat Movement, expressing solidarity with the Turks in their fight against the European powers. Gandhi advised the seventeen-year-old Syed to wear *khaddar* (home-spun cloth) and identify with the local people, as Gandhi himself did with the *harijan* ('untouchables'). Another role model was Khan Abdul Ghaffar Khan, often called the Frontier Gandhi, who led a campaign of civil disobedience mixed with social reform in the rural and tribal areas of the Northwest Frontier Province.[18] As a junior politician and a member of the Congress Party, G.M. Syed had access to these anticolonial leaders.

The Khilafat Movement meant his entrance into anticolonial politics. But true to his 'Syedism', his first political act was to found a *syed* committee to urge his fellow *syeds* to take their leading tasks seriously. Next, he founded a *hari* committee to protect the peasants from exploitation from Muslim landlords and Hindu moneylenders. At that time, Sindh administratively belonged to Bombay and in 1928 a movement was launched to call for provincial autonomy for Sindh. This movement was crucial for fostering a Sindhi political identity. As initially both

18. G.M. Syed, *The Case of Sindh: G.M. Sayed's Disposition for the Court* (Karachi, 1995), p. 18.

Hindus and Muslims were involved in this movement, which was supported by the Congress Party and the Muslim League alike, the arguments raised to prove Sindh's cultural uniqueness were not based on Islam. One rather referred to Arabic historical sources that identified the Indus delta as a separate country between Persia and *Hind* (India).[19] The archaeological discovery in 1926 of the remains of the Indus Valley civilization in a site known as Moedjo-Daro were also presented as proof of Sindh's historical uniqueness as the land of the Indus. In other words, a Sindhi nationalism already existed prior to the introduction of Muslim nationalism in the late 1930s and 1940s. This influenced G.M. Syed's notion of Pakistan when he allied himself with the Muslim League in 1938. For him, Pakistan was the restoration of a historical-geographical entity, a *Greater Sindh*, which he argued had once existed on the borders of the Indus and its tributaries.[20]

Sindh won its provincial autonomy in 1936. Muslim–Hindu riots first occurred in Sindh in 1939. G.M. Syed was arrested for being the leader of the rioting Muslim population of Sukkur, a town in Upper Sindh. Later he became the Minister of Education in the provincial government of Sindh and a leading figure in the Muslim League. He also established a school, including a boarding-house for students, in his home village, which became the first Anglo-vernacular school in the vicinity, where both English and Sindhi were used as languages of instruction. Over time, however, he became more of a politician than a social reformer. In his autobiography, which he wrote in the form of a deposition for the court, he mentions several mentors who warned him not to forget his task as a social reformer and spiritual leader. But he admits that he did not yet listen.[21] In 1945 he left the Muslim League, but he remained part of the Sindhi political elite, that almost exclusively consisted of landlords, *syeds*, and *pirs*, together with a few representatives of the up-and-coming Muslim trading castes (Memon, Khoja, Bohra) who had settled in Karachi – the port city, established by the British, and isolated from the province's heartlands by desert areas.

It was only in 1958 when G.M. Syed, in his own words, left party politics behind and returned to his true "faith"[22] of spiritually and economically liberating the rural poor. For some commentators, the

19. The most elaborate treatise arguing for Sindh's separate identity is a pamphlet called *A Story of the Sufferings of Sind*, first published in 1930 by Muhammad Ayub Khuhro in Hamida Khuhro (ed.), *Documents on Separation of Sind from the Bombay Presidency* (Islamabad, 1982), pp. 196–254. This text was an early expression of the notion of Sindh as the victim of a series of invasions – Arabic, Moghul, British, Punjabi, Muhajir – which is an important trope in Sindhi nationalism.
20. Riaz Ahmad, *Foundations of Pakistan* (Islamabad, 1987), vol. 2, pp. 442–443.
21. Syed, *The Case of Sindh*, pp. 47–49.
22. *Ibid.*, p. 34.

incentive for this came from the memory of an unhappy love affair with a
Turkish woman known as Mademoiselle Taraki, whom he had met in
Bombay. G.M. Syed himself indeed often told his visitors that he learnt his
first lessons about true love (*ishq*) from her, subsequently sublimating this
worldly kind of love (*ishq-i mijazi*) into a higher state of love (*ishq-i
haqiqi*) for Sindh and the divine. He gives a more profane explanation in
his autobiography. The military takeover in 1958 banned all political
activities and several politicians, including G.M. Syed, were put under
detention. For seven and half years he was under house arrest. In
retrospect, he considered this a blessing in disguise as it made him leave
"the thorny field of politics".

He made a study of the history of Sufism in Sindh, which resulted in the
publication in 1967 of a book called *Religion and Reality* – originally
written in Sindhi, but translated into English and Urdu. In this book he
presents an evolutionary theory of religion, distinguishing various stages
such as Hinduism, Buddhism, Christianity, Islam, "science", and finally
mysticism (*tasawwuf*) or "natural religion", which fully acknowledges the
oneness of being (*wahdat ul-wajud*). In his interpretation, mysticism goes
beyond doctrine and ritual. Hence, there is a mystical core in any religious
tradition that remains essentially the same. Mysticism, being universal and
eternal, can never be the basis of nationalism. Religious nationalism in any
form is a mistake and creates false communities. Although the love for
mankind as a whole is the truest form of love, akin to the love for God,
mysticism accepts the loyalty to one's family and homeland as genuine
incarnations of love. Naturally, nations are based on a shared love for the
homeland. Sindh is therefore a natural nation, but Pakistan is an artificial
nation. Moreover, he calls Sindh the cradle of mysticism with a long
history of religious tolerance and revolt against the tyranny of the *ulama*
and mullahs. In other words, it is Sindh's vocation to protest false
nationalism and promote mysticism.[23]

The book caused a scandal and met with several *fatwas* as well as legal
persecution. Nonetheless, it became the basis for the Sindhi revolt against
the military government in the 1960s, when groups of students and
intellectuals took to the streets to call for free democratic elections. After
G.M. Syed was released from detention in 1966, he continued his political
activities by promoting Sindhi literature, culture, and language. It was a
threefold campaign. On "the cultural front" he founded the Sufi Society of
Sindh (bazm-i sufia-i Sindh). He also initiated a foundation to promote
Sindhi language and literature (Sindhi Abadi Sangat). Finally, he tried to
arouse "political and social awareness" among Sindhi students. He noted
that "nations had been defeated politically and economically but their
intellectuals, working from the fastness of civilization, literature and

23. G.M. Syed, *Religion and Reality* (Karachi, 1986).

culture, not only converted political and economic defeat into victory but also overcame their victors".[24] These intellectuals, whom he called his "friends",[25] did not belong to the political establishment. They were rather the first generation of students from peasant and artisan background educated in the new secular educational institutions for which G.M. Syed himself was partly responsible. A central figure in this network of young intellectuals was Ibrahim Joyo.

IBRAHIM JOYO AND THE YOUNG SINDHI INTELLECTUALS

Ibrahim Joyo was born in 1915, twenty miles from the village where G.M. Syed was born. His father was a peasant but also acted as a middleman between the landlord and the other peasants. On top of this, he owned some land of his own. This gave him an important position in the village where the peasants and artisans were Muslims, and shopkeepers and traders were Hindus. The landlord, a *syed*, was also the spiritual leader. However, Joyo's father died when Ibrahim was two years old. Ibrahim, nonetheless, got the opportunity to go to the primary school in the village. After five years, he went to the school G.M. Syed had founded in his home village. G.M. Syed also arranged a scholarship for him that enabled him to go to the Sindh *madrassah* in 1932. There he stayed for two years, living in G.M. Syed's house in Karachi, known as Hyder Manzil. This house became a meeting place for students connected to G.M. Syed, and later, after 1958, it would become a center of the Sindhi movement emerging around G.M. Syed and Ibrahim Joyo.

It became Joyo's ambition to become a teacher at the Sindh *madrassah* himself and he managed to get another scholarship to do his bachelor in teaching in Bombay. During the two years he spent in Bombay, he got in touch with Marxist journalists and writers, writing in English, most of them from Bengal. They were opposed to both the Congress Party and the Muslim League. This was an important influence on Joyo's thinking. He became a critic of communal politics, that is, the religious identity politics that pitted Hindus against Muslims, and vice versa. True to Marxist doctrine, he considered religion an instrument of class politics and economic exploitation. For him, the main struggle was a class conflict, but capitalists as well as landlords used the religious sentiments of the people in order to keep the underprivileged masses divided. Back in Sindh, he became a teacher at the Sindh *madrassah*. He also started a magazine called *Freedom Calling*, which argued for supporting the British during World War II in return for independence.

24. Syed, *The Case of Sindh*, p. 160.
25. *Ibid.*, p.159.

In 1947 he published a little book called *Save Sind, Save the Continent (From Feudal Lords, Capitalists and their Communalisms)*, with a foreword by G.M. Syed. In this book he condemns the landlords (*zamindar*) and *pirs* for exploiting the peasants. He condemns the peasants for living like slaves, while on their part tyrannizing their women. "The only duty they know is to work like bullocks for their landlords and money-lenders, to touch the feet of their Zamindar-Masters and Pirs, and worship them literally as living gods, and lastly to instruct their children to do likewise".[26] This is particularly pitiful, he goes on, because these peasants are Muslims and Islam is a liberating religion. He thus gives his own twist to the notion, widespread among reformists of various kinds, that the true message of Islam has been forgotten with the result that the Muslims live in misery. For Joyo, however, the main fight is not with European powers. The main fight is against oppressive landlords, backward spiritual leaders, and Hindu moneylenders, a fight that can only be won if the Muslims return to the Islamic message of social justice and equality.

Besides, Joyo argues in his book, the recent Punjabi settlers, who came to Sindh after the completion of the irrigation works in the 1930s that turned vast desert areas into agricultural lands, are to blame for the misery of Sindh's peasants. He blames these settlers for being ignorant of Sindhi culture and especially of the eighteenth-century poet Shah Abdul Latif, who was the first poet to sing in the Sindhi language. He also blames them for obstructing the cultural decolonialization of Sindh after Sindh's provincial autonomy in 1936. He writes:

> Poor G.M. Sayed, when he was the Education Minister, had issued or was on the point of issuing orders that every non-Sindhee in Sind must learn *Sindhee* within a stipulated period of time. This, at that time, raised such a vehement noise everywhere among the circles concerned, as if somebody was asking them for giving up their religion.[27]

The "circles concerned" were of course the Punjabi settlers.

In short, in Joyo's analysis the notion of class struggle, Islamic revivalism, and early Sindhi nationalism come together in an optimistic belief in "the river of Progress",[28] in which the Sindhi Muslim peasants constitute the progressive potential, struggling against the reactionary forces of landlords, traditional religious specialists, and recent Punjabi immigrants. Recognizing the class and national differences between Muslims, he also criticizes Muslim nationalism, saying that "[t]o talk of Muslim nationalism would be as meaningless and self-contradictory as to

26. Ibrahim Joyo, *Save Sind, Save the Continent* (Karachi, 1947), pp. 103–104.
27. *Ibid.*, p. 131.
28. *Ibid.*, p. 139.

talk of world-Nationalism, for Islam represents Universalism, and can be embraced by any one of the hundred and one Nations of the world".[29]

At the time of publication the book failed to get much attention in Sindh as the group of leftists was still very small. Joyo saw it as his first task to form a revolutionary vanguard of young Sindhi students and intellectuals. "It is to their youth", he writes, "more specially their student community, and to their middle-class Intelligentsia, that a people always turns for rescue, in times of danger, sorrow or distress. In this respect, the people of Sind appear to be a little unfortunate",[30] as there was as yet hardly a Sindhi student community to speak of. His ambition to be a teacher was therefore ideologically informed. At the Sindh *madrassah* in Karachi, and later at Sindh University in Hyderabad, he left his ideological mark on several Sindhi students from peasant and artisan backgrounds.

One of them was Hyder Bakhsh Jatoi, who became the president of the Hari Committee in 1948. He also was a poet, writing poems in Sindhi in praise of the great river Indus or *Sindh*. Another student of Joyo was Rasul Bakhsh Palijo, who graduated from the Sindh *madrassah* in 1948. He became a schoolteacher in the town of Thatta and later became a lawyer defending Sindhi students and separatists in many controversial court cases. In the 1960s, Palijo was one of the most radical leaders of the Sindhi movement protesting against the military regime of General Ayub Khan. A third vocal leader of the Sindhi movement was Jam Saqi, leader of the Sindhi student movement in the late 1960s, who later became the leader of the Communist Party. Both Jam Saqi and his father had been students of Ibrahim Joyo, the father at the Sindh *madrassah* in Karachi, Jam Saqi himself at Sindh University near Hyderabad. Like G.M. Syed's house in Karachi, Joyo's residence in Hyderabad became a meeting place of Sindhi separatists and leftists from the 1960s onwards.

MYSTICISM AND MARXISM COMBINED

Till the mid-1960s, G.M. Syed's ideas about mysticism and Joyo's Marxism still seemed incompatible, as Joyo, a self-declared materialist,[31] had little patience with mysticism. Despite their close mentor–pupil relationship, the two men did certainly not agree on everything. Joyo was diametrically opposed to the "syedism" of his G.M. Syed. Like other reformists such as Muhammad Iqbal and Maulana Maududi, he condemned the devotion to spiritual leaders as a form of idol worship (*shirk*). On a personal level, however, Joyo always remained loyal to the man who had made his higher education possible. Joyo's admiration for G.M. Syed

29. *Ibid.*, p. 45.
30. *Ibid.*, p. 133.
31. Personal communication with Ibrahim Joyo.

was made easier because G.M. Syed himself dismissed uncritical commitment to the spiritual leader as wrong. His reform of mysticism was a
radical one, leading to the rejection of the various Sufi brotherhoods. As
Joyo told me in an interview, "G.M. Syed accepted no guides, only books."
In his personal conduct, however, he continued to behave like a *syed*,
wearing white clothes to express his purity and detachment from worldly
matters. Till the end of his life, the peasants working on his lands would
touch his feet asking for favours. This was unacceptable to Joyo.

When in 1966 his house arrest was lifted, however, G.M. Syed turned to
Joyo's group of young Sindhi students in order to return to politics. This
turned out to be mutually beneficial. G.M. Syed gave to his new friends his
charisma as a *syed*, a social reformer, and a political leader. In return he
received the revolutionary enthusiasm and street power of the young
intellectuals. This was the beginning of a new twist to Sindhi nationalism,
which combined both G.M. Syed's reformed Sufism and Joyo's interpretation of Marxism, resulting in a powerful and attractive ideology for
many young Sindhis.

G.M. Syed encouraged his new friends and "comrades" not to restrict
their activities to the university campus and schools. He sent them to the
many shrines of local holy men in the rural areas, especially on the annual
urs celebration, when the holy man's release from this world is celebrated
in colourful festivals that attract many pilgrims. These events were
important for several reasons. New intellectuals went back to the rural
areas from which they originated, bringing with them a new way of
looking at these places of pilgrimage. In the interpretation of G.M. Syed
and his group, the holy men were martyrs for the cause of mysticism,
Sindh, and the liberation of the peasant. Jam Saqi, the student leader, for
instance, wrote a book on one of these local holy men, the eighteenth-
century Shah Inayat of Jhok, calling him somewhat anachronistically a
"socialist Sufi". In Saqi's reading, Shah Inayat had been the leader of a
commune of liberated peasants, for which he was beheaded. This
reinterpretation of holy men as social reformers was a potential threat to
many local landlords, *pirs*, and *syeds*, who often claimed to be the
descendents (*sajjada nishin*) of holy men, who had inherited part of their
miraculous powers (*barakat*).

In Sindh, as elsewhere in South Asia, traditional Sufism consists of
various brotherhoods of holy men (*pir*), their descendents (*sajjada nishin*),
and their followers (*murid*). As the *sajjada nishin* are often landlords,
traditional Sufism is related to patron–client relations. By way of speeches,
songs, and discussions with fellow-pilgrims, however, G.M. Syed and his
group criticized this hierarchical structure of spiritual authority based on
inherited charisma. They condemned the patron–client relations that were
ritually confirmed and reproduced during the traditional *urs*. Instead, they
tried to turn the local holy men into historical heroes of Sindh and

prophets of mysticism, with whom the disciples could get in touch through the traditional practices of music and dance. In these mystical encounters they would be able to find the spirit to free themselves from their oppressors, that is, the landlord families, most of whom supported the military government.

Although these activities probably did spread some awareness among pilgrims and peasants about the causes of social inequality, the main effect of these activities was a deeper engagement with mysticism and Sindhi separatism among the Sindhi students and intellectuals themselves. The trips to the rural shrines became important rituals for the Sindhi left. Identifying with the rural *fakir* and other mystical figures who are so absorbed in the love for God that they are indifferent to pain and fear, they derived from these trips a romantic sense of passion and belonging, which was apparently more compelling than Ibrahim Joyo's belief in the inevitability of progress.

Zulfiqar Ali Bhutto, also a Sindhi, recognized the potential of this reformed Sufism when he founded the Pakistan People's Party to contest the elections of 1970. He, too, went to the rural shrines, sat down to talk to the peasants and pilgrims, and called himself a *fakir*. However, whereas G.M. Syed called for the independence of Sindh, Bhutto's ambition was to rule Pakistan, and when he did, he turned some of the shrines in Sindh into places of national, rather than provincial, importance. Attracted by Bhutto's rhetoric of socialism and mysticism, some of the Sindhi left-wing intellectuals joined Bhutto, but most of them were soon disappointed and returned to the Sindhi separatist movement of G.M. Syed. In 1973, the latter founded the Jeay Sindh Movement, which, two years after the foundation of Bangladesh, called for an independent Sindhudesh. From then on, G.M. Syed spent most of his life under house arrest. This seriously damaged the Sindhi movement. However, the notion of Sindh's unique identity rooted in a history of mysticism was spread widely. Today, it is commonly understood in Pakistan that Sindh is a place of religious tolerance and mysticism.

A brief note, then, on the question why Bhutto could successfully use the reformation of Sufism for his own project, while the separatist movement of G.M. Syed failed. Due to the Anglo-Saxon system of democracy, in which people vote in districts according to the winner-takes-all principle, people in Pakistan tend to vote for local power brokers rather than along ideological lines. In this way, landlord families have become the most powerful political class in Sindh. The Pakistan People's Party, in particular, relied for many years on the brokerage of local landlords within their districts. It is mainly for this reason that Sindh's new intellectuals and radical politicians have not been able to become an important political factor, even though many people in Sindh were sympathetic to their dual agenda of social reform and the revival of mysticism. Till recently, it was not uncommon for Sindhis to have a portrait of G.M. Syed in their house, often alongside a portrait of Zulfiqar Ali Bhutto or his daughter, Benazir. The former was widely admired as a true *syed*. When it came to voting, however, most people opted for his rivals, the Bhutto family of the Pakistan People's Party. After one of the many elections he lost, G.M. Syed remarked about the people of Sindh: "They sing and dance for me, but they don't vote for me."[32]

The lack of electoral success may have been the reason why the Sindhi separatist movement disintegrated into various smaller parties from the 1970s onwards. Nonetheless, the Pakistan People's Party adopted the discourse of peasant liberation and mysticism, for which G.M. Syed and Ibrahim Joyo were largely responsible. In the hands of the Pakistan People's Party, however, this discourse, once meant to bring to power an up-and-coming class of new intellectuals within an independent Sindhu-desh, served to confirm the political power of landlord families within Pakistan.

CONCLUSION

The new intellectuals I have described called themselves secularists because of their rejection of Muslim nationalism. Following G.M. Syed's distinction between religion and mysticism, they rejected the political relevance of religion, that is, religious doctrine and ritual, as well as the authority of the *ulama*, the mullahs, and the *pirs* and *syeds*. I have, nonetheless, called their ideology a specific form of Islamic reform or revival. Whereas some Islamic reformers revived the tradition of *ijtehad* or the individual interpretation of Islamic sources, and others returned to the sovereignty of the *shariat* or Islamic law, the Sindhi movement built upon the Sufi notion of *wahdat ul-wajud* or the oneness of being. Like the other variations of Islamic reform, the claim was to return to the original meaning of the concept, to rationalize it, and to purify it from the corruption of later innovations (*bidat*). In practice this meant an attack on the hierarchy of religious authority. Whereas other forms of Islamic reform undermined the authority of the *ulama* and the mullahs, the Sindhi form criticized the Sufi brotherhoods and their leaders, that is, the *pirs* and *syeds* who claimed to be the descendents of the founder of the brotherhood. In Sindh, the *pirs* and *syeds* used to be the most powerful religious specialists, more important than the *ulama*.

In this article I have focused on the network of new intellectuals responsible for this peculiar form of Islamic reform. For want of space I have not analysed the wider debates on Islam, nationalism, and ethnicity as

32. Personal communication with Hamida Khuhro.

they have evolved after independence in the process of nation and state building.[33] Like most other Islamic reformists, the students, teachers, lawyers, journalists, poets, and social workers who joined the Sindhi movement received their education in secular educational institutions. Most of them were among the first of their social milieu to be trained in these institutions. Their secular education took them out of their environment and into the city – the Sindh *madrassah* in Karachi and, after independence, the University of Hyderabad. Moreover, they did not only benefit from new education opportunities, they also actively promoted secular education as a means to reform society. Apart from politicians and intellectuals, they also were, and self-consciously wanted to be, teachers, founders of schools and boarding houses, and educational reformers.

Secular education enabled them to look at the villages from which they came in a new way. It also gave them the tools to develop their own kind of Islamic reform. Of particular importance was the reformation of the *urs* celebration at local shrines. For the new leftist intellectuals, the *urs* no longer was an occasion in which the authority of the landlord *qua pir* or *syed* was confirmed. For them, it rather became an event to commemorate the martyrs of Sindh and its peasants.

Although critical of the state and the state ideology of Muslim nationalism, the Sindhi intellectuals were influenced by other forms of Islamic reform as well as the discourse that links the nation to the religious community. In their own unique ways, they were searching for the essence of Islam, finding it in mysticism, and defining the distinct character of the Sindhi nation on the basis of this mystical essence of Islam. They were, in Gramsci's term, on the defensive, that is, responding to a dominant discourse of religious nationalism, appropriating it to argue for the uniqueness of the Sindhi people within Pakistan. They did so in opposition to an authoritarian regime, initially a military government, followed by a democratically elected regime that was, however, hardly less oppressive than the military rule that preceded it – witness G.M. Syed spending years under house arrest.

However, state oppression was not the main factor that rendered the Sindhi movement powerless. Paradoxically, the movement suffered more from the gradual incorporation of its ideas into official nationalism. In the 1970s, the Pakistan People's Party under the leadership of Zulfiqar Ali Bhutto managed to cut the grass from under the feet of G.M. Syed and his followers by reconciling the latter's ideas on ethnicity and mysticism with the notion of religious nationalism. This perhaps shows how close G.M. Syed and Ibrahim Joyo remained to the dominant discourse of Muslim

33. See Verkaaik, "Ethnicizing Islam", and *Migrants and Militants* for an elaboration of these debates.

nationalism and Islamic reform, despite their efforts to show that Pakistan was a mistake and despite the uniqueness of their interpretation of Islamic reform. In their opposition to state discourse they remained inextricably connected to it.

IRSH 49 (2004), Supplement, pp. 87–109 DOI: 10.1017/S0020859004001658

Unemployed Intellectuals in the Sahara: The *Teshumara* Nationalist Movement and the Revolutions in Tuareg Society*

Baz Lecocq

SUMMARY: In the past four decades the Tuareg, a people inhabiting the central Sahara, experienced dramatic socioeconomic upheaval caused by the national independence of the countries they inhabit, two droughts in the 1970s and 1980s, and prolonged rebellion against the state in Mali and Niger in the 1990s. This article discusses these major upheavals and their results from the viewpoint of three groups of Tuareg intellectuals: the "organic intellectuals" or traditional tribal leaders and Muslim religious specialists; the "traditional intellectuals" who came into being from the 1950s onwards; and the "popular intellectuals" of the *teshumara* movement, which found its origins in the drought-provoked economic emigration to the Maghreb, and which actively prepared the rebellions of the 1990s. By focusing on the debates between these intellectuals on the nature of Tuareg society, its organization, and the direction its future should take, the major changes in a society often described as guarding its traditions will be exposed.

INTRODUCTION

"In this still untamed Sahara – among the camel herdsmen, young Koranic students, government officials, and merchants now anticipating a more peaceful and prosperous future – we were seeking rhythms of life unbroken since the time of Muhammad, 1,300 years ago."[1]

When the Tuareg rebellions in Mali and Niger ended in the second half of the 1990s, journalists set out to look for the unchanging character of Saharan life, ruled by tradition and ways as old as mankind. They quickly discovered that the "veiled blue men of the desert" no longer travel by camel caravans, but in four-wheel drives and trucks, that their feet are no

* Research for this article has been funded through grants offered by the Amsterdam School for Social Science Research, and the Netherlands Organization for Scientific Research (NWO–SIR 12–3958, NWO–SIR 11–1840 and NWO–CNRS F 24–823). I would like to thank Greg Mann, the members of the Sahel Club, and Rosanne Rutten for their comments and suggestions. Of course, all errors are mine.
1. Donovan Webster, "Journey to the heart of the Sahara", *National Geographic*, 195:3 (March 1999), pp. 6–33, 11.

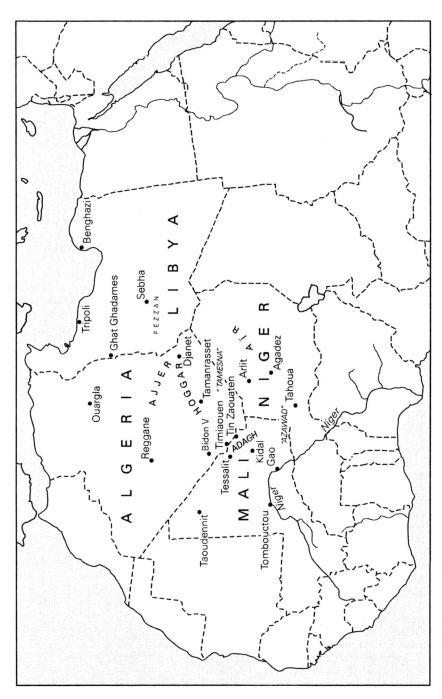

Figure 1. The Tuareg world.

longer scorched by burning sand as they wear sneakers, that their
mysterious eyes are no longer visible above their veil as they wear
sunglasses, that, in short, the Tuareg are as much touched by modern
existence as the next person.

The Tuareg are a pastoral nomad people inhabiting the central Saharan
mountain ranges of the Ajjer in Libya, the Hoggar in Algeria, the Adagh in
Mali, the Aïr in Niger, and the interior bend of the Niger river in Mali,
Niger, and Burkina Faso. They speak a Berber language, called Tamasheq,
and trace their origins to various places in the Maghreb and Libya. At the
advent of colonial conquest, the Tuareg held political control over a vast
stretch of the Sahara, and had the military upper hand over neighbouring
peoples to the south. After fierce resistance against colonial conquest and
pacification between 1893 and 1917, the Tuareg signed their peace with the
French. Due to a lack of economic interest in the area, the colonial
administration largely left them to their own devices as long as they did not
disturb *la paix française*. A certain fascination for the nomad Tuareg,
epitomizing nomadic freedom and chivalry in an orientalist fashion, led
French colonial administrators to endeavour to "conserve" their way of
life. As the anthropologist Jeremy Keenan formulated it: "The idea of a
Tuareg reserve, in which the traditional form of society would, as far as
possible, be protected and allowed to regulate its own internal affairs, was
never far removed from the directives of policy."[2]

In the last four decades, Tuareg society underwent drastic changes. First,
the newly independent states which encompassed Tuareg populations put
their modernity drives at full speed. They perceived the pastoral nomad
way of life of the Tuareg as backward and undesirable. Nomads should be
sedentarized and educated. In 1963, a first small-scale rebellion broke out
in Mali against these modernization policies, which the Tuareg perceived
as a "recolonization" of their society. It was bloodily crushed, after which
the survivors retreated into Algeria.[3] A second, even more important
impetus to change were the droughts that struck the Sahel in the 1970s and
1980s. These virtually annihilated Tuareg herds which still formed the
economic basis of society. The victims of these droughts were confronted
with insufficiency of relief aid and state corruption in its distribution, as it
was diverted and sold.[4] Those who were still able-bodied left for the urban
centres of the Maghreb and West Africa, looking for work. Here, they
were confronted with illegality, discrimination, and, from the late 1980s
onwards, expulsion. Thus, a generation of Tuareg, born in the 1950s, grew
up with forced sedentarization and education, social economic destruction

2. Jeremy Keenan, *The Tuareg: People of Ahaggar* (London, 2002), p. 137.
3. See Baz Lecocq, "'That Desert is Our Country': Tuareg Rebellions and Competing
Nationalisms in Contemporary Mali (1946–1996)", (Ph.D., Amsterdam University, 2002).
4. See Hal Sheets *et al.*, *Disaster in the Desert: Failures of International Relief in the West African
Drought* (Washington DC, 1974).

by drought and state agents, and social economic marginality in the nation-states ruling their land. This led to strong resentment. As one of my informants put it:

> I grew up seeing all this, and in my youthfulness I took a really, really strong hatred. In those years an incredibly grave obligation fell upon us. It was they who owned us, like hostages. All young people of my age in that period had the same hatred, the same sentiment of being re-colonized, and that caused a great feeling of hate in us.[5]

In June 1990, a small group of young Tuareg men started an armed uprising against the Malian state. In 1992, their example was followed by colleagues in Niger. These are generally known as the Tuareg rebellions. The Malian rebellion first formally ended in 1992, but violence continued between various Tuareg rebel factions and the Malian army. The conflict reached its height in 1994, with inter-ethnic conflicts between Tuareg rebels and a vigilante movement of the neighbouring Songhay people. After petering out at the end of 1994, the conflict was formally ended in March 1996. In Niger, a first peace was signed in October 1994, followed by treaties signed with breakaway factions in April 1995, January 1997, and, finally, June 1998.

The rebellions are generally described as low-intensity conflicts, because of the sporadic battles and the small absolute number of deadly victims (a few thousand), and internally displaced persons and international refugees (perhaps 250,000). However, if one considers that the rebellions took place in two of the world's poorest countries, in those parts of those countries generally considered the least favoured, that the conflict area is a naturally fragile environment, collapsed under ecological disasters which had totally disrupted local society and economy, one can imagine these rebellions to be of the gravest kind possible. Yet, the rebellions were started with the intention of improving living conditions through national independence, and to save Tuareg society from oblivion by altering its socio-political structures. These goals were set by a small group of young intellectuals and informal leaders of the generation born in the 1950s. A small group of these men had started to prepare for armed conflict since the late 1970s.

In this article, I will first describe these new Tuareg intellectuals. They can be divided into roughly two groups: the Western-educated, generally

---

Figure 2 (see opposite page). Two young *ishumar* have their picture taken somewhere in Libya in 1972. The young man in black is Iyad ag Ghali, the future leader of the rebellion in Mali (1990–1996), then eighteen years old. Note the flared trousers, the "soul" boots, and the Libyan *gandoura*, as well as the absence of a turban.
Photograph courtesy of Mohamed Lamine ag Mohamed Fall, the other person in the picture.

5. Interview with Mohamed Lamine ag Mohamed Fall, Kidal, 27 December 1998.

called *évolués*, and a group of autodidacts generally called *ishumar*. I will
then describe the subjects of their reflection and the debates between them
from the 1970s to the 1990s. These debates centred around two major
themes: nation and society. The *ishumar* were largely responsible for the
rethinking of the Tuareg nation and its desired independence from the
existing nation-states. The *évolués* focused on the nature of Tuareg society,
as based on pastoral nomadism and social hierarchy expressed through
social strata in which one was born, and tribal affiliation. Both groups of
intellectuals expressed the need to change society from hierarchical tribal
pastoralism to one based on equality between members, and a diversified
social economy. Disagreement on the importance of both subjects and
mutual resentment were not exceptional. On both issues however, the
younger generation of intellectuals united in their confrontation with an
older elite of tribal leaders and "traditional" Muslim intellectuals who had
interests in a social and political (but not an economic) status quo. It is not
exaggerated to describe the conflicts as a generational conflict between an
upcoming and an established elite. I will describe how before, during, and
after the rebellion, both groups of young intellectuals developed, and how
they tried to change society. In the end, we will see that most of their
attempts proved ineffective.

TRADITIONAL AND POPULAR INTELLECTUALS

Until the late 1940s, Tuareg society knew but one type of intellectual, of
the sort that Gramsci described as "organic". In Tuareg society these are
the so called *ineslemen* or *alfaqiten*, Muslim religious specialists serving as
mediators and spiritual guides. They could also be seen as "traditional"
intellectuals in the Gramscian sense. They are, however, part of the
political elite. The second group of these "organic intellectuals" consists of
the tribal chiefs, who function as tribal councillors and mediators between
authorities and population. Together these groups form the ruling elite,
creating and enforcing social and civil law. As Tim Carmichael remarks
with reference to the colonial Swahili Coast, Gramsci's conception of law
corresponds with that of many Muslim and African societies, where "there
is no effective division between religious and civil societies, and where law
is subsumed under religion".[6] These two groups of *organic* intellectuals
will be presented here as the *traditional* elite. They can be characterized on
a political level as conservative.

The *évolués* can only partly be described in a Gramscian sense as
"traditional". They have received higher education, by which most often is

6. Tim Carmichael, "British 'Practice' Towards Islam in the East Africa Protectorate: Muslim
Officials, Waqf Administration, and Secular Education in Mombasa and Environs, 1895–1920",
Journal of Muslim Minority Affairs, 17 (1997), pp. 293–309, 294.

meant "Western" university education, and they see themselves as independent from the ruling elite or from institutionalized traditional politics. They are, however, at least partly enmeshed in existing power structures. The *évolué* group only came into existence from the late 1950s onwards. After Malian and Nigerien independence in 1960 the new regimes saw educating the Tuareg as a necessity to the modern development of the nation.[7] Therefore, in the 1970s their number increased significantly as the young children sent to school in the 1960s came of age. I will here present this particular group as a "modern elite" which takes an intermediate position between the conservative tribal leaders and another group of intellectuals (and new leaders), which is the most important to this article.

This last group, generally called *ishumar*, are truly "popular intellectuals", fitting the description given in this collection. The *ishumar* are mostly autodidactic intellectuals whose reflections developed through the experiences of international travel, smuggling, and (un)employment in various industrial sectors previously unknown in Tuareg society. Their reflections turned largely around the modernization of Tuareg society and the need for political independence through revolutionary action. The latter discourse, typical for this group in Tuareg society, developed largely through exposure to mediatized revolutionary discourse in Algeria and Libya, which they compared to and measured against their personal experiences. This political reflection would ultimately lead to the Tuareg rebellions in Mali and Niger.

The *ishumar* can be perceived as an elite, first of all because they saw themselves as such. From the 1980s onwards, those *ishumar* involved in the preparation for armed rebellion perceived themselves as a revolutionary military vanguard which would lead their people to independence. Second, they can be seen as an *intellectual* elite among their fellow immigrant workers, as they put their thoughts on migration, modernity, and politics into words: the poems and songs of the *teshumara* movement. They were the ones who produced knowledge, even if part of this knowledge concerned experiences they had in common with their less articulate audience.

The categorization of these groups is, of course, more academic than real. These groups partly overlap. Part of the *évolués* shared in the *teshumara* experience, joined the rebel movements, and came originally from an organic intellectual milieu. One example is the famous Tuareg poet, Mahmoudan Hawad, a member of the Ikazkazen clan, which is part of the ruling elite in Niger. Living in chosen exile in France, Hawad started

7. Unfortunately, the English language has no standardized name for the inhabitants of the Republic of Niger. Many erroneously refer to them as Nigerians, which would make them inhabitants of Nigeria, which is another country. I will here use the term Nigerien.

his intellectual career as an *ashamor*, but during the rebellion he published many a polemic in Nigerien (and French) newspapers in the finest *évolué* tradition.

TESHUMARA: THE ORIGINS OF A NEW INTELLECTUAL REVOLUTIONARY ELITE

Participants in the Tuareg uprising against the Nigerien and Malian governments in the 1990s often refer to it as *ath-thawra*, which in Arabic means "revolution". However, it can be argued that the "revolution" took place before the rebellion, and consisted of the changes society underwent prior to the uprising. The major changes were a partial shift from a pastoral nomad society and self-sufficient economy, to an urban existence of wage labour and the introduction of new consumer items. These major changes brought along shifts in gender relations, cultural forms of expression, education, and politics. It was also the change from a society living in a geographically limited (if large) and coherent region, to a diaspora around West Africa, the Maghreb, and, to some extent, Europe.

The Tuareg name for the movement that actively promoted this revolution is *teshumara*, a derivative of the French *chômage*: unemployment. Those who followed this new way of life were called *ishumar*: unemployed.[8] An *ashamor* was first of all someone who had (partly) abandoned pastoral life in favour of employment in other economic sectors. In large parts of the Tuareg world, this meant migration, since economic alternatives hardly existed within society. An *ashamor* would travel in between jobs, during which period he was unemployed.

The *teshumara* was a direct consequence of the droughts that hit the Sahara and Sahel in the 1970s and 1980s. For centuries, the Tuareg had carved their existence out of the desert as pastoral nomads and caravan traders, fully dependent on their livestock for their livelihood. The droughts left them with less than 20 per cent of their former herds in cattle, small ruminants, and, especially camels, still alive, and thus with a strong need to look for other means of existence. Especially among the small group of contemporaneous Western-educated Tuareg intellectuals, the drought led to rethinking pastoral life. Many reached the conclusion that pastoral existence had no future.

> Pastoralism as we have always practised it is no longer an honourable option in our days. For different reasons it is condemned to be abandoned or at least to be

---

8. The masculine plural is *ishumar*; masculine singular: *ashamor*; feminine singular: *tashamort*; feminine plural: *tishumarin*. *Teshumara* is the indicative noun: "unemployment", or "the way of unemployment", meaning both the movement and the culture it produced.

restructured. It is not a goal in itself, and a Tuareg is not in the least predestined to be born and die as a pastoralist.[9]

At present, the Sahara on the whole rises from a kind of medieval lethargy to wake up and to open up to a modern world. [...] And the nomads? They too are condemned, not to disappear, but to become something different. They are condemned to disappear as nomads, but not as human beings. The question inevitably asked, is to know what the nomads are and what they will do, now that they have lost the major part of their herds.[10]

As few new means of existence could be found in Mali or Niger, many former herdsmen moved to the Maghreb and elsewhere in West Africa. Employment was found in various occupations, such as salaried herding, agriculture in the oasis towns of the Sahara, construction work and masonry, car mechanics and even fishery. Most jobs were temporary, and many moved from town to town, from job to job. As most jobs were to be found in the cities, the *teshumara* was an urban culture, taking shape in the booming Saharan cities of Algeria and Libya, such as Tamanrasset, Ghat, Ghadames and Sebha.

A profitable but dangerous activity was smuggling.[11] During the 1970s and 1980s, most smuggled goods consisted of basic foodstuffs, bought in southern Algeria where prices were subsidized and sold in Mali and Niger to the refugees and victims of the droughts. With the advent of the rebellions, the smuggling in arms, petrol, and cars took off to sustain the rebellion. After the rebellions, this transnational traffic network would become integrated in a larger trans-Saharan trafficking network generally known as the "Marlboro Road" after its main merchandise.

As a last, but certainly not least, professional occupation soldiery should be mentioned. This profession was, however, not taken up by many; one should think in terms of hundreds, and it was not taken out of economic interest, but out of political motives. The *teshumara* was more than a social economic culture. It ultimately evolved as a nationalist political movement seeking Tuareg independence. This movement is generally known as *tanekra*, Tamasheq for uprising, which will be treated more fully below.

It should be emphasized that not only young men migrated. Young women also travelled to the cities of Southern Algeria looking for a better life. They often traveled alone. The mobility and independence of Tuareg women made many Algerians look upon these female immigrants in disapproval.[12]

9. Anonymous I, *Quand le chef travaille, le peuple le suit* (unedited ms., personal archives, n.p., n.d. (1990)). Document circulating in Niamey in 1990 among Tuareg *évolués* [hereafter, *Quand le chef travaille*).

10. Acherif ag Mohamed, "Les possibilités agricoles dans le Cercle de Kidal", (Mémoire de fin d'Études, ENSUP Bamako, 1977), p. 37.

11. See Georg Klute, "Die Rebellionen der Tuareg in Mali und Niger" (Habilitationschrift, Universität Siegen, 2001).

City life also changed the simple everyday habits of society. To a Tuareg, the ideal repast consists of fresh milk and fat meat, with three glasses of sweet tea for dessert, but the diet changed. Cereal products and vegetables were added, fresh milk was substituted with milk powder, and butter with olive or peanut oil. While most women in the Maghreb kept their customary dresses, the male *ishumar* dress code changed sharply from customary dress. Especially telling were the changes in wearing the male turban and veil, through which individual male honour is expressed. The customary veil and turban are a complex, multi-layered wrapping of various cloths, sometimes as long as 20 metres. In general, the less of the face is visible, the more a man is guarding his honour. The *ishumar* deliberately expressed the turmoil they found their society to be in, and their desire for radical changes in the way they wore their turban. The multiple layers were abandoned for a single cloth, the length of which was reduced considerably to about 4 metres. This shortened turban was wrapped around the head in an uncaring fashion, yet carefully leaving the face exposed, expressing their chosen status as young and irresponsible men and their rebellious state of mind. But it also explicitly expressed the notion that society had lost its honour and found itself in turmoil.[13]

When the *ishumar* gained enough money, new consumer items became available to them, such as watches, sunglasses, cassettes, cassette players and guitars. The last three items were especially helpful in forming *ishumar* cultural expression. The *ishumar* developed their own musical genre: *al-guitara*, a particular style of guitar rock.[14] Musical inspiration was found in the repertoire of Jimmy Hendrix, for his virtuoso solos, and Dire Straits for the simplicity and clarity of their chord schemes. Despite these influences, *al-guitara* developed into an original sound with strong influences of local musical genres.

The first to make *al-guitara* music was a group of men from the Malian Adagh mountains who called their band, Taghreft Tinariwen, "Let's Build up the Countries", better known as Tinariwen, or "The Deserts". In the coming decades, the songs by Tinariwen or its individual members would accompany the *teshumara* and *tanekra* resistance movement, as well as the rebellion at its various stages. Tinariwen's musical sound remained long subordinate to its message, which was one of reflection on Tuareg existence.

12. Rachid Bellil and Badi Dida, "Evolution de la relation entre Kel Ahaggar et Kel Adagh", *Les cahiers de l'IREMAM*, 4 (1993), pp. 95–110.

13. Hélène Claudot-Hawad, "Visage voilé et expressivité", in *idem, Les Touaregs. Portrait en fragments* (Aix-en-Provence, 1993), pp. 29–43; and Susan Rasmussen, "Veiled Self, Transparent Meanings", *Ethnology*, 32 (1991), pp. 101–117.

14. Nadia Belalimat, "'Le Chant des fauves': Poésies chantées de la résistance touarègue contemporaine" (Mémoire de Maîtrise, Université Paris X, Nanterre, 1996).

We are mangled between the Arabs and the West,
But even more so by Mali against whom we fight.
I have a question for my brothers in my nation,
Consider the situation you are in.[15]

But slowly the message changed from one of despair to one of hope for a better future through common action:

We pull up our trousers and fasten our belts,
We no longer accept this maltreatment we endure.[16]

Through their songs, but also through the individual poems of other *ishumar*, the social and political messages of the *teshumara* were transfused in Tuareg society. Put simply, the message was: "*We, the Tuareg people have suffered under oppression and droughts since African independence in the 1960s. Independence left our country divided between various nation-states. Since then, we have moved away from kin and country to the Maghreb. We need to reunite and liberate our country, so that we can become prosperous again.*" This idea was already expressed in one of the oldest *al-guitara* songs:

Friends, hear and understand me.
You know, there is one country,
One goal, one religion.
And unity, hand in hand.
Friends, you know
There is only one stake to which you are fettered
And only unity can break it.[17]

Musicians would perform at *ishumar* parties, where those who had cassette recorders recorded the sessions, which were then copied by new listeners. Possession of cassettes was dangerous and could lead to imprisonment. During the rebellions, cassettes were spread more easily, but as both rebellions, especially in Mali, evolved in an internal struggle between clan or status-group based movements, the music changed as well. Some musicians would put their poetic talent to the service of one particular status-group or clan, while others wrote songs calling for reconciliation and

15. From "We Are Mangled by the Arabs", by Keddu ag Ossad (Irreguenaten), n.d., in Belalimat, "Chants des fauves", song 11. All poems cited in this article are part my own corpus, or that of two other unpublished works: Klute, "Rebellionen", and Belalimat "Chants des fauves", or published works. Translations into English are mine, based on my own versions in Tamasheq as well as transcriptions and translations in French and German by others. Poems cited will be referred to by title (often the same as the first lines of the song) poet, tribal origins, date/year of composition, corpus, or previous publication.
16. From "We Pull Up Our Trousers and Fasten Our Belts", by Cheick ag Aoussa (Irayaken), 1983, in Klute, "Rebellionen", annexe rebel songs, song 7.
17. From "Friends, Hear and Understand", by Intakhmuda ag Sidi Mohamed (Kel Essouk), 1978, Klute, "Rebellionen", poem 1, Belalimat, "Chants des fauves", poem 1.

reunification. Possession of cassettes containing one particular message or the other could then also lead to repercussions. In turn, these repercussions could lead to new poetry, spread on new cassettes.

A famous example is a long poem by Ambeyri ag Rhissa, a well known and highly respected Western-educated intellectual from Kidal, who condemned the rebellion and who was therefore taken hostage by the rebels for a considerable period. He then put his experiences into a poem, which was thereafter distributed on cassette. After the rebellion, the poem was sometimes broadcast on local radio, to remind the inhabitants of Kidal of the disruptive effects of the internal conflicts. After the rebellion, *al-guitara* became "mainstream" in both Mali and Niger, and even abroad. Tinariwen has put out two CDs, *The Tisdas Sessions* (the title is in English and Tamasheq) in 2000 and *Amassakoul* in 2003, available at your CD store, while they tour the European "world music" festivals. Some other former *ishumar* groups, notably Tartit (in Belgium), are even permanently based in Europe.

ISHUMAR AND *ÉVOLUÉS*: EDUCATIONAL DIFFERENCES

The *teshumara* was not the only path to change open to the Tuareg. It was particular to those who migrated to the Maghreb. Tuareg who moved to coastal West Africa had different influences transforming their way of life. Already, in colonial times, a number of *ineslemen* had migrated to the Hedjaz, where they took up religious professions. This migration continued after independence. From the 1980s onwards, a major access to a then already globalizing world, especially in Agadez, Tamanrasset and the Tassili mountains, was the arrival of tourists, which opened new vistas to those who spoke French as guides, drivers, and tour operators.

A more important alternative to the *teshumara* was formed by the path of formal education. In colonial times, both the Tuareg elites and the administration were hesitant towards Western education. The first primary schools in the Sahara open to Tuareg children were only created in 1947, and as late as 1955, Claude Blanguernon, head of education in Algerian Tamanrasset, still did not believe in the need to bring the Tuareg to a high level of education. He argued that, "It won't be good since the instructed nomad will find himself cut off from his tribe, his customs and, fatally, he will not be able to remain a nomad."[18]

Most Tuareg believed that French education would turn their children away from Islam, and therefore were reluctant to send them to school. Therefore, fixed quotas of children to be educated per tribe were set by the French colonial governments. Most noble families reacted to this measure

18. Claude Blanguernon, "Le Hoggar et ses écoles nomades", *Documents Algériens*, 15 (Algiers, 1955), p. 6.

by sending the children of their servants to school instead of their own. As in most other West African societies, Tuareg society had forms of servitude and dependency, persisting throughout the colonial period, despite the official abolition of slavery by the authorities. These servants remained with their (former) masters, obeying their wishes, in this case to be educated. This educational lack of effort from both sides changed in independent Mali. In the administrative *cercle*, Kidal for example, only one school had existed since 1947. Under the Keita regime between 1960 and 1968 an additional five schools were built.[19] The number of Tuareg *lycéens* too rose over the years, with equally growing numbers entering higher education at Bamako's *Ecole Nationale Supérieure* or *Ecole Nationale de l'Administration*. A number of Tuareg followed higher education outside Mali, mostly in Algeria but sometimes as far away as Riyaadh, Rabat, Khartoum, Nouakchott, Kiev, Moscow, or France.

This newly created intellectual elite with Western standards could enter the state administration, or they could offer their services to Western NGOs, which abounded in Northern Mali and Niger, especially after the droughts. Like their *ishumar* kindred, these *évolués*, as they are generally called (a highly pejorative term, nevertheless locally employed) lived in cities, where they were exposed to new cultures and ways of thinking, new consumer goods, new cultural expressions, and forms of organization.

To the *ishumar*, education meant something different than reading, writing, and calculus. *Teshumara* and formal education were not mutually exclusive, although their efforts in these matters were hardly sustained, and most of their interests were in practical skills such as mechanics, masonry, or electronics, which they acquired on the job. But to them, education meant political education and awareness about the situation Tuareg society found itself in. The nicknames the *évolués* received from their *ishumar* counterparts are revealing. They were called the *ondit* or *entoucas*, after the French expressions *on dit que* and *en tout cas*, which they often employed even when speaking Tamasheq.[20] They were accused of having knowledge but not using it for the benefit of their people, or even of outright betrayal of the Tuareg cause. Finally, they were accused of being acculturated.

I heard you are educated,
We have not seen your benefits,
Our history is known to all
[...]
And you tell me you live normally,
An organized, quiet life.

19. Ibrahim Litny, "Systèmes éducatifs et société touarègue: les Kel Adagh du nord du Mali" (Mémoire de diplôme, EHESS, 1992), pp. 157–158.
20. Nadia Belalimat, "Qui sait danser sur cette chanson, nous lui donnerons de la cadence: Musique, poésie et politique chez les Touaregs", *Terrain*, 41 (2003), pp. 103–120, 112.

Since your birth you run in vain,
Surrounded by enemies.
The easy life always escapes you,
Unless you make some effort to engage yourself,
To reach that truth that belongs to you.[21]

While the *ishumar* developed a more and more radical political outlook, calling for armed revolution and independence, the Western-educated Tuareg had a far more moderate standpoint with regards to the state and the necessity of violence. The *évolués* reproached the *ishumar* with being ignorant of the realities of this world, uncivilized, and engaged on an irrelevant cause. Changing society was necessary, but not along the vague and half-conceived ideas of the *ishumar*. The educated, in their turn called the *ishumar*, *mazbuten*, from their favourite colloquial Arabic expression *mazbut*: "right", "OK".[22]

Whereas the *ishumar* spoke out against the *évolués* in their poetry, their "victims" remained rather silent. Most documents by *évolués*, written prior to the rebellion, do not refer to rebellion because of either contempt for the subject, or ignorance of the intentions of the *ishumar*, or knowing of their intentions and not wanting to jeopardize the cause. After all, the *évolués* wrote in French, a language understood by their future adversaries. It was only during the later years of the armed conflicts, when the national idea had already been mitigated or totally abandoned, that some openly spoke out against the initial cause in a post-fact "told-you-so" fashion.

In his book, *A Peace of Timbuktu*, on the rebellion in Mali and its ending, United Nations Development Programme (UNDP) coordinator, and former employee of the NGO Norwegian Church Aid (AEN), Ibrahim ag Youssouf, gives ample space to describe the whereabouts of his former AEN colleague and fellow *évolué*, Zeidane ag Sidi Alamine. From late 1994 onwards, Zeidane directed the rebel movement, Front Populaire de Libération de l'Azawad (FPLA), previously headed by *ashamor* and Chad veteran, Ghissa ag Sidi Mohamed. Zeidane played a significant role as peace-broker between the, by then, highly embroiled movements and the Malian government in the final peace of March 1996. Fellow *évolué*, Ibrahim ag Youssouf, describes Zeidane as, essentially, "a man of peace" who had always been against the rebellion and who had integrated the movement to stop the conflict.[23]

On the other hand, a number of educated Tuareg lived an *ashamor* existence for a part of their lives, especially those who pursued an

21. From "I Heard You Are Educated and Understand", by Tinariwen, (Kel Adagh), Libya, 1986, Belalimat, "Chants des fauves", no. 10, Klute, *Annex*, no. 11.
22. Interview with Moussa ag Keyna. Leiden, 4 October 2001.
23. Richard Poulton and Ibrahim ag Youssouf, *A Peace of Timbuktu: Democratic Governance, Development and African Peacemaking* (Geneva [etc.], 1998), pp. 70–80.

educational career abroad as migrants in Algeria or Libya. They too were confronted with semi-legality, discrimination, expulsions, and the other *ishumar* experiences. The differences between *évolués* and *ishumar* were therefore not always so large, especially during the 1970s and 1980s. A number of these educated *ishumar* would become influential members of the *tanekra* movement during one period or another. Especially the European-based students would come to hold a special position during the rebellion, as they dispersed information on the rebellion in Europe and provided contact between the rebels and various organizations. Good examples of these are the newsletter, *Lettre Touarègue*, written and diffused as photocopies by Ibrahim ag Litny, then a student at the Ecole des Hautes Etudes en Sciences Sociales in Paris, between February 1993 and January 1994, and the newsletter, *Temoust Survie Touareg*, written by Bilatan Attayoub, a Lyon-based computer engineer, which was also published on the Web.

The best example of Tuareg Western education and cosmopolitanism intertwined with political activism is probably the best-known Tuareg ever: Mano Dayak. Born in the Nigerien Aïr mountains in 1950, Dayak was forcibly integrated in a French school when he was eight years old. He continued his scholarly career, studying anthropology in Paris and Indianapolis, and upon return to Niger, began a tourist agency through which he met his future French wife. He was one of the key organizers of the Paris–Dakar car rally, and collaborated with Bertolucci in the making of the blockbuster movie, *The Sheltering Sky*. Although Dayak had never been a true *ashamor*, many of his employees had, such as later rebel leader and minister in many a Nigerien government, Ghissa Boula. After the rebellion broke out in Niger, Dayak started his own rebel movement, the Front de Libération Temust, with the help of his employees and, most likely, his connections in France. Like no other, Dayak knew the importance and possibilities of favourable media exposure to indigenous peoples' insurgency movements. It was partly through his media contacts and his cooperation in mediatizing the Tuareg rebellions in Mali and Niger, that the conflict became seen in a light favourable to the Tuareg cause.[24]

Despite these examples, however, animosity between these educated Tuareg and the "true" *ishumar* could run high. It would come especially to the fore during the rebellions, when the rebels had no choice other than to let the educated negotiate with the Malian and Nigerien governments in their place, as the rebels saw themselves unfit to do so, or had been deliberately sidetracked by the authorities. With these disputes between *ishumar* and *évolués*, I have come to the political debates on the structure of Tuareg society.

24. Michel Vallet, "In Memoriam: Mano Dayak", *Le Saharien*, 136 (1996), pp. 50–53. Dayak's autobiography, ghost-written by a German and a French journalist, served especially well in mediatizing the conflict: Mano Dayak, *Touareg, la tragédie* (Paris, 1992).

POPULAR VERSUS TRADITIONAL INTELLECTUALS

Ishumar and *évolués* might have had their internal differences, but on one thing they could generally agree: the need to change society and social structure. In spreading this ideal, they found the traditional intellectuals, the tribal leaders, and *ineslemen* religious specialists in their way. The latter two groups did not share the vision that society needed to change.

Debates in the 1970s and 1980s between both groups of intellectuals focused on two key issues. The first was the relation between Tuareg society and the postcolonial states they lived in, within which the traditional elite functioned, and from which they acquired part of their legitimacy, and which the new elite perceived as detrimental to Tuareg social and cultural survival. The second key issue was the nature of Tuareg society itself, with its tribal structures and social inequalities expressed in status groups and tribal hierarchies. Again, where the traditional elite of tribal leaders and *ineslemen* found themselves at the apex of this system, a position they did not deem necessary to relinquish, the new elites objected to this system both on ideological and practical grounds.

Nation and state

As has been noted above, the *teshumara* social cultural movement brought forth a political nationalist movement generally called *tanekra*, which means "insurgency". In September 1979, about seventy *ishumar* gathered in the Libyan city of El Homs under the aegis of the Libyan government, to discuss their revolutionary ambitions. The congress of El Homs led to the creation of al-Jabha ash-Sha'biyya li Taghrir Sahara' al-Kubra al-'arabiyya al-Wasta: the Popular Front for the Liberation of the Greater Arab Central Sahara (FPLSAC). The FPLSAC was endowed with a political bureau, and a military training camp at Ben Walid in early 1980. Both the camp and the office were closed in late 1981, following a shift in Colonel Khaddafi's political strategies. It should be stressed that the Libyan government outlawed the FPLSAC after the closing of the Ben Walid camp in 1981. Upon closing the camp, the recruits were offered the opportunity to enrol for the Palestinian cause in Lebanon. About 200 recruits volunteered and served with the Popular Front for the Liberation of Palestine in the Bekaa valley and Beirut until Israel ousted the Palestinian forces from Lebanon in 1982.[25] In 1983, the Libyan government again recruited Tuareg fighters, this time to fight for Libyan interests in Chad.

These two groups of men would form the *tanekra* movement, the inner

---

25. Based on various interviews with former rebels. Written evidence of their time in Lebanon is left in correspondence of this group with the PLO, documented in Raphael Israeli (ed.), *PLO in Lebanon: Selected Documents* (London, 1983), pp. 192–201.

core of officers and organizers of the rebellions of the 1990s. It was this
movement which formulated the nationalist outlook on the world that
found its expression in the Tuareg rebellions of the 1990s. The *tanekra*
vision of colonial conquest, rule, decolonization, and their effects on
society, are nicely summed up in the following text written by a member
évolué:

> The colonizers and their successors have all stressed the stratification of Tuareg
> society, opposing Imajighan [nobles], Imrad [free], and Ineslemen [religious].
> They have put one against the other, and one group against the other. For a
> moment all fell into these sordid traps, forgetting their Tuaregness [*targuité*],
> their identity and the hatred their enemies festered for them. It is this hatred and
> the exclusion, of which we all are victims, which in the end binds us and makes us
> conscious of our destiny as a community.[26]

The calamities striking the Tuareg in the postcolonial period – an
abortive rebellion in Mali in 1963, two droughts, and general (perceived)
discrimination by the state – made it all the more clear to the *ishumar* that
Tuareg independence was necessary. Some of these calamities would not
have struck if independence had been given to the Tuareg straight away in
1960, or so they thought. The *tanekra* movement was all about regaining
independence, expressed in ideas on territory and the Tuareg nation. As in
almost all nationalist discourses, Tuareg ideas on nation and country
focused on concepts of land and nation, in Tamasheq, *akal* and *temust*.
Within the *tanekra* movement the term *akal*, ground or territory, came to
embody the territory of *all* Tuareg on which an independent state was to
be formed. *Temust*, from *imas* "being", originally meant "identity" or
"self". It acquired political meanings in the *teshumara*. Cultural unity was
stressed through elements that had always been criteria of unity within the
Tuareg world, notably the Tuareg language. "The foundation of our
identity is TAMAJAQ. Our language, the central axis of our society, is the
most precious we have to preserve. We can lose everything, if we can save
the Tamajaq [*sic*], we save our specificity. Nothing distinguishes a people
more from another people than language!"[27]

Disregarding the obvious paradox in defending one's identity and
language in *French* (more or less proving the point of the *ishumar*, who
composed their lyrics in Tamasheq, against the *évolués*), a few things are
striking when looking at the Tuareg national idea as it was imagined in the
1970s and 1980s by the new intellectual elite. The first is that a people
which organized society and politics on the basis of fictive kinship ties,
expressed in clans, based its nationalist ideal first and foremost on

26. Anonymous II, "De la marginalisation des Touaregs au Niger", (unedited ms., Paris, 1994),
p. 14.
27. Anonymous I, *Quand le chef travaille*.

territorial notions (*akal*). There were very specific reasons that "soil" was taken as the binding national factor, instead of "blood". The nationalists of the *tanekra* perceived kinship relations in politics as a major obstacle to successful political unification of the nation.

Indeed, the clan structure, as well as the existing divides between independent states, kept hindering the nationalist movement throughout its existence. The Tuareg from Algeria and Libya, the Kel Hoggar and Kel Ajjer, never joined the liberation movement. Already, during the 1980s, Tuareg from Mali and Niger, once united in the FPLSAC, broke up along the lines of the nation-states they sought to overthrow, Mali and Niger, to continue in two "national" movements that started revolts independent of each other (in Mali in 1990 and in Niger in 1992) with hardly any communication between the two. In both cases, the movement would split along lines of clan affiliation soon after the outbreak of revolt, proving the failure of the nationalist ideology.

Society, caste, tribes, and chiefs

The second key issue between old and new elites, as described above, was the hierarchical organization of Tuareg in caste and clans, at the apex of which stood the tribal chiefs. The clan and caste system was an abhorrence to the *ishumar*. They derived their identity from a common experience of marginalization within their host societies and within Mali and Niger, in which tribal or clan affiliation had no meaning. At the margins of Algerian and Libyan society, the *teshumara* formed a network of men and women who largely depended on trust in each other for economic and social survival. Coming as they did from all parts of Mali and Niger, and from all the various tribes, tribal affiliation could not serve as a common factor establishing social coherence and group loyalty among *ishumar*. On the contrary, the constant competition over hierarchy between clans could only sow discord among their ranks. It should therefore be abolished. One of the main rules of the *ishumar* was that one should never mention someone's clan affiliation. Only using someone's name or nickname was allowed.

The idea that feelings of clan affiliation should be suppressed had been enhanced by the nationalist and socialist political discourses the *ishumar* had been exposed to in Mali, Algeria, and Libya. In Algeria, national unity and an Algerian identity were created during and after the war of independence at the expense of other solidarities. That this identity was contested by both advocates of Islam and Berber culture made the FLN's nationalist discourse all the more insistent on the unity of the Arab working masses of Algeria. At the primary schools founded by the socialist Keita regime in Mali, the idea of equality had been vehemently propagated. The Keita regime had depicted the chiefs as colonial feudal lords working against the interests of the laborious Malian masses. Indeed, to many Tuareg, those tribal chiefs who owed their legitimacy to state appointment had grown synonymous with the collection of taxes, the forced education of children and other forms of coercion.

Ironically, although tribal societies are often portrayed as premodern, they are in fact essentially modern. They were created during the first few decades after colonial conquest. The tribe and the *fraction* were based on the French comprehension of the Tuareg social political system. The term *tribus* was believed to be the proper translation of the term *ettebel*, or clan federation, the highest level of Tuareg political organization. *Fraction* was seen as the proper translation of the term *tewsit*, or clan. After independence, the new Malian administration set out on an active policy to modernize society on a basis of "tradition", and to undo parts of the administrative colonial heritage. Paradoxically, to do so part of the colonial structure was now formalized by law. The new regime believed that in "traditional" African society the village had been the pivot of society, and therefore proclaimed the village to be the basic unit of Malian political, economic, and administrative organization. Parallel to the village, the *fraction*, an essentially colonial structure, became the basic "traditional" unity of administrative, political, and economic organization in nomad societies, which did not have villages.

Despite the inherent modernity and constant modernization of the tribal system, to many Tuareg intellectuals, tribalism is seen as a premodern obstacle to modern life. Ironically, to transform the structure the new elites feel compelled to use it. By installing the *fraction* and its institutions *de jure*, the procedures and conditions of creation and dissolution became standardized. The main condition to form a new fraction is that one needs 100 potential members, who agree upon a designated chief and elect among themselves a *fraction* council (often consisting of the initial organizers of the new *fraction*). The potential chief and his council can then demand the necessary administrative forms, fill them in, and submit their demand.

The formalization made it possible for others than the chiefs or the administration, such as former rebel leaders, to create *fractions* to the detriment of traditional leadership. The procedure became very popular shortly after the second rebellion and still is today. In 1974 there were 65 fractions in the *cercle* Kidal, a number that had been more or less stable since the 1940s. In 1996 their number had almost doubled to 114.[28] "It won't be long before everybody is his own fraction" as one of my interlocutors cynically observed. The new fractions are often based on the social and political dynamics within a *tewsit* as clan, and between various internal tendencies.

As for the position of the tribal chiefs, their vision on the rebellions

28. *Journal officiel de la République du Mali*, spécial 3 (Bamako, 26 November 1996).

became clear soon after the rebellions broke out. In September 1990, two months after the outbreak of the rebellion in Mali, the tribal chiefs made a declaration, broadcast on radio and television, in which they qualified the rebels as "bandits and traitors, committing unimaginable follies disturbing the tranquillity and stability regained after years of merciless drought", and "denounced and condemned with their last energy the hideous acts the bandits perpetrated".[29] That these chiefs had indeed something to fear from the rebels, was most clearly demonstrated by the abduction of Intalla ag Attaher, the paramount chief of the Kel Adagh of northern Mali, by the rebel movement ARLA in March 1994. In response, Intalla created a heavily armed bodyguard, which functioned as a vigilante movement of its own.

As elsewhere in postcolonial Africa, "traditional" tribal leaders had remained intermediaries between population and government in both Mali and Niger. Yet, the fate of tribal leaders in Mali and Niger differed sharply after independence. In Niger, independence brought to power the Nigerien Progressive Party, which was dominated by the traditional chiefs. A coup d'état in 1974 by Colonel Seyni Kountché did not alter their position. In Mali, independence was brought by the staunchly Marxist US–RDA, whose policy to the Tuareg chiefs remained ambiguous throughout its reign. Its desire to do away with these "feudal remnants of colonialism" entirely were abrogated by the need to have them collaborate in the implementation of policies. Thus, although the chief-taincies were formally abolished in 1961, the chiefs retained informal power in collaboration with the government. After the 1968 coup d'état and the creation of the single party UDPM in 1979, which was less hostile to traditional leaders, a number of Tuareg tribal chiefs or their sons managed to have themselves "elected" as representatives of their constituencies. Thus, the traditional elite regained power in national politics and managed to fortify their position in Mali, whereas they had never really lost it in Niger. It can therefore easily be concluded that the old elite had nothing against a system it owed its existence to.

Still seen by the respective governments as both the legal (as members of parliament) and legitimate representatives of the Tuareg population, some chiefs managed to play an important role in brokering peace in Northern Mali. After the conflict in Northern Mali degenerated in 1994, tribal chiefs in the Niger Bend area played a crucial role in establishing a final peace. Through their efforts, these chiefs regained their status as the true protectors in and of Tuareg society. They shared this position with those *évolués* who had taken over leadership within the rebel movements and

---

29. Declaration made by the Malian fraction chiefs and Tuareg ranks of the Gao region, 12 September 1990; personal archives.

who had negotiated earlier peace deals. Gradually, the true *ishumar* military commanders of the rebellion lost their influence.

THE OUTCOME

So what came of all the proposed changes to society and the nationalist zeal of the new intellectual elites? As most nationalist insurgency movements in Africa, the Tuareg separatist movements failed to reach their goals. When the rebellion broke out in Mali in 1990 and in Niger in 1992, it was received with some enthusiasm by the Tuareg population, who saw the military violence in a "traditional" way as a restoration of lost collective honour endured during the colonial and postcolonial periods. This was perhaps especially true in Niger, where rebellion broke out in 1992, only after initially peaceful attempts to settle Tuareg grievances. Even when army retaliations on the civil population intensified, support did not wither away, and was even strengthened. But with the continuation of the conflict after initial peace agreements were signed, popular support for the rebellion died down in both Mali and Niger. The Tuareg population (not unjustifiably so) accused the rebel elite of being out for personal gain to the detriment of the common people. Another group strongly denouncing the rebellion were the traditional intellectuals, the tribal chiefs, and the *ineslemen* or religious specialists. It is, of course, not surprising that the chiefs were against the rebellion as they were perfectly aware that one of its aims was to undermine their position.

However, partly as a result of the rebellions, both Niger and Mali, which were military dictatorships at the outbreak of the rebellions, underwent a process of democratization and administrative decentralization. The communal elections of June 1999 in Mali were the first ever in which Tuareg could vote other Tuareg into power at local level. The rather bitter and intense struggle for votes between some of the candidates was an indication of the enthusiasm for this relative form of political independence.

The idea that society needed to change was not shared by society and probably not even by all *ishumar* in their hearts. Many rebels fought more out of loyalty to fellow tribesmen who had initiated the rebellion, than out of full understanding. As one informant put it:

> You know, of all the fighters who had been trained in Libya, perhaps only twenty percent understood the goal. The others had understood nothing, they just went along. With the Tuareg, there is this thing we call *teylelil*. If there is one who has a goal, the rest follows automatically. Without knowing what the goal is, without thinking. That is *teylelil*. But we are also *jâhil* [unknowing, uneducated]. Give a *jâhil* a gun and the gun controls the man, not the man the gun.[30]

30. Interview with Lamine ag Bilal, Gao, 20 June 1999.

The internal hierarchy between clans and tribes was especially hard to root out. Both rebel movements in Mali and Niger underwent a process of fragmentation in a mixture of clan affiliation and political differences between various *ishumar* and *évolué* intellectuals.

With this fragmentation, the unending internal fights, the continuing army retaliations, the creation of vigilante movements by neighbouring ethnic groups, and the general insecurity in the Tuareg regions, support by the population declined to zero, while more and more attention was again paid to the traditional intellectuals, the tribal chiefs. Thus, the balance of power between traditional and new elites was reset. After the decentralization of Mali in the late 1990s and the introduction of local democracy, the struggle over political power between both elites continued through more peaceful means.

CONCLUSION

In the past half-century, dramatic socio-economic and political transformations in Tuareg society (brought about by ecological and political changes in the region) have led to the emergence of new intellectual and political elites. These new intellectuals have sought to understand and influence these changes with the aim of ensuring the continuing existence of the Tuareg as a people. Those most consciously thinking about and modelling these changes, were the *ishumar* or "unemployed". From their concrete experiences and way of life as migrant labourers (who were unemployed part of the time) in Libya and Algeria, these "unemployed" developed a political outlook that may be described as nationalist and, in a way, socialist. Members and adherents of this informal network or movement of popular intellectuals organized a more formal movement, the *tanekra* or uprising, which sought to materialize these nationalist and social aspirations through armed resistance against the state.

The initial political aims of the rebellions were twofold. The first was to win independence for a nation-state to be created. This goal was quickly abandoned in favour of demands for more autonomy, which was eventually granted in both Mali and Niger through the decentralization of the national political structure. The second was to enforce social political changes in Tuareg society itself, by abolishing the clans and tribes and by breaking the power of the traditional tribal chiefs and Muslim specialists (*ineslemen*). This second goal was never reached. Soon after the outbreak of the conflicts, the united rebel movements in both Mali and Niger broke up along the lines of clan affiliation. Specific tribes or status groups (castes) were represented by their own movement. When these movements started to fight among themselves, leading to the degeneration of the conflict and to general insecurity in northern Mali and Niger, the traditional elites were instrumental in brokering a final peace.

Nevertheless, the rebellions that broke out in 1990 in Mali and in 1992 in Niger, formed the culmination of years of conscious and active revolutionary nationalist struggle. They also formed the culmination of decades of profound changes in Tuareg society. The initial ecological and economic causes of these changes were perhaps unintended, but the changes they provoked were actively and consciously shaped by an intellectual and cultural elite in search of modernity. Thus, one could argue, the "revolution" in Tuareg society had taken place before "the revolution" broke out.

IRSH 49 (2004), Supplement, pp. 111–132 DOI: 10.1017/S002085900400166X
© 2004 Internationaal Instituut voor Sociale Geschiedenis

Between Sovereignty and Culture: Who is an Indigenous Intellectual in Colombia?*

JOANNE RAPPAPORT

SUMMARY: Recent studies of Latin American indigenous intellectuals affiliated with social movements demonstrate that, while the hold that national intellectuals have as mediators between the state and civil society may be precarious, intellectuals from subordinated minorities are intermediaries between the national society and minority groups, successfully articulating ethnic strivings within national arenas and building ethnic discourses in local communities. But in order to comprehend the success of indigenous intellectuals, it is necessary to inquire into how their discourse is developed internally. To achieve this, we must pay close attention to the heterogeneity of the indigenous movement, in which an array of different types of intellectuals interact and debate issues in a range of ethnic organizations. This article explores the complexities of the negotiation of ethnic discourse by intellectuals within the Regional Indigenous Council of Cauca, a Colombian indigenous organization, focusing on a conflict in which indigenous cultural activists and politicians are at loggerheads over the nature of indigenous political autonomy.

* The research upon which this article is based was conducted from 1995 to 2002 in Cauca, Colombia, thanks to the support of an international collaborative grant from the Wenner-Gren Foundation for Anthropological Research, as well as support from the Graduate School of Georgetown University. My research was conducted within an international collaborative team composed of Colombian academics (Myriam Amparo Espinosa and Tulio Rojas Curieux of the Universidad del Cauca); foreign scholars (David D. Gow of George Washington University, and myself); and indigenous intellectuals (Adonías Perdomo Dizú of the Resguardo Indígena de Pitayó and Susana Piñacué Achicué of the Consejo Regional Indígena del Cauca (CRIC)), who came together to engage in a dialogue focused on our distinct theoretical orientations, methodological approaches, and political commitments. I am indebted to the other members of the team for their acute insights into Caucan ethnic politics and their commentaries on my own work. I also entered into a close collaboration with members of the bilingual education program of CRIC, and owe a great debt to Graciela Bolaños, Abelardo Ramos, and Inocencio Ramos, for their astute observations and critiques, as well as for their immense hospitality. This article is drawn from a longer book manuscript, *Intercultural Utopias*, written while I held a National Endowment for the Humanities fellowship at the National Humanities Center during the 2002–2003 academic year. I thank Michiel Baud and Rosanne Rutten for their very helpful suggestions, which have made this article more persuasive.

INTELLECTUALS IN LATIN AMERICA

Some observers assert that post-Cold-War Latin American intellectuals are in crisis, having lost their status as mediators between strong Latin American states and weak civil societies. In their traditional role as importers of ideas from abroad – what Brazilian literary critic Roberto Schwarz has called "misplaced ideas" – intellectuals have simultaneously stood in for international thinkers and for local constituencies. In so doing, argues Renato Ortiz, they reinterpret local and international ideas, creating national philosophies: "If intellectuals can be defined as symbolic mediators, it is because they fabricate a link between the particular and the universal, the singular and the global."[1] Such globalizing factors as migration and the expansion of transnational markets on the one hand, and the rise of subordinated groups in rapidly decentralizing states on the other, have obviated the need for such "keepers of truth". However, Nicola Miller argues that, on the contrary, twentieth-century Latin American intellectuals were never effective mediators between civil society and the state because they were encompassed by the state through containment, cooptation, or suppression. She reasons, moreover, that their voices – whether in favor or in opposition – were muted by the anti-intellectual policies of most Latin American states, which relegated them to the lower rungs of the bureaucracy; the implicit acceptance on the part of many intellectuals of the modernizing discourse of the state also contributed to their silencing.[2]

Recent studies of intellectuals affiliated with indigenous movements in Latin America indicate that the crisis of national intellectuals is not being experienced by those from subordinated minorities, whose objective is not to create a national consciousness, but to build social movements.[3] Their numbers have increased exponentially in the past two decades as indigenous organizations have taken center-stage, not only in countries such as Bolivia, Ecuador, and Guatemala, with majority or near-majority

---

1. Jorge G. Castañeda, *Utopia Unarmed: The Latin American Left after the Cold War* (New York, 1993), p. 182; Renato Ortiz, *A moderna tradição brasileira: cultura brasileira e indústria cultural* (São Paulo, 1998), p. 139; Roberto Schwarz, *Misplaced Ideas: Essays on Brazilian Culture* (London, 1992); George Yúdice, "Intellectuals and Civil Society in Latin America", *Annals of Scholarship*, 11 (1996), pp. 157–174.
2. Nicola Miller, *In the Shadow of the State: Intellectuals and the Quest for National Identity in Twentieth-Century Spanish America* (London, 1999); Beatriz Sarlo, *Scenes from Postmodern Life* (Minneapolis, MN, 2002), pp. 142, 147–148.
3. Diane M. Nelson, *A Finger in the Wound: Body Politics in Quincentennial Guatemala* (Berkeley, CA, 1999); Esteban Ticona Alejo, *Organización y liderazgo aymara, 1979–1996* (La Paz, 2000); Kay B. Warren, *Indigenous Movements and their Critics: Pan-Maya Activism in Guatemala* (Princeton, NJ, 1998). I use the term "indigenous movement" to refer to the myriad local, regional, and national organizations of native peoples in Latin America whose objective is the defense of ethnic rights.

native populations, but in nations like Colombia, where only 2 per cent of the population is indigenous, but where their influence increasingly pervades the national consciousness. In particular, indigenous organizations have posed concrete alternatives to the nineteenth-century notion of a homogeneous Latin American nation-state, opening a space through their organizing strategies and through civil disobedience in which ethnic pluralism could be imagined. It is the intellectuals of these organizations who are fashioning discourses and institutional structures through which indigenous people have begun to play a significant role in national life, through participation in the writing of new national constitutions, in the creation of legislation that enhances minority participation in political process, and in the development of ideologies that inject cultural difference into education, healthcare, and environmental planning. In other words, intellectuals attached to the indigenous movement have served a mediating function, but their positioning within emergent popular organizations and ethnic movements has enhanced their voice, rather than muting it. They are organic intellectuals in a Gramscian sense, nourishing the imaginings of emergent sectors.

As I will illustrate in this article, however, it would be a mistake to focus exclusively on indigenous intellectuals as individuals who lay claim to indigenous identity. First, the collective nature of indigenous identity, articulated both through community structures of authority and through indigenous organizations, ties being "indigenous" to collective aspirations. Second, as I will demonstrate, not all the intellectuals affiliated with the indigenous movement identify as indigenous, although they support and sustain indigenous organizations. Gramsci's theory of intellectuals provides a background to these related issues.

Gramsci rooted his interpretation of intellectuals in the historical contexts in which intellectual work of all sorts maintains the hegemony of certain social classes or fosters the emergence of new sectors. Gramsci's notion of the intellectual is not so much focused on individuals, as on the relationship between intellectuals or groups of intellectuals and the social sectors in whose name they speak. Gramsci distinguished between those whom he called traditional intellectuals, who work within existing hegemonic sectors in order to maintain them – teachers and priests are good examples – and organic intellectuals who nourish the imaginings of emergent groups. For Gramsci, the notion of organic was not confined exclusively to those intellectuals who emerge from a given class. Instead, he emphasized that what is at stake is the creation of relationships between members of a class and intellectuals from another social sector who have chosen to ally themselves with an emergent group in the course of a struggle for hegemony. In other words, the creation of intellectuals involves not only fostering their emergence within a particular class, but also the assimilation of traditional intellectuals into that group, thus transforming them into organic intellectuals.[4] As I will demonstrate, Gramsci's typology, which is inclusive in the sense that it envisions the movement of intellectuals across groups, is fundamental to an understanding of the indigenous movement, where intellectuals of native backgrounds interact with intellectuals from the dominant society in organizations that are consciously pluralist, looking to forge alliances with other subordinated groups in the construction of a new notion of nationhood in which ethnic difference is a source of strength, not weakness.

A HETEROGENEOUS MOVEMENT

During the past eight years, I have been involved in a collaborative ethnographic relationship with a group of organic intellectuals in the southwestern province of Cauca, Colombia, specifically, activists affiliated with the bilingual education program of the Regional Indigenous Council of Cauca (CRIC), one of Colombia's most prominent indigenous organizations, which unites the Guambiano, Kokonuko, Nasa, Totoró, and Yanacona ethnic groups under a common cause.[5] Many of these cultural activists come out of rural indigenous communities called *resguardos*, communal landholding corporations with title granted in the colonial period by the Spanish crown and governed by annually elected councils, or *cabildos*. Their activist aspirations have led them to the provincial capital of Popayán to pursue political and cultural activities in the organization's regional headquarters.

Many cultural activists are Nasas who come from areas characterized by subsistence farming and the use of indigenous languages, places like the *resguardos* of Caldono on the western slopes of the Central Cordillera, a few hours from Popayán, or from the isolated communities of Tierradentro, four hours of hard travel to the west.[6] Correspondingly, they tend to

4. Antonio Gramsci, *Selections from the Prison Notebooks* (New York, 1971). Anthropologist Kate Crehan provides a useful gloss on Gramsci's notion of the role of the intellectual, which I have used in this brief synthesis of his argument; Kate Crehan, *Gramsci, Culture and Anthropology* (Berkeley, CA, 2002), ch. 6.

5. There is a broad panoply of local, regional, and national indigenous organizations in Colombia, CRIC being one of the oldest of these, founded in 1971. These groups frequently espouse conflicting discourses and ideologies, recruit from rival ethnic groups, and are commonly at odds with one another, although in the course of mobilizations against the state, they come together in a single voice. See David D. Gow and Joanne Rappaport, "The Indigenous Public Voice: The Multiple Idioms of Modernity in Indigenous Cauca", in Kay B. Warren and Jean Jackson (eds), *Indigenous Movements, Self-Representation, and the State in Latin America* (Austin, TX, 2002), pp. 47–80.

6. Subsistence agriculture has always been supplemented by short-term labor migration by men during the coffee harvest, or by women, who work as domestic employees in neighboring cities and towns. However, in recent years these communities have entered the global economy

define "indigenous" according to the cultural characteristics of their home communities, where the native language is Nasa Yuwe, where shamanism provides a widespread alternative to Western medicine, and where the majority of the population supports the *cabildo*. Having received the bulk of their training as apprentices within the indigenous organization, the task of these activists is to produce a discourse of cultural revitalization that reconstructs local culture-bearers as modern ethnic actors. The major focus of their work is the creation of an educational infrastructure in which such ideas can be operationalized. This dual task involves a combination of community organizing with ethnographic, educational, and linguistic research.

Culturalist intellectuals employ discourses that diverge significantly from those of indigenous politicians, who are much less apt to make recourse to cultural forms and are more motivated to cast their objectives in a universal political language that is comprehensible to their allies in other social movements and to the state officials with whom they negotiate. CRIC's most forceful political leadership springs from northern Cauca, where in the early and mid-twentieth century, Nasas migrating from insular areas like Tierradentro sought employment on cattle ranches and in sugar plantations, and where Nasa lifeways have taken on the cadences of urban Colombian culture, given their proximity to the metropolis of Cali and the small city of Santander de Quilichao. While many of these leaders maintain a strong indigenous identity, they have opted for a regional organizational culture and discourse, as opposed to local ones. Thus, many of these men – for their ranks are largely male – are highly pragmatic social actors who pay little attention to the culturalist discourse of their colleagues. In fact, CRIC's cultural activists see themselves as the cultural conscience of the movement, and are constantly seeking to instill in the political leadership a deeper appreciation of the nuances of cultural difference. It is important to note, however, that cultural activists, like indigenous politicians, are intensely political, wedded to organizational strategies and CRIC's program of land claims, defense of the *resguardo* system, and support for *cabildos*. What is different about the two groups is the discourse that each employs to achieve these common objectives and the political space in which each moves.

Given their objectives, indigenous activists – whether cultural workers or politicians – are only intellectuals to the extent that they remain conscious of their ethnic identity, because this is what distinguishes them from those members of native communities who have acquired university

through the cultivation of coca and opium poppies. The Nasa have a long history of struggle against their Spanish and Colombian overlords, and thus brought to the indigenous movement a legacy of grass-roots organizing. There is, moreover, a critical mass of speakers of Nasa Yuwe, which has resulted in a Nasa leadership in cultural affairs in the Caucan movement.

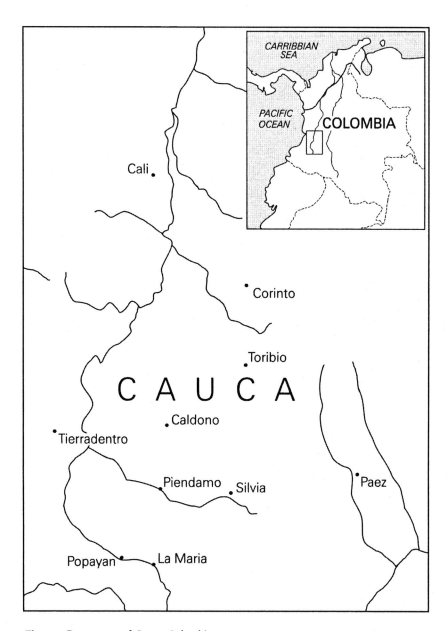

Figure 1. Department of Cauca, Colombia.

degrees and become professionals at large in the dominant society.[7] That is, these activists see being indigenous as what makes their intellectual work meaningful, in contrast to other intellectuals, whose personal identities are not at the center of their role as intellectuals. In addition, it is through their identity as members of a collectivity that they function as intellectuals; their intellectual roles are articulated through participation in *cabildos*, in CRIC, or in related organizational settings, and not simply by virtue of their research and writing activities. The objectives of the organic intellectuals of CRIC thus revolve around their identity as native peoples and their service to the movement; their work is not harnessed towards the creation of academic knowledge, but to promote local activism infused by a contestatory indigenous ideology. Culturalist intellectuals achieve this by encouraging local schools to function as organizing venues and as incubators in which cultural forms can be revitalized. CRIC schools function as a base from which an ethnic ideology that originates from below can be articulated in dialogue with regional cadres. CRIC politicians – who are also organic intellectuals, but are more active in policymaking than in research and grassroots organizing – harness this discourse in their overtures to unorganized indigenous sectors and allies in other social movements, in their conversations with sympathizers, and in their negotiations with the state.

True to their calling as cadres who emerged from the native sector, indigenous public intellectuals in Cauca are generally loathe to call themselves by such an elitist epithet. Lacking the traditional status and tools of trade of those deemed by the dominant society to be intellectuals, they prefer to see themselves as activists who are engaged in intellectual concerns. That is, they consciously dissociate themselves from those who identify as intellectuals in Colombia.[8] Likewise, the ways in which they conceptualize their cultural calling defy elite images of how indigenous culture functions. For many external observers, the cultural constructs that

7. For the latter, indigenous identity is not a necessary part of their intellectual endeavor, but instead, is frequently a hindrance to professional advancement.

8. However, indigenous intellectuals increasingly interact in academic venues with scholarly researchers. They are students in undergraduate and graduate courses, they present papers at scholarly meetings, and they circulate their observations through publications aimed at both an academic and a non-academic reading public. See, for example, Abelino Dagua Hurtado, Misael Aranda, and Luis Guillermo Vasco, *Guambianos: hijos del aroiris y del agua* (Bogotá, 1998); Bárbara Muelas Hurtado, "Relación espacio-tiempo en el pensamiento guambiano", *Proyecciones Lingüísticas*, 1:1(1995), pp. 31–40; Rocío Nieves Oviedo and Abelardo Ramos Pacho, "Expresión del espacio en nasa yuwe", *Lenguas aborígenes de Colombia: Memorias 2 (II Congreso de CCELA)* (Bogotá, 1992), pp. 175–183; Marcos Yule, *Nasa üus yaht'n u'hun'i/"Por los senderos de la memoria y el sentimiento Paez": nasa yuwete twehn'i/"tradicion oral Nasa (Paez)"* (Toribío: Programa de Educación Bilingüe Intercultural/PEBIN/Proyecto Nasa Toribío, 1996). CRIC also publishes a broad range of books, pamphlets, and magazines, which circulate among bilingual teachers, as well as in pedagogical circles in Colombia and in the NGO community throughout Latin America.

emerge from the indigenous movement are essentialist, in the sense that they appear to project coherent, unchanging, and primordial models of native uses and customs. Or they are "strategically essentialist," harnessing primordial sentiments to counter charges of inauthenticity by the powers that be.[9] But, to the contrary, culture, as it is conceived by the indigenous sector, is dynamic and highly permeable. Indigenous intellectuals endeavor to create ethnic imaginaries out of utopian strivings that do not represent native uses and customs as they are lived, but project their revitalization in the future.

COLABORADORES

However, we cannot view indigenous intellectuals as self-sufficient. As we examine indigenous public intellectuals and their role in social protest, we commonly lose sight of the fact that they do not work alone, but in association with intellectuals from the dominant culture who have abandoned the task of the national intellectual who mediates in favor of the hegemonic state, to contribute to social movements that they feel will transform national society. The fact that CRIC is part of an indigenous movement does not mean that all of its militants are members of native ethnic groups. To the contrary, the day-to-day work of the organization is carried out by intercultural teams that include not only Nasas, Guambianos, and members of other indigenous groups, but also leftist intellectuals from urban centers – whom I shall call *colaboradores*, as they call themselves – who have dedicated themselves to indigenous politics and who bring much-needed skills to the movement.

Among the ranks of the *colaboradores* are university professors, who work closely with native activists and whose intellectual priorities have merged with those of their indigenous colleagues, resulting in a relationship that has shifted the paradigms used in the academy. But the relationship of these metropolitan intellectuals to the indigenous movement is uneasy, since they are outsiders to indigenous communities and to the political discipline of the indigenous organization.[10] Furthermore, the

9. Gayatri Chakravorty Spivak and Elizabeth Grosz, "Criticism, Feminism, and the Institution", in Sarah Harasym (ed.), *The Post-Colonial Critic: Interviews, Strategies, Dialogues* (London, 1990), pp. 1–16.
10. Diane Nelson, in *A Finger in the Wound*, and Kay Warren, in *Indigenous Movements and their Critics*, describe an almost adversarial relationship between Guatemalan urban intellectuals and the indigenous movement, and point out that few non-Maya intellectuals support Maya cultural aspirations. The Colombian case is considerably more fluid than the Guatemalan one. Many non-indigenous intellectuals in Colombia are highly supportive of indigenous organizations and have routinely worked as their allies. This does not mean, however, that external supporters are fully trusted by indigenous activists who, like other minorities, are wary of members of the dominant group, however supportive they may seem. Hence, the uneasiness between them.

theoretical discourses that they employ, while frequently of interest to indigenous intellectuals, emerge from and are most pertinent to academic agendas, and are geared not toward promoting activism, but with an eye to producing academic writing; this makes this sector essentially untrust-worthy – almost cannibalistic – for indigenous activists. Academics are traditional intellectuals who are not organic to indigenous organizations, but are sympathetic to them; they could almost be said to be in transition between traditional and organic status, given that, in the Gramscian model, traditional intellectuals could be potentially absorbed within the cadre of organic intellectuals.

More active interlocutors are the *colaboradores* who work full-time for ethnic organizations, whose everyday lives transpire in an indigenous milieu, and who submit to the risks and the discipline of ethnic organizations; *colaboradores* are, essentially, intellectuals from the domi-nant culture who are organic to the indigenous movement. Many of the most prominent members of this group function as interlocutors who stimulate discussion within the organization, but they rarely, if ever, publish their ideas in formats other than internal documents and reports. This sector is almost totally ignored in the literature, perhaps because *colaboradores* do not fit neatly within the essentialist models that we have created for analyzing indigenous organizations.

Despite the adherence of *colaboradores* to movement objectives, their discourses only partially mirror those of indigenous intellectuals, for the conceptual models that they employ originate in part in the worlds from which they have come, just as do those of academic interlocutors. In fact, their origins outside of the communities and their use of external ideas mark their ambivalent membership within the movement as "outsiders within".[11] But, in spite of their close association with indigenous intellectuals, they are not, in any sense of the word, a vanguard of the sort that intellectuals in leftist parties hoped to constitute. *Colaboradores* see themselves as adherents to an existing movement, playing an equal – and increasingly, a subaltern – role to the *cabildos* and the indigenous activists that form the backbone of the organization. If necessary, *colaboradores* can find a home outside the indigenous movement; while for the most committed, it would be painful to disengage from the indigenous movement, there are many other organizing venues in which they can incorporate themselves and further their political agendas, unlike the indigenous intellectuals who recognize that their very survival as indigenous people is what is at stake in the movement.

Gramsci's theory of intellectuals is useful in making sense of the internal role of *colaboradores* in indigenous organizations. In fact, if we are to take

11. Patricia Hill Collins, *Black Feminist Thought: Knowledge, Consciousness, and the Politics of Empowerment* (New York, 1991), p. 11.

Gramsci to heart, we cannot study the indigenous movement without paying attention to the role of outsiders within, because they have achieved organic status alongside indigenous intellectuals. But, notwithstanding the utility of Gramscian thought for making sense of the relationship between indigenous intellectuals and *colaborador* outsiders, Gramsci does not supply us with sufficient conceptual tools to contend with the internal complexities of intellectual work in Cauca, nor, I suspect, in other locations.

The category of the organic intellectual provides a key to comprehending the interactions of the organization with external actors, but does not shed light on negotiations internal to the regional organization, or between CRIC and the local sphere of action, where a multiplicity of indigenous organic intellectuals operate, frequently at loggerheads with one another. There are considerable differences in the discourses employed by the cultural activists of CRIC's regional office and affiliated teachers or *cabildo* members working in local venues: while the former look toward leftist theorists, particularly those writing about bilingual education or grassroots development, to stimulate their construction of indigenous proposals, the latter are more concerned with fostering an exchange with other indigenous groups and with other subordinated minorities (such as Afro-Colombians) in the peasant sector. It is within the dynamic that unfolds between regional and local indigenous intellectuals, and among the different sorts of intellectuals who operate in these spaces, that ethnic projects are constituted, not in the imposition of one sector on top of another.

COSMOVISION

There is another significant group of local intellectuals: shamans – in Nasa Yuwe they are called *thê' walas* – whose discourses are rooted in an exchange with the spirit world, and whose knowledge provides a potent language for the politicized construction of cultural forms. I call these individuals *sabedores* or "knowers", in acknowledgment of the recognition that the movement has given them as the source of the organization's cultural imaginings and their role as brakes against what the movement perceives as its ideological colonization by external forces. Unlike most activists, who choose to function as intellectuals – even if they do not accept to be labelled as such – *thê' walas* are chosen against their own wishes. After a lengthy period of illness and persistent visions, they come to the realization that they hold powers which, if not harnessed through ritual, threaten to engulf them. Shamans are very much more attuned to oral tradition and sacred geography than are other indigenous intellectuals and thus have a great deal more to bring to the table. Many cultural activists, in contrast, know little more about things spiritual than what they have read in movement publications or heard in workshops, that is, their knowledge is second-hand. While both groups employ an intuitive methodology that combines culturally self-conscious reflection with the collection of empirical information, the intuitions of the *thê' walas* are grounded in empirical knowledge they acquire through the interpretation of bodily signs – vibrations and pulses that they feel in their extremities – which non-shamans cannot fully comprehend and no-one can fully verbalize.

It is through the reappropriation of shamanic knowledge, called "cosmovision" by indigenous militants, that cultural activists hope to derive a new indigenous political strategy. Shamanic learning functions as a source of historical models and conceptual structures capable of transforming the priorities and objectives of the organization. The rituals that shamans conduct maintain harmony and balance in the universe, knowledge of which orients the development of the indigenous jurisprudence and legal procedures that are currently under construction, as Colombian indigenous people adapt customary law to the needs of their changing communities. The very notion of harmony embodied in ritual provides, in the opinion of culturalist intellectuals, a new model for behavior within the organization, a non-Western code of conduct. The oral narratives and origin stories with which shamans are intimately familiar provide the movement with a historical basis for asserting their difference. In fact, many of the key narratives in the oral tradition recall the efforts of colonial hereditary chiefs to establish *resguardos* – communally-controlled indigenous territories – and entreat *cabildos* and the regional organization to defend them as bastions of indigenous autonomy.

But there is another, more utopian facet of the cosmovision project. The wealth of shamanic lore must ultimately be converted into re-authenticated indigenous lifeways – ritual made familiar by repetition, house gardens tilled by local hands, healing practices replacing Western medicine – so that local people begin to live their cultural difference in their everyday lives, making the personal political, to appropriate a slogan from the 1960s. For this reason, it is highly significant that CRIC linguist Susana Piñacué translates cosmovision into Nasa Yuwe as *fxi'zenxi* – *vivencia* or everyday experience.[12] The hope is to reintroduce into indigenous communities lifeways that slowly become habitual, unremarkable, unselfconscious, in short, authentic.

Whether they are entirely successful in this goal depends to a great extent upon the indigenous community in which cosmovision is introduced, however. People from Tierradentro, where shamanic practice is

12. Susana Piñacué Achicué, "Liderazgo, poder y cultura de la mujer nasa (páez)", in Joanne Rappaport (ed.), *Retornando la mirada: una investigacion colaborativa interetnica sobre el Cauca a la entrada del milenio* (Popayán, forthcoming).

accepted as an alternative to Western medicine and where shamans have always been active in *cabildos*, are more receptive to the discourse of cosmovision than are the Nasa of northern Cauca, who are closely integrated into the regional *mestizo* culture. Tierradentro shamans have been engaged for a number of years in collective research into cosmovision and played an important role in maintaining community cohesion after a 1994 earthquake that forced many villagers to resettle in distant locations. Correspondingly, there has been a recent burst of attempts to incorporate shamans even further into daily activities and political organizing in Tierradentro. In other regions, however, where shamans have not traditionally played a role in everyday life, cosmovision is far from becoming a *vivencia*, although it is a popular discourse among local teachers and catechists. In short, the cosmovision project is still a utopia, but one that cultural activists see as feasible and necessary.

CONFLICTING DISCOURSES

The remainder of this article will explore how negotiations among intellectuals organic to the indigenous movement take place on the ground, because it is only through such case studies that we can make sense of how multiplicity ultimately results in a persuasive organizational discourse. I will examine a recent confrontation in which tensions between various groups of indigenous intellectuals came to a head, a scenario in which the negotiation by intellectuals of a movement discourse is most readily apparent.

For the past three years the provincial administration of Cauca has been led by a Guambiano activist, Governor Floro Alberto Tunubalá. His election to the governorship of Cauca was made possible by the emergence of an alternative public sphere that grew out of a coalition of urban and rural social movements, with the indigenous movement at its vanguard.[13] His administration reflects the diversity of the electoral coalition, bringing together in common cause indigenous activists, urban intellectuals, unionists, and peasant leaders. But what happens when *cabildo* members – who are prominent members of this contestatory public sphere – come into conflict with an indigenous-led state? For the next few pages, I will explore the antagonisms that flared when a group of community leaders attempted to impose what they called *derecho mayor* – their "greater

13. On the notion of the alternative public sphere, see Nancy Fraser, *Justice Interruptus: Critical Reflections on the "Postsocialist" Condition* (New York, 1997), ch. 3. Unfortunately, the coalition was not strong enough in the 2003 gubernatorial elections to prevail against the traditional Liberal Party candidate, who won the election, but has since been barred from assuming office for irregularities in payment of contracts when he occupied another post. The National Electoral Council has ruled that new elections must take place (*El Tiempo*, 23 December 2003, "Cauca, sin gobernador").

right" as the original Americans – over the national law that the Tunubalá administration was bound by oath to uphold. This dispute, which erupted in the summer of 2002, magnifies the heterogeneity of the indigenous movement and brings into focus the complex and intertwined relationships of local and regional activists, *colaboradores*, and indigenous state representatives. As I will illustrate, this was a encounter between the culturalist vision of indigenous intellectuals and the discourse of sovereignty of native politicians, but with a telling twist: it is almost impossible to separate out the threads of who is a politician, who is a cultural worker, who is affiliated with a regional apparatus, who is a local, who speaks in the cadences of sovereignty, who can legitimately speak of cosmovision, and who is an intellectual.

Taita Floro Tunubalá – as most indigenous Caucans call him, using a Guambiano term of respect – is in his late forties. A model of the new brand of indigenous leadership, he has partially completed a university degree and has spent a great deal of time outside Cauca, serving as a national senator and as a development consultant.[14] But Taita Floro also enjoys local legitimacy, having been elected to two terms as governor of the *resguardo* of Guambía, which is affiliated with the Indigenous Authorities of Colombia (AICO), an organization that operates parallel to CRIC and in Cauca, is largely confined to Guambianos. Indeed, Taita Floro's affiliation with Guambía defies any easy distinction between local and regional actors, given that the *resguardo* of Guambía controls this regional organization, which has its own political line in comparison to other Caucan ethnic groups, which are aligned with CRIC.[15] When in the public eye, Taita Floro's "Guambianoness" is accentuated, much to the consternation of the provincial elite: he wears the trademark blue kilt, black poncho, and fedora hat of his ethnic compatriots. He is equally fluent in Spanish and in Guambiano, although he speaks Spanish with a distinct Guambiano accent.

Taita Floro entered the governor's palace in Popayán with the support of AICO and CRIC, who came together in an unprecedented alliance in the wake of a series of occupations of the Pan-American Highway at a site

14. The 1991 Colombian constitution provides two senate seats for indigenous people, who run under the rubric of various indigenous organizations and political parties, but are chosen by the electorate at large. Taita Floro was one of the earliest indigenous leaders to hold such office.

15. AICO espouses a grass-roots organizing model based on *cabildos* and does not have a central committee. There are no *colaboradores* inside AICO, although there have been outsiders working in solidarity with the organization, positioned on the outside (they are called *solidarios*). Historically, AICO supported the reincorporation of reclaimed lands within the *resguardo* structure, while CRIC did not always follow this model; this difference, which was fundamental in the late-1970s, is no longer at issue. On the ideology of AICO, see María Teresa Findji, "From Resistance to Social Movement: The Indigenous Authorities Movement in Colombia", in Arturo Escobar and Sonia Alvarez (eds), *The Making of Social Movements in Latin America: Identity, Strategy, and Democracy* (Boulder, CO, 1992), pp. 112–133.

called La María to protest the lack of basic services to indigenous communities, a coalition that that gave rise to his campaign. But his largest voting base was among non-indigenous urban dwellers who had tired of the stranglehold that the two mainstream political parties had on Caucan politics. Taita Floro has made his mark on Cauca. His efforts at organizing the governors of surrounding provinces in opposition to the US-inspired fumigation policies of Plan Colombia, and his encouragement of the manual erradication of ilicit crops attest to his broader political commitment beyond the boundaries of indigenous territories, as does the general development plan drafted by his administration, which promotes community organizing in nonindigenous areas and in the cities, in the hopes of dynamizing the *mestizo* and Afro-Colombian populations; one of Taita Floro's central concerns has been the paucity of participation in these sectors, evidenced in the high proportion of community development proposals his administration received from indigenous communities, which far surpassed the relative weight of the native population in Cauca. Taita Floro appropriates methods from his indigenous constituency, such as community assemblies and the notion of the *minga* or Andean communal work party, as tools to revitalize the public sphere in non-native rural and urban areas.

While Taita Floro is the child of the indigenous movement, he is also the governor of Cauca, serving a much broader constituency than the roughly 30 per cent of the provincial population that identifies itself as indigenous. Hence, he feels a pull between two conflicting allegiances and sets of administrative priorities. Furthermore, as governor, he is subject to the restrictions of the Colombian state and he cannot make decisions that contravene its rules and regulations. Taita Floro regularly experiences, in the flesh, the tensions between leading an indigenous community and representing the state. In June and July 2002, one such contradiction emerged, when the indigenous authorities of the municipality of Caldono blocked the Pan-American Highway at La María, demanding that Taita Floro dismiss their municipal mayor.

CONFLICT IN CALDONO

Caldono is a large municipality encompassing six Nasa *resguardos*. Located to the north of the provincial capital of Popayán, Caldono is part of what indigenous activists call the "inside", those insular spaces in which contact between indigenous people and the national society are limited. Activists see these places as more culturally authentic and as embodying a set of lifeways that should be emulated by the indigenous organization through cultural planning and a heightened attention to ritual activity.[16] Several of

16. While it is the place of activists to promote the "inside", they expressed to me the feeling that

the municipality's *resguardos* were home to intense land struggles in the early years of CRIC, when communities occupied haciendas lying within *resguardo* boundaries and incorporated them into their communal land base. In the course of this struggle, experimental schools were founded as organizing venues in which leaders could harness popular political sentiment for building CRIC from the grassroots up. These *resguardos* retain a vivid memory of Juan Tama, the mythico-historical hereditary chief of the Nasa, who left them a *resguardo* title that dates to the early eighteenth century and provides the narrative upon which contemporary oral tradition is based. This colonial document unites the various communities of Caldono into a single historical unit.[17] In recent years, CRIC regional activists returned to Caldono to run for office in their respective *cabildos*, bringing with them a militant culturalist position that they had developed in the course of their work in bilingual education and a renewed interest in regional consolidation, using Juan Tama as a model.

Caldono's municipal seat was designated a *zona de población* under Law 89 of 1890, the law that, until the 1991 constitution, defined the organization of the *resguardo* system and its nature as a vehicle for the assimilation of native peoples into the dominant society. The *zona de población*, as decreed in Law 89, was an urban district established in the midst of communal indigenous territory, home to a *mestizo* settler population that was not subject to *resguardo* jurisdiction. Such settlements were meant to diffuse national culture within the indigenous hinterland and to form the core of potential *mestizo* localities. As a result of this historical circumstance, the town of Caldono is still largely *mestizo* in character and there is considerable hostility between the urban center and *resguardos*. There are also various satellite towns with *mestizo* peasant populations and considerable Guambiano settlement throughout the municipality, making this an ethnically heterogeneous region. Until the Indigenous Social Alliance (ASI), an indigenous political party, successfully ran Nasa candidates in municipal elections in the 1990s, the mayor was a *mestizo*, running a tight and ethnically segregated bureaucracy characterized by clientilistic political practices.[18]

intellectuals live on a cultural "frontier" from which they make forays "inside" and "outside", thus mediating the two constituencies; see Joanne Rappaport, "Los nasa de frontera y la política de la identidad en el Cauca Indígena", in *idem* (ed.), *Retornando la mirada.*

17. Juan Tama's title, written in 1700 but brought into the Colombian notarial record in 1881, can be found in the Archivo Central del Cauca, Popayán, "Título de las parcialidades de Pitayo, Quichaya, Caldono, Pueblo Nuevo y Jambalo", partida 843. On the importance of Juan Tama to colonial Nasa political aspirations and his continued prominence in contemporary oral tradition, see Joanne Rappaport, *The Politics of Memory: Native Historical Interpretation in the Colombian Andes* (Durham, 1998).

18. José María Rojas, *La bipolaridad del poder local: Caldono en el Cauca indígena* (Cali, 1993).

But in 2000, ASI lost out to a *mestizo* politician, Gerardo Iván Sandoval, whom the *cabildos* accused shortly thereafter of having usurped lands destined for purchase by the *resguardo* of La Laguna. They also charged him with misuse of municipal funds and of supporting an upstart *resguardo* in the locality of Plan de Zúñiga, which the other communities refused to recognize. Beginning in late May, 2002, the *cabildos* sought Sandoval's resignation on the grounds that he was "unfit to govern them". They convoked a "permanent assembly", a state of belligerency marked by constant public meetings, enlisting CRIC's executive committee to assist them in persuading Taita Floro to remove the mayor from office.[19]

On 26 June 2002, the *cabildos* occupied the Pan-American Highway at La María, commanding their indigenous compatriots to join them in the struggle. Many *cabildos* from across Cauca half-heartedly sent representatives. La María was the site of a tent city, fed by a huge communal kitchen and patrolled by an indigenous civic guard armed only with staffs and made up largely of teenagers, young adults, and elderly women. Hundreds congregated n the large public space overlooking the highway, listening to the addresses of council representatives. Below, the road was blocked off by the civic guard and by hundreds of parked trucks, with Colombian soldiers lining the route. Before being allowed into the meeting space, visitors were subject to frisking by the guard and their identity papers were inspected.

COSMOVISION AS A ROUTE TO SOVEREIGNTY

In the years before the 2002 highway occupation, regionally based cultural activists had made considerable inroads into the *cabildos* of Caldono. One of the first was Luis Carlos Ulcué – originally from the tropical colonization zone of Caquetá, but whose parents were born in Caldono – who was elected to the governorship of Pueblo Nuevo in the late 1990s. Luis Carlos came into conflict with its piously Catholic population when he advocated a return to reconstructed Nasa rituals intended to replace Christian practices. Since then, cultural activists and their allies have been elected to high posts in *cabildos*, to the zonal organization uniting Caldono's *cabildos*, and to CRIC's executive committee. The influence of cultural activists is evident in the councils' discourse, which revolves around cosmovision.

The councils united against the municipal mayor, pointedly affirming their ethnic ascendency and sovereignty by calling themselves the "indigenous communities of the ancestral territory of the Nasa People

19. Autoridades Tradicionales del Territorio de Caldono, 2002. "Nuestra posición cultural y política: resolución de la Asamblea Permanente del Territorio Ancestral del Pueblo Nasa (Indígena) de Caldono", Caldono, Cauca: mimeo.

of Caldono" and by asserting that they "affirm[ed] and ratif[ied] the teachings of the elders about our Laws of Origin [and] the Greater Right [Derecho Mayor], founded in and lived through cosmovision". Here, for the first time in a public and intercultural space, a group of indigenous politicians was employing the discourse of cosmovision in its purest form – which is no accident, since the *cabildo* rosters included cultural activists-turned-local authorities.

In a widely circulated broadside, they argued, for example, that the Greater Right whose hegemony they sought, was a law originating at the center of the earth, and was meant for all people because all living beings were born from the Mother Earth. They asserted that their territory was at once cosmic and earthly, harmonized by rituals that ensured equilibrium among its inhabitants and ruled by the laws of the creator ancestors. They couched their demand for political autonomy in a discourse that combined the political language of self-determination with an acceptance of the role played by the spiritual world in orienting indigenous authorities. Their denunciation of the municipal mayor accused him of having violated ancestral law and of "trampling our dignity and integrity as Originary Peoples, charged with and pledged to the conservation and preservation of Harmonic Life in what we call planet Earth". Their condemnation was delivered "in the name of the Earth, the Sun, the Water, the Moon, and the cosmic, earthly, and subterranean spirits". The broadside was signed by the governors and captains of the six *cabildos*. Beside their signatures, the names of their offices were listed in both Nasa Yuwe and Spanish: the captains were called *sa't nehwe'sx*, combining the word for hereditary chief (*sa't*) with that of legitimate authority (*ne'hwe'sx*), underlining the cosmic roots of their authority.[20]

While cosmovision has been a goal of the cultural activists who, for half a decade, have held *cabildo* office in the municipality, the culturalist approach had never before received the overwhelming reception that it did in 2002, when a critical mass of the Caldono indigenous community followed its traditional authorities into confrontation over the mayorality. The notion of the Greater Right that coalesced them was not, however, part of the local discourse; in fact, while the Guambianos have articulated this notion in their political demands for the past twenty-odd years, it had never before been expressed by CRIC-affiliated communities. The novelty of the discourse was, indeed, apparent in the speeches delivered at the gathering at La María. Most of the traditional authorities who spoke could say little about what constituted the Greater Right and they dwelled, instead, on how indigenous legislation – even the 1991 constitution – was an imposition by outsiders.

Finally, for lack of material to cover, the organizers were forced to bring

20. Caldono, "Nuestra posición cultural y política", pp. 2, 4.

in speakers from the outside, most notably, regional cultural activist, Inocencio Ramos, and – to my surprise – myself. Our presentations were preceded by a brief, very self-conscious, and abbreviated shamanic cleansing ceremony, consisting in chewing a small packet of herbs which, mixed with alcohol, was blown in the air, while two *thê' walas* mediated with the spirits; some participants criticized the ceremony as too public and inappropriate, given that it was conducted in broad daylight. I was first on the podium, taking the opportunity to speak about how Juan Tama – the hereditary chief and founder of the *resguardos* of Caldono, who has become an icon of the Caucan indigenous movement – had laid the basis for the Greater Right. Inocencio took the Nasa translation of "constitution" – *eç ne'hwe'sx* or "the principal book" – and proceeded to explain why the Greater Right was more primordial than the constitution. The Greater Right could be translated as *mantey neesnxi*, which he cast in Spanish as an ancient ethical system that makes people *nasnasa* or "more Nasa". The staff of office carried by *cabildo* members, Inocencio pointed out, was inhabited by the guardian spirit, or *ksxa'w*, thus transforming it into an object that embodies harmony and is emblematic of the cosmic roots of politics. He concluded that the language of the Greater Right is ritual in nature, aimed at redistributing energy to achieve equilibrium.

What was striking to me about this assembly was the tremendous discursive gulf that yawned between the indigenous politicians from other parts of Cauca and the Caldono-based cultural activists-cum-traditional authorities. The politicians spoke in the cadences of sovereignty, reiterating their support for Taita Floro and the need to build a coherent proposal for a new political system. The culturalists insisted upon the preeminence of cosmovision. Both are well-developed discourses of the indigenous movement, but their narrative tropes did not resonate with one another in this context. As a result, although the presentations persuasively synthesized the theoretical foundations of the Greater Right and the political conditions that had made its introduction necessary, no-one reached even the most preliminary of conclusions as to what implications this reasoning held for everyday political practice. It was as though two parallel intellectual and political projects, both springing from a single movement, had come into momentary contact to propel a community into action. The gulf between philosophy and practice was sensed by the representatives of other *cabildos* who had come to the assembly and who, in a debate mediated by CRIC officers, attempted to persuade Caldono to retreat from the radically indefensible position it had assumed.

A CONFRONTATION WITH TAITA FLORO

Taita Floro appeared at La María some six hours after the communities occupied the highway, accompanied by an entourage that included the then-Secretary of Government (a former member of the Quintín Lame Armed Movement, an indigenous guerrilla organization), representatives of the regional legal apparatus, and advisors. Unlike at earlier meetings in La María, where his electoral campaign hosted public events and where he was treated as an exemplary member of the indigenous community, now Taita Floro found himself representing the Colombian state, invited into the large open-air public meeting space to address the assembly and then banished to an out-building while the *cabildos* mulled over their response to him. Taita Floro told the Caldonos that they had placed him in an untenable position. As a former governor of Guambía, he intimated that he understood and fully supported their demand for recognition of their Greater Right as originary peoples – in fact, he asserted that, as a Guambiano, he knew more about the Greater Right than they did. But as governor of Cauca, he not only represented the indigenous communities that had propelled him into office, but also was the governor of the *mestizo* town-dwellers and peasants of Caldono, who for the most part, supported the municipal mayor and feared the asendancy of the *cabildos*.

Taita Floro's quandary is underlined by Ernesto Laclau in his explication of the dynamics of the coalition politics of new social movements.[21] Laclau reasons that the organization that assumes the leadership of a coalition is forced to place its own demands on the back burner in the interests of representing a communal platform. In the process, its organizational dynamic is muted and weakened. But the long-term unity of the coalition is also placed in danger, because its survival is premised on the vitality of the component organizations and, in particular, of the coalition leadership. Were Taita Floro to take up the Greater Right as his banner – which is precisely what Guambiano *cabildo* governors do – he would risk alienating the *mestizo* members of the coalition that elected him. When he showed reluctance to engage the *cabildos* of Caldono to the exclusion of his peasant constituency, he was seen by the Caldonos as a sell-out. The movement's very objective of refashioning the state, then, requires that the indigenous agenda must, necessarily, fall by the wayside.

But it is not only the exigencies of the coalition that forced Taita Floro to take the position he did – so did the requirements of the Colombian state. As he explained to the assembly, his options were limited by the office he held. A *cabildo* governor simultaneously fills executive, judicial, and legislative functions, Taita Floro told the congregation, but the governor of Cauca does not – cannot – encroach upon the prerogatives of other branches of government. He could not force Iván Sandoval to resign, but was obliged to let accepted legal procedures take their course. What went unaddressed was the intense political pressure being exerted by Taita Floro's political opponents among the regional *mestizo* elite, who had lost

21. Ernesto Laclau, *Emancipations* (London, 1996), ch. 3.

the governorship to the popular coalition and eagerly awaited his downfall as a result of the confrontation with Caldono.[22] This was what most concerned many influential *colaboradores*, who immediately deployed respected public figures to evaluate the legality of the Caldonos' demands and defuse the situation.

In short, Taita Floro was about to become a casualty of the contradictions between community and state that indigenous politicians are discovering as they assume public office. He was from the community, but no longer of it.[23] At stake was his own political future in the eyes of his indigenous and *mestizo* constituents and the broader Caucan society. At stake, also, was the legitimacy of the indigenous movement as the vanguard of a broader popular coalition, as well as the extent to which its paired discourses of sovereignty and culture were at all relevant to other coalition members.

Ultimately, Taita Floro achieved a middle road: he persuaded the Caldonos to open the Pan-American Highway to traffic and assembled a commission to work with them at laying the groundwork for future legislation to establish "indigenous territorial entities", the geo-administrative units of the Colombian state governed by indigenous people that are proposed in the 1991 constitution, but have never been legislated into existence by a recalcitrant Congress.[24] The *cabildos* of Caldono are now engaged in that process, attempting to harness the discourses of cosmovision and sovereignty into a new politics of indigenous citizenship. Thus, the 2002 confrontation at La María did not end in failure for any of the parties involved. Taita Floro effectively defused a dangerous conflict, the regional culturalist intellectuals ensconced in local councils were provided with a space in which to ground their utopias in political practice, and even the municipal mayor and his supporters were given a temporary lease on life (at least, until the ponderous state bureaucracy makes public its decision on his continued tenure).

CONCLUSION

While the Gramscian model helps us to conceptualize the differences between the articulation of intellectuals with social movements and the mediating function that Latin American intellectuals have filled between civil society and the state, we need to go beyond it to make sense of how intellectuals impact upon the face of indigenous politics. That is, we must

22. *El Liberal* (Popayán), 25 July 2002, p. 1, and 26 July 2002, p. 1.
23. I am indebted to Arquimedes Vitonás, a Nasa anthropology student and currently the municipal mayor of Toribío, for clarifying this concept for me.
24. Enrique Sánchez, Roque Roldán, and María Fernanda, *Derechos e identidad: los pueblos indígenas y negros en la Constitución Política de Colombia de 1991* (Bogotá, 1993).

inquire into how the very heterogeneity of the movement is itself a fertile ground for the construction of a native political ideology. What I am proposing contrasts with existing work on Latin American indigenous movements. Scholars generally tend to describe these organizations as homogeneous with generic "indigenous" memberships. As a consequence of our inattention to the complexity of the membership of these organizations and the multiple discourses engendered by them, however, we frequently come up short. We deny ourselves the conceptual space needed to interpret the relationship between the internal multiculturalism of these organizations and the pluralist demands that they project to the dominant society. Instead, we have persisted in essentializing them, producing the image of a package of separatist demands lodged in the nostalgic appeal to a primordial culture, which in no way reflects their intellectual dynamism or the protagonist role that they are playing throughout the continent.

The creation of a typology of intellectuals organic to the indigenous movement, which is what I did in the first half of this article, only takes us so far. In order to comprehend how an organizational voice emerges, we must conceptualize the different discourses of the various sectors within the movement, and we must study how they are engaged in the course of negotiations both internal and external to the movement. For me, one of the most useful tools for arriving at this conceptualization is the distinction between culturalist projects and discourses of sovereignty, between an inward-looking emphasis on the revitalization of cultural specificity and an emphasis on universal languages of minority rights that discursively and practically links the indigenous movement to other progressive social sectors and makes possible negotiation with the state. As Bruce Albert so cogently argues in his interpretation of the discourse of Davi Kopenawa, a Brazilian Yanomami leader, the only way that the indigenous movement can hold its own in an ethnically heterogeneous political field is if it looks simultaneously toward political universals and cultural specifics.[25]

It is at the intersection of these two discourses that the articulation of the cultural project with the movement's political objectives can be most fruitfully explored. This calls for a comparative analysis of the positioning of indigenous intellectuals in local and regional venues, as well as an understanding of the fluidity of their discursive practices within the diverse political contexts in which they operate. Accordingly, we must explore the alliances, dialogues, and disjunctures among the indigenous

25. Bruce Albert, "O ouro canibal e a queda do céu: uma crítica xamânica da economia política da naturaleza" (Brasília: Série Antropologica no. 174, Departamento de Antropología, Universidade de Brasília, 1995), p. 4. See also Allen Chadwick, *Blood Narrative: Indigenous Identity in American Indian and Maori Literary and Activist Texts* (Durham, 2002); Les Field, "Complicities and Collaborations: Anthropologists and the 'Unacknowledged Tribes' of California", *Current Anthropology*, 40 (1999), pp. 193–209.

cultural activists who move in the regional sphere, regional and local indigenous politicians, *colaboradores*, local native intellectuals, and sha-mans. While their ultimate aim is to construct a movement that speaks to the dominant society in what appears in the course of mobilizations as a single voice, their objectives emerge out of the heterogeneity of their agendas, their methodologies, and their discourses.

It is through the confrontation of discourses of diverse intellectuals – politicians, cultural activists, shamans, *colaboradores* – that a communal voice is achieved in the Colombian indigenous movement. The mediating function that they fill between community and national society, or between indigenous movement and the state, is made infinitely complex by the heterogeneity within their ranks. If we are to comprehend the discourse of indigenous movements, then, we must pay heed to this heterogeneity, recognizing it as the ground upon which politics is constructed.

IRSH 49 (2004), Supplement, pp. 133–157 DOI: 10.1017/S0020859004001671
© 2004 Internationaal Instituut voor Sociale Geschiedenis

Critics and Experts, Activists and Academics: Intellectuals in the Fight for Social and Ecological Justice in the Narmada Valley, India

PABLO S. BOSE

SUMMARY: The following article examines the role of popular intellectuals in the rise of the Narmada Bachao Andolan, a mass-based movement opposed to the building of large dams in the Narmada Valley of central India. In particular, it focuses on two of this struggle's most prominent public figures and spokespersons, Medha Patkar and Arundhati Roy. The article examines the relationship between these individuals and the movement itself – how issues have been framed by Patkar and Roy for local, national, and international audiences, how support for the anti-dam struggle has been mobilized, and how each of these figures are themselves perceived and portrayed. The article will also examine some of the challenges faced by the movement and its leaders, not only from proponents of the dam projects, but also from other social activists and intellectuals. The latter have raised questions about representation, voice and strategy, as well as insider/outsider authenticity and legitimacy in the anti-dam movement, issues that this paper considers in some detail. Finally, the article draws on the Narmada case to ask some broader questions regarding popular intellectuals and social movement organizing and strategy.

INTRODUCTION

This paper examines the role of popular intellectuals in the rise of a mass-based social and ecological justice movement mobilized against the building of large dams in the Narmada Valley of central India through the latter half of the twentieth century. This movement has enjoyed widespread support both nationally and internationally and has drawn upon a vibrant and longstanding local tradition of opposition to hydro-electric dam projects in order to raise questions about the nature and purpose of economic and social development in the region. In doing so, it has broadened its message, its appeal, and its constituency, fostering in the process regional, national, and even transnational networks of solidarity and support with regards to issues of sustainable development.

The story of Narmada is well known within the fields of development and social movement studies, a tale of diverse local communities and organizations coming together to challenge development authorities, state

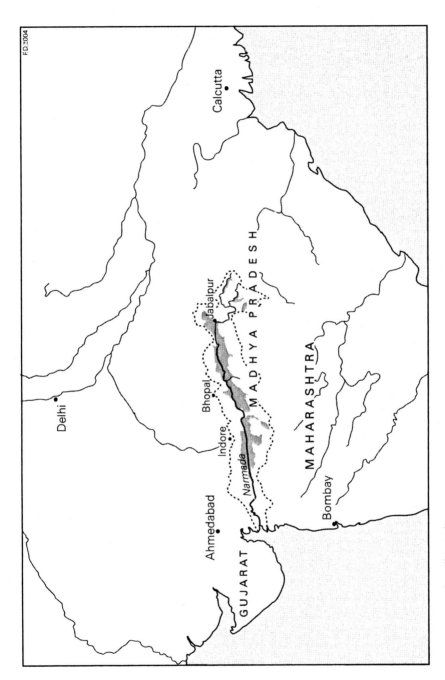

Figure 1. Narmada Valley, India.

and national governments, and even the World Bank on their plans to redraw the social, physical, and economic landscapes of the region. What is less recognized is the complicated, confusing, and at the same time integral role played by popular intellectuals in this history.

There are two types of intellectuals particularly visible in the Narmada Valley – what Michel Foucault might distinguish as "critics" and "experts".[1] The latter are a ubiquitous presence in the Narmada Valley, the legions of engineers, scientists, and administrators who have worked to plan, implement, and legitimize the Narmada Valley Development Project of an intricate series of interlinked dams. The "critics" are also numerous – including environmental activists, social workers, university students, and labour organizers, as well as spokespeople and leaders from amongst the townsfolk, villagers, marginalized groups, and landless labourers who inhabit the proposed submergence zone.

It is many of these critics, with their multiple roles and diverse backgrounds, who I conceive of as the "popular intellectuals" of the Narmada conflict. They have helped to voice the concerns and opposition of local populations to the proposed project. They have also, through their empirical research, critical reflection, and careful analysis sought to understand the complex processes of nationalism, international development, and globalization that are intertwined and affect life in the Valley. Through organizing solidarity campaigns, broadening access to information, writing in scholarly journals and the popular press, making films and penning novels, they have intervened actively and directly in the political struggle gripping the Narmada region. They have challenged the state on its legitimizing claims of working "for the common good"; they have held private corporations and multilateral development agencies accountable for their actions. Indeed, as indicated earlier, their critique has extended beyond this set of projects to question the validity and efficacy of postcolonial development strategies within India itself. Popular intellectuals in the Narmada Valley have been instrumental in fostering links with other social justice struggles both within the subcontinent and internationally, helping to found the National Alliance of People's Movements in India, and forming strong solidarity ties with indigenous people's movements and social justice networks across the world.

The following paper focuses on one such set of "critics", gathered together under the umbrella of the social justice organization known as the Narmada Bachao Andolan (NBA), or the "Save Narmada Movement". This essay will examine the context and work of the NBA in four parts. In the first section, I provide a brief overview of the Narmada case and the rise of opposition to dams in the region in the form of the NBA. The next

1. Michel Foucault, "Truth and Power", in *idem* and Colin Gordon (ed.), *Power/Knowledge: Selected Interviews and Other Writings 1972–1977* (New York, 1980), pp. 126–132.

section focuses on two particular popular intellectuals – the NBA's leader, Medha Patkar, and one of its leading supporters, the novelist, Arundhati Roy. Both have become increasingly identified as the public faces of the Narmada struggle, much more so even than the many thousands of villagers scheduled to be displaced by the dams. I will look at how Patkar and Roy have attempted to frame the Narmada struggle, situating it within a broader political context, and linking it to other national and global issues. The third section will look at a series of public debates amongst Indian intellectuals and activists regarding the NBA and its leaders and supporters; in particular, at criticisms levied at Patkar and Roy, and the response that both they and others gave to such charges. In the final section, I will explore some of the broader questions that the Narmada case raises regarding the idea of "intellectuals" and their relation to progressive movements and social change. What role might "popular intellectuals" have to play in such struggles? What possibilities and problems might confront them and the movements on whose behalf they work?

NARMADA VALLEY DEVELOPMENT PROJECTS AND THE "SAVE NARMADA MOVEMENT" (NBA)

The Narmada is the fifth largest river in India, running for over 1300 km through the states of Madhya Pradesh, Maharashtra, and Gujarat, and spilling out into the Gulf of Cambay. Plans to build a series of dams in the Narmada Valley were first drawn up following India's independence in 1947. Construction began in the early 1960s; however, disputes over project costs and benefits between various riparian states resulted in delays of over a decade as a federally appointed Water Disputes Tribunal sorted things out, announcing its award in 1978 after 10 years of deliberation. The final outcome of the project envisions the construction of 30 major dams, 135 medium dams, 3,000 minor dams, and over 30,000 microharvesting (conservation) schemes throughout the Valley; 250,000 people will be directly displaced, while over a million will see their livelihoods disrupted or erased. This project is paralleled in size and scope by the Three Gorges Dam Projects in China.[2]

Proponents of the Narmada Valley Development Plan (NVDP) speak of the benefits it will bring, primarily in terms of drinking water, irrigation, and hydroelectric power.[3] Gujarat, as the main beneficiary of the planned

2. For excellent overviews of the Narmada controversy see William F. Fisher (ed.), *Toward Sustainable Development: Struggling Over India's Narmada River* (London, 1995), and Sanjay Sangvai, *The River and Life* (Mumbai, 2000).
3. C.C. Patel, "Surging Ahead: The Sardar Sarovar Project, Hope of Millions", *Harvard International Review*, 15 (1992), pp. 24–27; Mahesh Pathak (ed.), *Sardar Sarovar Project: A Promise for Plenty* (Gandhinagar, 1991); Sardar Sarovar Narmada Nigam Ltd website, available at http://www.sardarsarovardam.org.

dams, will potentially see the irrigation of over 1.8 million hectares of land, the provision of drinking water to 135 urban centres and 8,215 villages, the generation of over 200 megawatts (MW) of hydroelectric energy, and flood protection for 210 villages as well as the major city of Bharuch. The remaining energy production from the project will be divided between the states of Madhya Pradesh (800 MW) and Maharashtra (400 MW). Additionally, the perennially drought-stricken state of Rajasthan stands to potentially gain the irrigation of over 75,000 hectares of desert land.

Critics of the project point on the other hand, to massive social and ecological (as well as financial) costs.[4] These include the flooding of 245 villages in order to create the dam's reservoir, as well as the lands of another 140,000 farmers to make way for irrigation canals. Thousands more may be affected by the project, including farmers and fisher-folk downstream from the dam, whose livelihoods will be disrupted. It is also worth noting that a majority of those destined to be affected by the NVDP are from indigenous or "tribal" groups (known in India as *adivasis* – a term that has been both a political rallying point *and* a point of contention for such groups). Such groups are often displaced by large-scale development projects because their traditional homes and livelihoods are situated within resource-rich or previously under-developed areas.

In addition to these serious social costs, critics of the NVDP point to the heavy ecological and financial burdens that the planned projects will place on the region. The environmental impacts of the planned dams include the loss of dense forests, the extinction of rare and endangered wildlife, possible risk of tectonic instability and resulting earthquake activity, an increased danger of siltation and salinity, the loss of topsoil, and an increase in health risks from waterborne diseases such as malaria.[5] The full cost of the terminal dam alone is estimated to reach 200 billion rupees (roughly $4.6 billion), and its completion date is anticipated as some time in 2040.[6] This dam project currently consumes 80 per cent of the irrigation and water budget of Gujarat (which, as primary beneficiary also bears the brunt of the financial costs) and draws much needed resources away from other water conservation efforts.

Given these considerable social, financial and environmental costs, it is unsurprising that there has been a long and sustained opposition to the dam projects within the Narmada Valley. Protests accompanied the very onset of the project in 1960, as the inhabitants of six villages were displaced

4. Mridula Singh, *Displacement by Sardar Sarovar and Tehri: A Comparative Study of Two Dams* (New Delhi, 1992); Uday Turaga, "Damming Waters and Wisdom: Protest in the Narmada River Valley", *Technology in Society*, 22 (2000), pp. 237–253.
5. Claude Alvares and Ramesh Billorey, *Damming the Narmada* (Penang, 1988); K. Sankaran Unni, *The Ecology of River Narmada* (New Delhi, 1996).
6. Y.K. Alagh, Mahesh Pathak, and D.T. Buch, *Narmada and Environment: An Assessment* (New Delhi, 1995), p. 35.

in order to house dam builders and officials in a new "construction colony" named Kevadia. These villagers have yet to be adequately compensated.[7] Since those early days, many different groups have rallied against the project. Farmers and merchants, labour organizations, social workers, and even the occasional mainstream politician have all at various times joined the protests.[8] However, perhaps the most vigorous and effective opposition has been mounted over the past two decades.

Opponents of the NVDP have criticized the plans on multiple grounds. They have decried the lack of transparency in all stages of the project design, from planning to implementation to mitigation. They have critiqued in particular the lack of public participation in all of these processes. While state governments, engineers, and technical experts quarrelled among themselves during the 1960s and 1970s, the villagers and farmers whose lands were to be submerged were kept mainly in the dark. By 1985, as rumours ran rampant about their fate, inhabitants of the valley began to organize in order to demand greater access to information, and as a way of negotiating more equitable compensation packages with the various state governments.[9] Several of these groups coalesced in 1987 into the NBA, an umbrella organization that brought together villagers, labourers, farmers, social and environmental activists, writers, scientists, academics, and a host of others to protest the project.

The NBA helped to raise other questions and concerns regarding the NVDP. They highlighted the fact that many of the anticipated gains from the dams are based upon inaccurate or exaggerated data, pointing out that technical flaws render the existing estimates of power generation, drinking water availability, and irrigation efficiency grossly exaggerated.[10] The effect of this opposition has been to move the issue beyond the local context and to challenge the project at national and even international levels. The NBA, through mass public protests and a series of strategic alliances with international NGOs, convinced the World Bank (one of the major financial backers of the project as of 1985) to launch an independent review of the dams, which, after a thorough re-evaluation, denounced the plans and recommended that the World Bank withdraw from the project (which it did in 1994).[11]

---

7. Singh, *Displacement by Sardar Sarovar and Tehri*, p. 31.
8. Amita Baviskar, *In the Belly of the River: Tribal Conflicts over Development in the Narmada Valley* (Delhi, 1995), pp. 196–239.
9. Rahmahtullah Khan, "Sustainable Development, Human Rights and Good Governance – A Case Study of India's Narmada Dam", in Konrad Ginther, Erik Denters, and Paul J.I.M. de Waart (eds), *Sustainable Development and Good Governance* (Dordrecht, 1995), pp. 420–428.
10. "Rehabilitation Status of Sardar Sarovar Project as of February 2002", briefing notes prepared by Narmada Bachao Andolan; "Who Pays? Who Profits? A Short Guide to the Sardar Sarovar Project", flyer prepared by Narmada Bachao Andolan.
11. For an overview of the work and findings of the independent review, see Bradford Morse and Thomas Berger, *Sardar Sarovar: Report of the Independent Review* (Ottawa, 1992).

Nevertheless, despite the World Bank's departure, as well as that of other former financiers such as the Overseas Economic Cooperation Fund of Japan, plans for the project proceeded unabated, with the government of Gujarat taking the lead as chief proponent. Unable to draw on funds from the international development-financing community, Gujarat turned instead to investors and proceeded to finance the project through a series of bond issues, spending close to 100 billion rupees by 2000. The costs of building the dam mounted steadily as construction ground to a halt with a federally-mandated moratorium imposed in 1994.

The following six years saw court battles fought between the NBA, the riparian states, and the central Indian government – legal arguments that focused primarily on issues of resettlement and environmental impacts. While these cases wound their way through the Indian legal system, the NBA at the same time continued its strategy of media and protest campaigns against various elements of the NVDP (such as the building of the Maheshwar Hydroelectric Project, a subsidiary dam in the scheme). On 18 October 2000, in a controversial split decision, the Supreme Court of India ruled in favour of the states and central government and allowed construction of the dams to resume.[12] By mid-2001 the height of the Sardar Sarovar Project (also known as the SSP, this is the terminal dam in the entire scheme) had been raised by several metres, despite the fact that several thousand families were yet to be rehabilitated. Even faced with such concerns, a year later the central government of India reaffirmed its commitment to the NVDP and the designs of Gujarat and the other partner states. In November 2002, the then Indian Water Resources Minister, Arjun Charan Sethi, proclaimed the SSP to be a "national project", one that the National Democratic Alliance government would support fully.[13] At the point of writing this article, the Indian Supreme Court has authorized the increase of the dam height by a further ten metres, considered to be a considerable victory for the dam proponents. Despite such proclamations, the NBA and its supporters continue their struggle against the building of the dams.

In the following section, I will look more closely at two of the leading voices on the NBA side of this struggle: Medha Patkar and Arundhati Roy. I will focus on their roles as popular intellectuals and framing specialists – as writers and orators, political strategists and legal petitioners, as commentators and critics – exploring how they conceive of themselves and their relationship to the anti-dam campaign, and in particular, how they attempt to frame the Narmada struggle within the context of broader social justice struggles both nationally and internationally. Beyond the two

---

12. Pablo Bose, "Judgement not Justice: The Supreme Court of India's Decision on Narmada and the Sardar Sarovar Projects", *Harvard Asia Quarterly*, 5 (2001), pp. 12–23.
13. "Sardar Sarovar Being Treated As National Project, Says Govt", *Outlook India*, 18 November 2002.

individuals I have chosen to profile, there are many others who are important to the struggle in the Narmada Valley, from both within and outside the region, who have lent their voices to the anti-dam campaign and who might be construed as popular intellectuals. They include academics, scientists, writers, civil servants – people like the activist and scholar, Vandana Shiva, or the Gandhian social activist, Baba Amte – as well as large numbers of village and community leaders who have helped to organize and mobilize the population in the Valley throughout the years. Such people act as interpreters and mediators, communicators and translators; they enable dialogue between disparate groups, across communities and across differences. But my focus remains on Patkar and Roy because they are seen by many to be leaders and eloquent spokespersons for the struggle.

FACES OF THE ANTI-DAM MOVEMENT – PATKAR AND ROY

Medha Patkar

Medha Patkar has been the guiding force throughout the history of the NBA. Even before the Narmada issue came to dominate her life, Patkar had a strong background in social activism. Born and raised in a middle-class family in Bombay (Mumbai), her father a noted trade-unionist, her mother a social worker, Patkar's own schooling included an MA in Social Work from the Tata Institute of Social Sciences. Patkar originally went to the Valley in 1984 to pursue research on social inequality amongst tribal groups in northeastern Gujarat for a Ph.D. (also at the Tata Institute of Social Sciences). Soon she was to abandon her formal studies, settle in the Valley, and work with local community groups to help articulate their concerns and questions regarding the dam projects. Her work has gained her both praise and notoriety both within and outside India. In 1992 she was awarded the Right Livelihood Award (also known as the "alternative Nobel Prize") for her efforts; in 1993 the Goldman Environmental Prize, an annual award of $125,000 presented by a US-based charitable foundation.[14] Later, she participated as one of the twelve official commissioners of the World Commission on Dams, specifically on behalf of the NBA and the National Alliance of People's Movements, but more broadly as a representative of grass-roots campaigns for human and political rights.[15] In 2002 she acted as a "debt prosecutor" at the 2002 World Social Forum in Porto Alegre, Brazil, and she has also been a

14. The Richard and Rhoda Goldman Foundation has presented, since 1990, six annual awards of $125,000 each to "environmental heroes" as recognition for "their efforts in sustained and important environmental achievements"; http://www.goldmanprize.org.
15. The WCD Commissioners; http://www.dams.org/commission/commissioners.htm.

speaker at academic conferences and activist demonstrations across the globe.[16]

There are three main ways in which Patkar has worked to frame and articulate issues in the Narmada Valley. Firstly, she has helped to raise questions regarding the costs and benefits of the proposed projects in the NVDP such as the Sardar Sarovar Project (SSP). Secondly, she has worked not only to challenge the specifics of dam construction in the Narmada Valley and the shortcomings of particular projects, but indeed to critique the prevalent model of industrial development as a whole. Thirdly, she has attempted to link the struggles in Narmada with emerging global social justice movements against neoliberalism and globalization.

Patkar's work to evaluate critically and challenge the claims of project planners stems from her original studies in the Valley on the potential impact of the large dams on local communities. Very soon she began to realize that measures designed to mitigate such impacts were, at best, inadequate or lacked enforcement; at worst they simply did not exist. Widespread confusion and a serious absence of information characterized the situation in the Narmada Valley in the early 1980s, following the announcement of the Narmada Water Dispute Tribunal's decision. In these early years, Patkar worked with the residents of thirty-three villages in the state of Maharashtra in an organization called the Narmada Dharangrast Samiti (Narmada Displaced People's Organization).[17] The goal of this organization was mainly to work with state governments to provide better rehabilitation and resettlement packages. Such efforts were not uncommon in the Valley; indeed, numerous NGOs and social justice organizations worked steadily to improve compensation programmes for the displaced.

But over the course of her work on improving rehabilitation and resettlement packages, Patkar began to question the long-term sustainability of such an approach. As new studies called into question the true nature of the costs and benefits of the NVDP, and the displacement experiences of other dam "oustees" in India made compensation promises by governments appear suspect, Patkar and like-minded others in the Valley made a crucial break with their erstwhile NGO allies. Gujarat-based groups such as ARCH-Vahini had taken (in their view) the pragmatic or realist view that since the dams were going to be built anyway, their responsibility as social activists was to secure the best compensation for the displaced possible. Accordingly, such NGOs – often exerting political pressure by using nonviolent methods such as demonstrations and fasts (similar to tactics that the NBA also employed) – helped

16. "You Need a Thorn to Remove a Thorn", interview with Medha Patkar by Dilip D'Souza, *International Indian Woman*, Dubai, 31 December 1995.
17. Baviskar, *In the Belly of the River*, pp. 202–203.

to create some of the most comprehensive rehabilitation and resettlement packages in India.[18]

Indeed, the work of ARCH-Vahini and other NGOs like it was hailed as "crucial", "immensely important", and "vital" by the World Bank's independent review.[19] But the same report pointed out the limits to what such an approach might achieve in the face of much larger, systemic flaws in the project plans. True, the pragmatist NGOs had achieved considerable gains in improving potential compensation for those to be displaced by the dams. But, as Patkar and others pointed out, these gains were relatively minor in the grand scheme of the NVDP; the best packages had been negotiated between Gujarat and oustees in that state – yet only a fraction of the villages to be submerged were located in that region and the other states had yet to offer similar compensation, and little or no mechanisms existed for implementing, monitoring, or enforcing proposed regulations to safeguard the displaced.

Patkar and her allies, therefore, joined together in the coalition that was to become the NBA, and declared their outright opposition to the projects. It is here that Patkar began to articulate the second element with which she framed the Narmada issue: questioning the very model of development that demanded the construction of the NVDP. No longer did she simply call into question the viability and desirability of a particular dam or series of hydroelectric projects, but indeed of an entire vision of development. In an open letter to the Indian Prime Minister, Patkar argued that:

> The assessment of large dams like the Sardar Sarovar cannot be made on the basis of the displacement-rehabilitation issue alone; other equally important aspects like the displacement and destruction, cost-benefit analysis and a realistic analysis of benefits are some of the necessary parameters. It would be irrelevant to discuss merely the rehabilitation aspect while disregarding the strong challenge from our organisation to the claims regarding the benefits from the dam. The dam will not solve the serious problem of water and drought of Kutch-Saurashtra regions while the distribution of the benefits too is not equitable and just. Knowing this, it becomes important to ask as to why the adivasis, peasants, and labourers should sacrifice their life and resources. Instead of spending most of the irrigation allocations of Gujarat on this single project, we appeal to concentrate all the attention, resources and power for true, sustainable, decentralised alternatives without the problem of displacement.[20]

In Patkar's view, what the NBA was questioning was the very "process of

---

18. John R. Wood, "Changing Institutions and Changing Politics in Rural Water Management: An Overview of Three Zones in Gujarat", in Tony Beck, Pablo Bose, and Barrie Morrison (eds), *The Cooperative Management of Water Resources in South Asia* (Vancouver, 1999), p. 203.

19. Morse and Berger, *Sardar Sarovar*, pp. 129–131.

20. Letter from Medha Patkar to the Prime Minister of India, A.B. Vajpayee, 28 September 1999, NBA Press Release, 10 October 1999.

development planning, right from deciding the development goals as well as managing the natural resources".[21]

She argued that those most affected by the NVDP had been ignored by previous planning processes, including the Water Disputes Tribunal as well as the official political and bureaucratic apparatus. Their participation had been neither sought nor welcomed. She complained that local people lacked access to information regarding the very plans that would impact their lives, and that what was publicized generally consisted of highly exaggerated benefits and promises. Patkar argued that this was part of a systematic process of deceit and domination that kept people ignorant, and by which elite sections of society were able to exploit others, particularly the rural poor:

> The point is that the communities which are based on the natural resources are compelled to sacrifice those resources in the name of development, with the principle of eminent domain that the state resorts to. The state takes away these natural resources from the communities, the fish workers, the farmers, or manual labourers. It certainly stands by the marketized, industrialized, urbanized communities, and that small section of the society then uses these resources or the benefits drawn out of these resources at the cost of all those who loose theirs. This society certainly doesn't give a real share in the benefits to those who sacrifice their land, water, forests. This is considered as a part and parcel of development and the tradeoff that is necessary.[22]

Patkar also criticized the role that the state – and in particular in India, the developmental state – had played in *not* safeguarding the rights and lives of the very people in whose name it was carrying out massive development projects. She argued that the state did not act as a neutral arbiter between competing interests, nor did it protect oppressed minorities from manipulation and exploitation. In somewhat Gandhian terms, Patkar characterized the state, instead, as concretized violence, as an institution that employs its security apparatus to intensify accumulation by elites.[23]

Her critiques of the Indian state did not lead Patkar to abandon the national political sphere as an arena of struggle. Nor did the reframing of the Narmada debate as one on development rather than on the short-comings of one dam, lead her to abandon her specific criticisms of the Sardar Sarovar Project. Instead, what Patkar and the NBA did was to pursue a multi-faceted approach to their campaigns, adopting a "compre-hensive, polito-economic, social ideology, which may not come merely from Gandhi or Marx, but a combination of various [analyses], tools that

21. Medha Patkar, interviewed by Venu Govindu, Friends of River Narmada, 9 August 1999.
22. *Ibid.*
23. Medha Patkar, interviewed by Sonya Thimmaiah, Friends of River Narmada, 6 May 2001.
24. Medha Patkar, interviewed by Venu Govindu, Friends of River Narmada, August 1999.

all of them have offered to us".[24] At the local level, the anti-dam campaign continued to study the project planners' designs and their possible impacts, intervening with direct action and media campaigns when required. Nationally, Patkar in particular focused the attention of India's urban middle class on Narmada as a crucible for the nation's postcolonial development strategy by repeatedly asking why certain sacrifices were being sought and for whom. The NBA worked within the structures of the state – launching court petitions, negotiating at times with local politicians, participating fully in debates within the public sphere – as well as pursuing their direct-action strategies of political protest (including fasts, marches, rallies, sit-ins) in ways deemed sometimes illegitimate by the state.

But perhaps Patkar's most important move – both tactically and theoretically – in framing the issues of the Narmada Valley was to link them more explicitly with similar struggles elsewhere in the country and around the world. The campaign that the NBA launched against the World Bank, for instance, was successful in part because of the direct challenge that the protests by the displaced made against the Bank's President and officers in New Delhi, but also because of alliances that the NBA was able to form with international NGOs. Patkar in particular worked with the Environmental Defence Fund (Washington DC), International Rivers Network (Berkeley, California), and Friends of the Earth (Japan) during this period, and personally made appeals to various political bodies (including the Japanese Diet and the United States Congress).[25] The anti-dam movement also received considerable support from a North-American based support network comprised of diasporic South Asian students and young professionals that calls itself "Friends of River Narmada", hosts a website, and conducts media campaigns in the United States and Canada.[26]

Such alliances have been crucial to the success of the NBA, argues Amita Baviskar.[27] She suggests that the NBA has protected itself by tapping into a worldwide discourse of relatively affluent middle-class environmentalism, whereas other movements in the same region that have explicitly organized on behalf of indigenous or workers' rights have been much more brutally repressed by the state. It is noteworthy that the NBA has made its strongest international alliances with NGOs such as the International Rivers Network, Friends of the Earth, and Environmental Defense Fund, rather than Amnesty International, or Human Rights

25. Lori Udall, "The International Narmada Campaign: A Case of Sustained Advocacy", in Fisher, *Toward Sustainable Development*, pp. 201–227.
26. Friends of River Narmada's website can be viewed at http://www.narmada.org.
27. Amita Baviskar, "Environmental Identities: The Politics of Nature and Place in India", Asian Environments Series, York Centre for Asian Research, York University, Toronto, Canada, 24 November 2003.

Watch. Such connections, though they have proved fruitful, have also helped to buttress criticisms that the NBA works on behalf of external, middle-class interests, rather than those of local people, an issue that will be addressed further below.

One of Patkar's greatest assets has been an ability to speak with equal facility to a range of audiences – local communities, grass-roots activists, international NGOs, national and international politicians, academics and scientists, and a host of others. Patkar's skills with translation across experiences and idioms has thus greatly enhanced the NBA's strategy of building networks and coalitions of support. Within India, for example, the NBA has helped to found the National Alliance of People's Movements (NAPM), a group that brings together diverse local struggles such as hawkers in Bengal, mining communities in Orissa, fisherfolk from the coasts of India's south, and people affected by displacement-inducing development schemes all across the subcontinent.[28] Patkar sees such linkages as crucial to the success of the movement in the Narmada Valley:

> At another level, the NBA has always been relating to the wider struggle. NBA to NAPM, that process does not merely [mean] going to different struggles and then saying, "We support you, and you support us." It means building a comprehensive ideological position and taking local to national action. Now with globalization and liberalization, which we are opposed to completely, we need to link up struggles like Narmada with other struggles. All these years we have been fighting a centralization that is undemocratic, unsustainable and unjust. And now it is the same centralized power and structure that has been hijacked to a global level. We have to fight that also.[29]

The connections that Patkar has attempted to draw between the struggles in the Narmada Valley and those elsewhere within India and the rest of the world has had several effects. From a tactical perspective, such connections have helped the anti-dam movement to mobilize effective support networks, when needed, to confront specific threats to its cause. For example, during the campaign carried out between 1999–2002 against the building of the first privately-constructed and operated dam in the NVDP, the Maheshwar Hydroelectric Project, the NBA was able to draw on allies such as the German NGO, Urgewald and the North American-based Friends of River Narmada to bring pressure to bear upon German and US partners in the project.[30] These NGOs confronted financiers, utility corporations, and engineering firms on their involvement in the project, highlighting the social and environmental costs of this project in particular. Simultaneously, the NBA carried out protests, rallies, and other direct action to pressure the Indian partners and local develop-

28. Medha Patkar, interviewed by Venu Govindu, Friends of River Narmada, August 1999.
29. *Ibid.*
30. Heffa Schücking, "The Maheshwar Dam in India", Urgewald briefing report, March 1999.

ment authorities to rethink their plans. This two-pronged approach resulted in the eventual withdrawal of foreign partners from the project and an eventual suspension of construction activities.

In a strategic sense, however, Patkar's framing of Narmada as a global issue has been perhaps even more important. As mentioned at the outset, the Narmada case is well-known within international development circles. But it has equally become a test not only of development within India, but of development globally. By participating in processes such as the World Social Forum and the World Commission on Dams, and by explicitly declaring that the struggle in Narmada is part of a global struggle, Patkar has helped to redefine a locally oriented, place-based social movement in ways that might potentially move it away from a framework of local interest and towards one of international solidarity and support. Such a framing approach has been similarly undertaken, perhaps even more overtly, by the second popular intellectual in the Narmada case on whom I would like to focus, the novelist Arundhati Roy.

Arundhati Roy

Originally trained as an architect, Arundhati Roy was born in Bengal, raised in a small village in coastal Kerala, and is currently a novelist living in Delhi.[31] Her parents – a Bengali Hindu father and a Syrian Christian mother – divorced during her childhood, and Roy's mother became well-known for winning a public-interest litigation case challenging Kerala's Syrian Christian inheritance laws in 1986. Roy came to the Narmada Valley as an already established celebrity, a writer who won the Booker Prize in 1997 for her novel, *The God of Small Things*, a book that has sold six million copies and has been translated into forty languages. She donated the prize monies she received for this critically and commercially successful work to the NBA and has since been a passionate advocate for the struggle in Narmada, writing polemical essays, articles, letters, and books on the subject, and participating in marches, rallies, and other forms of protest.[32] While Roy's involvement with the Narmada issue has begun much more recently than Patkar's, her impact and notoriety has been considerable. Like Patkar before her, Roy has critiqued the NVDP on multiple levels – from problems regarding specific project plans, through broader issues regarding regional and national development policy, to global political and socio-economic struggles.

31. Arundhati Roy, interview by David Barsamian, *The Progressive*, 65 (2001), pp. 33–39.
32. Arundhati Roy's writings include Narmada-related publications such as: *The Cost of Living: The Greater Common Good and the End of Imagination* (New York, 1999); *Power Politics* (Cambridge, MA, 2001); and newspaper editorials such as "Lies, Dam Lies and Statistics", *The Guardian*, 5 June 1999; "The Greater Common Good I", *Outlook India*, 24 May 1999; and "The Greater Common Good II", *Outlook India*, 12 July 1999.

In *The Cost of Living* (1999), a book comprised of the essays "The Greater Common Good", and "The End of Imagination", which provide in tandem a critical examination of India's developmental and nuclear policies, Roy focuses specifically on Narmada and writes:

> In India over the last ten years the fight against the Sardar Sarovar Dam has come to represent far more than the fight for one river. This has been its strength as well as its weakness. Some years ago, it became a debate that captured the popular imagination. That's what raised the stakes and changed the complexion of the battle. From being a fight over the fate of a river valley it began to raise doubts about an entire political system. What is at issue now is the very nature of our democracy. Who owns this land? Who owns its rivers? Its forests? Its fish? These are huge questions.[33]

In her later book, *Power Politics* (2001), Roy sustains her critique, drawing a portrait of a clash between developmental visions by using a metaphor of two different vehicles on separate trajectories. One – occupied by a small minority – is on a road towards increasing opulence and privilege, while the other – by far the more crowded, and becoming increasingly so – is headed towards marginalization and oppression. She argues that "India lives in several centuries at the same time", and that the contradictions can be seen in the "road gangs of emaciated labourers digging a trench to lay fibre optic cables to speed up our digital revolution".[34] It is these sometimes grotesque contradictions that, Roy argues, need to be acknowledged in modern India (and indeed elsewhere around the globe) as it struggles on the edge of the social and ecological crises that mark the new millennium. These should not simply be swept away in the glare of a burnished modernity, or accepted as a cost of doing business. Cases such as the struggle in the Narmada Valley can teach important lessons about the real costs of modernist fantasies, Roy argues:

> Curiosity took me to the Narmada Valley. Instinct told me that this was the big one. The one in which the battle-lines were clearly drawn, the warring armies massed along them. The one in which it would be possible to wade through the congealed morass of hope, anger, information, disinformation, political artifice, engineering ambition, disingenuous socialism, radical activism, bureaucratic subterfuge, misinformed emotionalism and, of course, the pervasive, invariably dubious, politics of International Aid.[35]

Like Patkar, Roy has depicted the Narmada struggle as more than a site-specific or contained incident. The issues that Roy and Patkar speak about are similar ones, and if Roy does not have the long history of involvement with the Narmada issue that Patkar does, the extensive research she has

33. Roy, *The Cost of Living*, p. 4.
34. *Idem, Power Politics*, p. 1.
35. *Idem, The Cost of Living*, p. 4.

done on the facts of the case to buttress her arguments makes it clear that Roy has taken the time to look very carefully at the ways in which life in the Valley may be irrevocably altered by big dams. Both Patkar and Roy would argue that the NVDP is not an aberrant situation, in which poor design, implementation, corruption, or enforcement has undermined an otherwise reasonable system. It is the very theoretical underpinnings and normative frameworks of that system that need to be critically interrogated and overhauled.

But while Patkar and Roy's framing of the issues are often quite similar, their presentation of their arguments can be somewhat different. Patkar, as noted earlier, speaks to a range of audiences and in a range of voices, from impassioned political speeches to reasoned scientific and academic debates. Roy has written and spoken mainly to a middle-class audience, both within India and internationally, and her work has been perhaps more pointedly acerbic and political (so much so that she was slapped with a Supreme Court of India contempt charge, for which she served a token day in jail).[36] She has been criticized for her style of argumentation, as will be examined more closely in the next section. But Roy argues that there is little distinction between her work as a novelist and as an essayist and activist:

> I don't see a great difference between *The God of Small Things* and my works of nonfiction. As I keep saying, fiction is truth. I think fiction is the truest thing there ever was. My whole effort now is to remove that distinction. The writer is the midwife of understanding. It's very important for me to tell politics like a story, to make it real, to draw a link between a man with his child and what fruit he had in the village he lived in before he was kicked out, and how that relates to Mr Wolfensohn at the World Bank. That's what I want to do. *The God of Small Things* is a book where you connect the very smallest things to the very biggest: whether it's the dent that a baby spider makes on the surface of water or the quality of the moonlight on a river or how history and politics intrude into your life, your house, your bedroom.[37]

What Roy has done through her essays and her other writing has been to sustain, and perhaps even enlarge, the arguments that Patkar and the NBA have been making for over two decades: that the struggle in the Narmada Valley is part of a much greater fight for social and ecological justice that is going on across the world. By telling the story as she sees it to an audience that she is familiar with, Roy is trying to make visible a reality that has been all too often ignored. For example, while the violence, suffering, and displacement of over five million people that accompanied the British

36. For more on the contempt of court case, see Supreme Court of India Original Jurisdiction I.A. No. 14 of 199 Writ Petition (Civil) No. 319 of 1994, NBA (petitioner) vs. Union of India and Respondents.
37. Arundhati Roy, interview by David Barsamian.

Partition of the Indian subcontinent during Independence remains seared on the nation's soul, the fact that as many as fifty million people have since been uprooted and impoverished in the name of dam-building and other development projects is much less widely acknowledged.[38] Roy's writing seeks to reach those on whose behalf development and the project of modernity proceeds – the wealthy, the middle-class, and the urban privileged, in India as much as in the rest of the world.

The work that Patkar and Roy have undertaken, the context and connections that they constructed in publicizing the struggles in the Narmada Valley, have been largely successful in ways indicated above. But these efforts have not gone without challenge. In the following section, I will explore some of the criticisms that have been levelled in recent years at the NBA, and at Roy and Patkar in particular.

CRITICISM OF THE NBA, PATKAR, AND ROY – THE OMVEDT DEBATE

The work of the NBA and of Patkar and Roy has had its share of criticism over the years. Proponents of the projects have reviled the leaders of the NBA as glory-seekers, and militant martyrs, leading a manipulated flock down a destructive path. They have been called uninformed "eco-romantics", "backward radicals", and "alternative society counter-culture ideologues", adamantly and irrationally opposed to any development in the Valley.[39] They have been charged (and as noted in the case of Roy, convicted) with contempt by the Supreme Court of India for their criticism of its decisions. Some argue further that Patkar and Roy's position ultimately dooms the inhabitants of the Valley and robs them of the opportunity to better their lives, substituting a grand vision of revolution for small, practical, and achievable change in their daily existence.[40] Others critique Patkar and Roy for their supposed lack of insider legitimacy – they are not "from" or "of" the Valley in such a reckoning, and thereby ostensibly unqualified to express an opinion on its fate.

Some of these critiques can be dismissed as spurious or ill-conceived, others are simply false or the rhetorical flourishes of those who have a vested interest in the continuation of the NVDP. But in 1999, a more serious challenge to the work of the NBA and its leaders and supporters

---

38. Ashish Kothari, "The Development Debate", *Humanscape*, 6:11 (November 1999).
39. B.G. Verghese, *Winning the Future: Bhakra to Narmada, Tehri, Rajasthan Canal* (Delhi, 1994), p. 1.
40. John R. Wood, "Struggles within Struggles: Indian NGO Politics and the Narmada Dams Controversy", in Hugh Johnston, Reeta C. Tremblay, and John R. Wood (eds), *South Asia Between Turmoil and Hope* (Montreal, 1999), pp. 235–260.

was raised by Gail Omvedt, an American-born anthropologist who, along with her husband, has been actively involved in women's and farmers' organizations in the state of Maharashtra. Omvedt's scholarly and activist work has centred on new social movements, campaigns for women's empowerment, property rights, political representation, involvement in sustainable agriculture, anticaste, and environmental struggles.[41] In recent years she has been involved in a series of debates with self-identified leftist voices within Indian academia and polity regarding the purpose, nature, and implementation of liberalization and globalization, which she has argued in favour of as a qualified necessity. Omvedt's debates on these subjects have included strong criticisms of certain social movements and organizations, especially "radical" environmental movements and Roy and Patkar in particular.

The criticisms that Omvedt raised were certainly not new ones, and concern familiar debates regarding social movement strategy that often take place in activist and academic circles within India and elsewhere. However, Omvedt brought her questions up in a very public forum, with a series of open letters and articles published in the Indian English-language press. Omvedt's arguments were aimed primarily at Roy, with Patkar and the NBA as subsidiary (though significant) targets.

Omvedt raised several concerns. She criticized Roy's conflation of the nuclear issue with the developmental agenda of big dam building. In Omvedt's view, dams were not an unalloyed evil, and for the NBA and its supporters to oppose them on principle was both irresponsible and a betrayal of the ultimate need for sustainable development by villagers in the Narmada Valley. Omvedt argued that, in building the international alliances that the NBA felt were necessary for its survival and success, the anti-dam movement's "small local base" of landless labourers and small farmers and their concerns were being subsumed to the interests of a global, affluent upper-middle class of environmentalists. Omvedt went so far as to suggest that "the NBA has become the voice of the eco-romanticists of the world", of an environmental movement "caught in an extremist trap".[42] She argued that their haste to appease these middle-class interests had led the NBA to ignore the real needs of the marginalized in the Valley and elsewhere, and even to ignore smaller-scale alternatives to the big dams.

Omvedt strongly opposes Roy and Patkar's assertion that big dams are

41. Gail Omvedt's recent publications include *Reinventing Revolution: New Social Movements and the Socialist Tradition in India* (Armonk, NY, 1993); *Dalits and the Democratic Revolution: Dr Ambedkar and the Dalit Movement in Colonial India* (New Delhi [etc.], 1994); *Dalit Visions: The Anti-Caste Movement and the Construction of an Indian Identity* (New Delhi, 1995); "Reflections on the World Bank and Liberalization", *Bulletin of Concerned Asian Scholars*, 27 (1995) pp. 41–43; and "Caste and Hinduism", *Economic and Political Weekly*, 29 November 2003.
42. *Idem*, "Dams and Bombs – II", editorial, *The Hindu*, 5 August 1999.

evil; instead, she makes the argument that it is only poorly planned ones that have disastrous outcomes. Omvedt suggests that, for the NBA, "their main concern is to question the entire goal of development itself"[43] – a statement that Patkar and Roy would no doubt agree with wholeheartedly (though obviously not in the negative light in which Omvedt casts their views). Omvedt argues that their opposition to industrial development as a matter of principle has trapped Roy and Patkar into a static and unrealistic view of the past, fighting to preserve the "village life" of the Narmada Valley without acknowledging the multiple hierarchies, oppressions, and structural constraints which frame those living within. How can social change occur, Omvedt asks, with only backward-looking models?

But perhaps the most difficult questions that Omvedt raises have to do with the nature of the NBA and the anti-dam movement itself. She criticizes Patkar for failing adequately to acknowledge the organizing that had been done prior to her arrival in the Valley, and for insufficiently answering the questions of legitimacy and representation. Omvedt quotes an *adivasi* activist who had asked of the NBA, "Why is it that there is no top ranking *adivasi* leadership in the NBA?"[44] Omvedt complains that there has been no real answer given to this query, or her related question, "Why are all the leaders from the urban elite, and how democratic exactly is their relationship to the rural poor they are organizing?"[45] She points to the NBA's use of the term "tribal" as further evidence that the NBA leadership is out of touch with its grass-roots base – she mentions the negative connotations of the word and its disavowal by many who have been identified (and marginalized) by it.

Underlying all of Omvedt's attacks on Patkar and Roy, there is a sense that she is questioning the legitimacy of their leadership because they are outsiders to the Valley, urban interlopers in a rural dispute. In her eyes, there is a crisis of representation between the NBA and the farmers, labourers, merchants, and villagers. She suggests to Roy that:

> There is nothing wrong with going out to organize people, with throwing oneself into a cause or supporting a cause, with rallying world opinion. NBA has succeeded in giving great power to a "no-big-dam" position and in putting a big question mark before the whole issue of "development". You have every right to support them. But in doing so, please think about one thing: when you go as leaders to people in the valley, or when you represent people in the valley to the world outside, what are the consequences for them of the arguments you make? What does it mean when you put your own arguments, either explicitly or implicitly, in their mouths? Are you so sure your sweeping opposition to big

43. *Idem*, "The Trouble with Eco-Romanticism and the NBA", *Humanscape*, 6:11 (November 1999).
44. Waharu Sonavane, quoted in *ibid*.
45. Omvedt, "The trouble with Eco-Romanticism and the NBA".

dams is in their best interest, or that you are democratically representing their real feelings on the matter?[46]

The point Omvedt is making is crucial and one that is difficult for Roy, Patkar, or the NBA to answer: how does this movement address the issue of representation? In what ways does the leadership survey the desires and sentiments of its constituency? How does the NBA even know what their constituency is, given its fluid and amorphous nature? There are, after all, no party memberships in a people's movement, no annual dues paid by the rank-and-file, no real way of keeping track of support. The NBA must rely instead upon the support for their actions shown by local inhabitants of the Valley as well as outsiders, as evidenced by their participation in various rallies, marches, protests, and village and town-level public meetings. Such participation has been consistently shown throughout the history of the NBA. Still, Omvedt's caution is an important one.

As a respected scholar of social movements and someone with no vested interest in the continuation of the NVDP, Omvedt's observations were taken seriously and answered in a series of open letters and editorials by other activists and scholars.[47] Though they understood and sympathized with certain aspects of her critique, many were dismayed by the timing of her intervention, coming as it did when the battle over the Narmada Valley was reaching a crescendo in the court system. Others dismissed Omvedt's arguments as occasionally ill-informed and misleading, selectively choosing to highlight some facts and to minimize others. Some pointed out that, in her own polemic, Omvedt had conveniently ignored the NBA's study of positive alternatives to the big dams. They argued that, far from a "small local base", the NBA had a sizable grass-roots constituency, as evidenced by the tens of thousands who participated in rallies, marches, and protests organized by the NBA. Others took issue with Omvedt's defence of big dams, pointing to the extensive evidence indicating their deleterious effects. Some intimated that Omvedt's criticisms were driven by pique rather than reason, pique at the relative success enjoyed by the NBA over that of the anti-dam campaign that Omvedt had been involved with.[48]

With regard to the question of legitimacy and representation, Ashish Kothari of the environmental education and research NGO, Kalpavriksh – an intellectual and activist with his own long history of involvement with the Narmada issue – remarks:

46. *Ibid.*
47. For responses to Omvedt, see in particular, Kothari, "The Development Debate"; Nalini Nayak, "Response to Gail Omvedt's Open Letter to Arundhati Roy", National Fishworkers Forum Press Release, 11 August 1999; Himanshu Thakkar, "Sardar Sarovar and the Bomb", South Asia Network on Rivers, Dams and People Press Release, November 1999.
48. Ashish Kothari, "Dams, Bombs and Development", Opinion, *The Hindu*, 17 August 1999.

The question of why there is no "top-ranking *adivasi* leadership in the NBA", is important, and needs to be squarely addressed by NBA itself. But it is not a question restricted to the NBA, it can be asked of most recent movements in India. Perhaps it has to do with the history of displacement of *adivasi* identity, perhaps something else. Perhaps it has to do with the way in which the Indian and international media singles out "heroes" they are comfortable with, or who belong to their "class". What is absolutely clear, however, is that in the decision-making process in the valley itself, both *adivasis* and non-*adivasis* are highly involved, even though Medha and other "middle-class" activists do often have a stronger say.[49]

Issues of insider legitimacy and of appropriation and agency are crucial for all progressive social movements to consider. What exactly is being advocated? On whose behalf? On whose authority? These are questions that need to be, as Kothari puts it, "squarely addressed". By portraying the NVDP in the manner that they do, are Patkar and Roy accurately representing the perspective of the people about to be displaced by the dams? Do the inhabitants of villages like Jalsindhi and Manibeli and Domkhedi see their struggles as intimately linked to those of roadside vendors in Kolkata or street sweepers in Mumbai – or indeed to the urban poor in Cochabamba and the homeless in Chicago?

These are tensions that are perhaps the most difficult to resolve within any social movement, and the NBA is no different. Patkar, Roy, and their supporters would argue that they are intimately close to the people on whose behalf they advocate – much closer in fact than the governments and development agencies who themselves undertake their projects in the interest of the "greater good". Patkar lives and works and is prepared to die in the Valley if it is to be submerged by the dam. Roy has always claimed to be a writer and a reporter of events and situations, rather than the demagogue others accuse her of being. She states flatly, "I don't ever want to portray myself as a representative of the voiceless".[50] While Patkar and Roy have been identified as leaders by the media, and on occasion by themselves, their more crucial role has been that of critics, reporters, and translators, reaching diverse audiences in a variety of ways. It is also true that the struggle in the Valley cannot be reduced to simple dichotomies between "insiders" and "outsiders" – or indeed, between industrial development on one side and local communities on the other, as it is sometimes cast. The constituency of the NBA reflects many disparate backgrounds and interests, including both rich farmers who use technology-intensive and industrial agriculture, and hill *adivasis* who were once displaced and continue to be exploited by them.[51] The success and strength

49. Kothari, "The Development Debate".
50. Arundhati Roy, interview by David Barsamian, p. 39.
51. Baviskar, *In the Belly of the River*, pp. 219–222.

of the NBA has been in welding together these historically antagonistic groups by focusing them on the common goal of halting construction on the dam. In the final section of this paper, I will look at some of the lessons that can be learnt from the Narmada experience regarding popular intellectuals and social movements.

POPULAR INTELLECTUALS AND THE NARMADA VALLEY – PITFALLS AND POSSIBILITIES

The case of the anti-dam movement in the Narmada Valley demonstrates the pivotal role that popular intellectuals can play in the organizing, sustaining, and widening of specific struggles. It also shows the contested and evolving nature of intellectual labour in the service of progressive social movements. How are relationships with those outside the movement negotiated? How are internal differences resolved and decisions arrived at? In the words that Patkar and Roy use to describe their own efforts, in the critique of Omvedt, and in Kothari's response, there is a definite prescriptive element. That is, there is a strong – if relatively undefined – set of assumptions regarding what the role of the popular intellectual *should* be. In such a reckoning, popular intellectuals should support a movement, not supplant its objectives with their own. They should avoid vanguardist tendencies or speaking for others without their consent. And, above all, such intellectuals should remain committed and connected to their base of support at all times. In their articulation of particular problems, they should remember on whose behalf they operate, and to what effect. Indeed, the idea that Roy, Patkar, and the NBA have not remained faithful to such a set of assumptions lies behind many of the charges levied at them by their critics.

But the question of the place and purpose of popular intellectuals – or of intellectuals at all – with regard to social movements is not confined to the Narmada case; indeed, the question has long been debated within activist and academic circles. Some argue for Antonio Gramsci's idea of the "organic intellectual", knowledge-workers firmly grounded in the everyday struggles of the communities from which they arose, situated in a "philosophy of praxis" – of thought and action.[52] A related idea is that of Foucault's "specific intellectual", which similarly insists on the intellectual situating his or her work "within specific sectors, at the precise points where their own conditions of life or work situate them".[53] Issues of distance or disconnection between intellectuals and social movements may be overcome, then, when intellectuals are self-consciously embedded

---

52. Antonio Gramsci, *Selections from the Prison Notebooks*, Quentin Hoare and Geoffrey Nowell Smith (eds and tr.) (New York, 1971), p. 9.
53. Foucault, "Truth and Power", p. 126.

within particular contexts. Some have taken this to mean that popular intellectuals must therefore be representatives of a particular struggle on the basis of their identity rather than their function. In such a conception, indigenous movements would be led by indigenous intellectuals, workers' movements by workers, and so on.

The reality is of course that social movements across the globe are not, by and large, dominated by voices "from within"; that is, by intellectuals who have arisen from the social categories whose aspirations they claim to articulate. Instead, those who write about issues, give speeches to crowds, negotiate with governments, study the impacts of proposed plans, organize rallies and marches, and act as the face and voice of social movements are still overwhelmingly drawn from the upper and middle classes of educated elites. Does this "distance" or apparent lack of authenticity negate their contribution? Patkar strongly rejects such a position, pointing out the important role that the city-based intelligentsia has played in the anti-dam campaigns:

> In the Narmada movement, we have found that while the struggle had its main base in the valley, these [urban] kinds of support groups played a very different role. Analysing designs and plans, finding roots and targets of development, defining our strategies – these are roles that urban intelligentsia can take. Others can disseminate information through the media and so forth. And if you have strategies which cannot be restricted to village level action – when you have to come out on the streets – you need urban supporters. You need lawyers. As long as you need support from within the system to fight the system – just like you need a thorn to remove a thorn – you need such support. That has to be one front of the movement.[54]

Roy is equally vehement in her response, arguing that the charge of inauthenticity is misleading and misguided:

> You can't expect the critique to be just *adivasi*. You isolate them like that, and it's so easy to crush them. In many ways, people try to delegitimize the involvement of the middle class, saying, how can you speak on behalf of these people? No one is speaking on behalf of anyone. The point is that the NBA is a fantastic example of people linking hands across caste and class. It is the biggest, finest, most magnificent resistance movement since the independence struggle.[55]

One of the dangers of adhering too strongly to a set of prescriptive assumptions regarding the role of the popular intellectual is of focusing more on their background than on their function. Many have asked whether intellectuals from elite backgrounds can ever radically interrogate their own subjectivity, privilege, power, and authority enough to participate actively in movements for social transformation. This is a fair

---

54. "You Need a Thorn to Remove a Thorn", interview with Medha Patkar.
55. Arundhati Roy, interview by David Barsamian.

question. As anticolonialist struggles have long asked, "can an oppressed [group] rely on knowledge produced by others, no matter how progressive, who are members of an oppressor [group]?"[56] But to argue that only intellectuals who belong to underprivileged classes are able adequately to represent the latter's objectives is both misguided and short-sighted. Insisting on an authenticity of voice and representation suggests that a fixed, homogenous identity is possible. But identities are never so static, even if polarizing struggles such as that over Narmada might portray them as such. Kothari goes so far as to suggest that the category of middle-class urban activists is no longer "a valid real-life category"[57] for describing the leadership of the NBA, many of whom have dedicated their lives to the struggle and have settled in the region. Are the interventions of such activists deemed less valuable because of their lineage?

Part of the problem lies with the framing that popular intellectuals must utilize, whether out of necessity or as part of a longer-term strategy. Patkar, Roy, and the NBA have at times cast their struggle in terms of monolithic, reductionist, and stereotypical dichotomies – industrialization vs small-scale development, rich urban elites vs rural poor, modernity vs tradition. The use of such essentialist rhetoric has been strategic – both Patkar and Roy are well aware of the multiple oppressions within which the participants of the anti-dam movement operate, of gender, caste, class, religion, even language. They are equally aware that "locality" is not an inherently positive space, but may foster, instead, parochialism, inequality, and domination. When Patkar and Roy and the NBA rally their supporters around notions of the local, and against the "outside" influence of actors such as the World Bank and development planners, they run the risk that their rhetoric of "strategic essentialism" occasionally exceeds their reach.[58] Patkar and Roy do not claim to defend the status quo – as Roy says, "I've spent my whole life fighting tradition. There's no way that I want to be a traditional Indian housewife. So I'm not talking about being anti-development. I'm talking about the politics of development, of how do you break down this completely centralized, undemocratic process of decision-making."[59]

How Patkar and Roy framed the core issues of the protest is, therefore, double-edged in its effect. Aimed at multiple audiences, their message has straddled diverse and sometimes contradictory discourses on develop-

---

56. Nkululeko, quoted in Deborah Kasente, "The Gap Between Gender Research and Activism in Uganda", in Obioma Nnaemeka (ed.), *Sisterhood, Feminisms and Power: From Africa to the Diaspora* (Asmara, 1998), p. 227.
57. Kothari, "Dams, Bombs and Development".
58. For the term "strategic essentialism", see Gayatri Chakravarty Spivak, "Subaltern Studies: Deconstructing Historiography", in Donna Landry and Gerald MacLean (eds), *The Spivak Reader: Selected Works of Gayatri Spivak* (New York, 1995).
59. Arundhati Roy, interview by David Barsamian.

ment, social justice, human rights, community-building, and nationhood. What has been their strength in one arena – their emphasis on the very real connection felt by local inhabitants to their lands and livelihoods – has been used by others in other contexts to critique them for their romanticism and nostalgia. The framing process is not entirely under the control of Patkar, Roy, and the NBA, however. The presentation of the social movement by and to others is mediated by other actors, not least of which is the commercial mass media.[60] Within India, there is even a considerable difference in the reporting of the Narmada issue between the different regional and linguistic news media. Even beyond the press, narratives of struggles such as those in the Narmada Valley tend to be mediated by hegemonic discourses, ones that tend to privilege those who can speak in the dominant languages. This is part of the reason we hear so often from Patkar and Roy in their own words, articulate, passionate, and able to speak in a variety of languages and contexts. We catch only brief glimpses of the other people who live in the region, as the subjects of newspaper articles, academic studies and conferences, political rallies and films.

But despite these tensions and contradictions, Patkar, Roy and the NBA have been able to produce a considerable impact. Their ability to frame the struggle in the Narmada Valley over the building of dams at multiple levels simultaneously has enabled the movement to grow and survive. It has enabled them to challenge diverse and ever changing opponents, from local politicians to regional and national development authorities, from international financial institutions to multinational corporations. Their framing of the Narmada issue as both an ecological and a social justice issue has afforded the movement greater protection than others that have fought for human rights alone. Above all, the explicit linking of local, national, and international issues by Patkar and Roy has resulted in the type of multi-level "scalar politics" that is, according to Arturo Escobar, a necessary approach for contemporary social movements in the context of increasing globalization.[61]

60. Todd Gitlin, in his study of student antiwar activists during the 1960s, argues that the mass media keys on readily identifiable and "marketable" leaders of such social movements and transforms them into celebrities for audience consumption. For more, see Todd Gitlin, *The Whole World is Watching: Mass Media in the Making and Unmaking of the New Left*, with a new preface (Berkeley, CA, 2003).
61. Arturo Escobar, "Displacement, Development, and Modernity in the Colombian Pacific", *International Social Science Journal*, 55 (2003), p. 5, and *idem*, "Culture Sits in Place: Reflections on Globalism and Subaltern Strategies of Globalization", *Political Geography*, 20 (2001), pp. 139–174.

IRSH 49 (2004), Supplement, pp. 159–177 DOI: 10.1017/S0020859004001683
© 2004 Internationaal Instituut voor Sociale Geschiedenis

Framing Jihad: Intramovement Framing Contests and al-Qaeda's Struggle for Sacred Authority

QUINTAN WIKTOROWICZ

SUMMARY: This article emphasizes the credibility of popular intellectuals as a point of contention in framing contests. A movement group – a faction, clique, submovement, network cluster, organization, etc. – asserts its authority to speak on behalf of an issue or constituency by emphasizing the perceived knowledge, character, and logic of its popular intellectuals while attacking those of rivals. Four basic framing strategies relevant to the credibility of popular intellectuals are identified: (1) vilification – demonizing competing popular intellectuals; (2) exaltation – praising ingroup popular intellectuals; (3) credentialing – emphasizing the expertise of the ingroup intellectuals; and (4) decredentialing – raising questions about the expertise of rivals. Al-Qaeda's intramovement framing struggle with nonviolent Islamic fundamentalists over the permissibility of violence is used as a case study. In an attempt to assert its right to sacred authority, the movement portrays scholars who support its *jihad* as logical, religious experts of good repute while characterizing opposing clerical popular intellectuals as emotional, corrupt, naïve, and ill-informed about politics.

Over the past several decades, a dense ideological network of Islamic fundamentalists known as *salafis* has expanded dramatically to become one of the largest Islamist movements in the Muslim World. The term, *salafi*, is derived from the Arabic *salaf*, which means "to precede", and refers to the companions of the Prophet Mohammed. Because the *salaf* learned about Islam directly from the messenger of God, their example is an important illustration of piety and unadulterated religious practice. *Salafis* argue that centuries of syncretic cultural and popular religious rituals and interpretations have distorted the purity of the message of God, and that only by returning to the example of the Prophet and his companions can Muslims reach Paradise in the hereafter. The label, *salafi*, is thus used to connote "proper" religious adherence and moral legitimacy, implying that alternative understandings are corrupt deviations from the straight path of Islam.[1]

---

1. For more details about the *salafi* ideology, see Quintan Wiktorowicz, *The Management of Islamic Activism: Salafis, the Muslim Brotherhood, and State Power in Jordan* (Albany, NY, 2001), ch. 4.

The nodes of the network are constituted by religious scholars, who interpret sacred texts and outline the obligations of Islam in the modern context. These scholars are "popular intellectuals", in the sense that they provide interpretations of Islam and frames that guide *salafi* activism and collective action, which are seen as necessary to fulfill duties to God. The decentralized nature of religious authority in the Muslim world, however, means that no single individual or group of scholars enjoys theological hegemony or dictates how all *salafis* engage in collective action. Although *salafis* are united in their methodological approach to religious interpretation, which emphasizes the prophetic model and the paradigm of the *salaf*, the fragmentation of religious authority has engendered schisms within the *salafi* community, particularly over the issue of violence.

In the wake of the Soviet invasion of Afghanistan in 1979, there was initial agreement that violence in defense of an occupied Muslim country is an individual obligation (*fard 'ayn*), incumbent upon all able Muslims through verbal, financial, or physical support. Even after the Soviet withdrawal, there was agreement that violence was necessary to support Muslims in places like Bosnia and the Palestinian territories. This consensus, however, began to erode as "Arab Afghans" returned from the front and organized violence in their home states. *Salafi jihadis* continued to support the use of violence while "reformists" emphasized the necessity of individual spiritual transformation, propagation, and advice to the rulers and *umma* (Muslim community). Al-Qaeda is part of the *jihadi* faction.[2]

During the 1980s and 1990s as al-Qaeda developed, the initial debate between violent and non-violent *salafis* was over *takfir* – declaring a Muslim an apostate. The central axis of divergence was over whether one could judge a ruler in the Muslim world an apostate according to his actions.[3] Nonviolent groups argued that one can never know with certainty what is in an individual's heart, and that, so long as a ruler has a "mustard seed of *iman* [belief]", Muslims cannot rebel. The *jihadi salafis*, on the other hand, argued that the oneness of God (*tawhid*) demands that Muslims follow Islam in both belief and action. In other words, an un-Islamic action is just as revealing as an un-Islamic belief. As a result, the *jihadis* charged the Saudis and other regimes in the Muslim world with apostasy and called for a *jihad* to remove them from power.

In the late 1990s, although this debate continued, it became less relevant to Islamist struggles on the ground, as *jihadis* faced defeat and marginalization throughout the Middle East. This was particularly the case in the

2. See *idem*, "The New Global Threat: Transnational Salafis and Jihad", *Middle East Policy*, 8 (2001), pp. 18–38.
3. This brief history is taken from Quintan Wiktorowicz and John Kaltner, "Killing in the Name of Islam: Al-Qaeda's Justification for September 11", *Middle East Policy*, 10 (2003), pp. 76–92.

largest Islamist insurgencies in Egypt and Algeria.[4] In Egypt, leaders from both the Islamic Group and Islamic Jihad declared ceasefires and the violence came to a dramatic end. Elements from within the Islamic Group went so far as to issue a public apology for the violence. In a move that epitomized the recasting of the *jihadis*, a number of Islamists from both groups attempted to establish political parties (the Shari'a and Islah parties), though the regime rejected the requests for permits. Violent *jihadi* dissidents found themselves marginalized, and many left for Pakistan and Afghanistan to work directly with al-Qaeda.

In Algeria, a similar process occurred. The regime's decision to cancel elections in 1992, as Islamists were poised to control parliament, sparked an insurgency that has claimed more than 150,000 lives. Early in the conflict, the *jihadi salafis* united under the banner of the Armed Islamic Group (GIA) and attacked government officials and soldiers. In 1996, however, the GIA launched a series of civilian massacres that undermined the unity of the Islamist opposition: a number of *salafi* rebel groups (as well as non-*salafi* groups such as the Islamic Salvation Army) condemned the atrocities and issued unilateral ceasefires. The regime, in turn, responded to the ceasefires by using an amnesty program to reintegrate former Islamist fighters into society. Although a number of radical groups continue to operate, the violence has dropped substantially since the late 1990s. As a result, many Algerian *jihadi salafis* placed their networks, resources, and personnel at the service of al-Qaeda.[5]

For nonviolent *salafis*, these defeats made it clear that the *jihadi* vision to unseat incumbent Muslim regimes was at an end (at least in the short term), and so the issue of *takfir* became less prominent in debates over violence. Instead, the focus shifted to al-Qaeda's war against the US and its allies. In general, *salafis* share the same diagnostic frame: the US is waging a war of aggression against Islam and is responsible for many of the problems in the Muslim world. Differences emerge, however, over the proper response and course of action. *Jihadis*, once again, call for violence while the nonviolent *salafis* promote reform. Each side proffers an assortment of *fatwas* (religious jurisprudential opinions) and copious religious evidence to support its position.

This dispute is a "framing contest"[6] in which each contender not only asserts particular religious interpretations but also claims "sacred authority" – the right to interpret Islam and religious symbols on behalf of the

---

4. See, for example, Fawaz Gerges, "The Decline of Revolutionary Islam in Algeria and Egypt", *Survival*, 41 (1999), pp. 113–125.
5. See Quintan Wiktorowicz, "The GIA and GSPC in Algeria", in Magnus Ranstorp (ed.), *In the Service of al-Qaeda: Radical Islamic Movements* (New York, forthcoming).
6. Charlotte Ryan, *Prime Time Activism: Media Strategies for Grassroots Organizing* (Boston, MA, 1991).

Muslim community.[7] The *jihadis* and reformists operate in a competitive religious marketplace of ideas, and therefore must offer religious interpretations or "products" that can effectively tap into audience predispositions and personal understandings about religion and its application in the modern world. The target audience of framing efforts, however, is not an assortment of religious scholars capable of adjudicating complex theological debates. The vast majority of Muslims find it extremely difficult to weigh the considerable religious evidence marshaled by both sides of the framing contest. Under such circumstances, frame resonance has little to do with the theological arguments themselves, or the supportive evidence. Instead, audiences use the reputation and authority of scholars as heuristic devices to ascertain authenticity. As a result, both the *jihadis* and the reformists assert the legitimacy of their scholars and concomitant authority to issue *fatwas*.

Using interviews, *fatwas*, and speeches by Osama Bin Laden, and other al-Qaeda representatives, this article examines the framing strategies used by al-Qaeda to assert its right to sacred authority and promote *jihad*.[8] Rather than focusing on popular intellectuals as ideological producers or frame articulators, I emphasize the credibility of popular intellectuals as a point of struggle. Four basic framing strategies relevant to the credibility of popular intellectuals are identified: (1) vilification – demonizing competing popular intellectuals; (2) exaltation – praising ingroup popular intellectuals; (3) credentialing – emphasizing the expertise of the ingroup intellectuals; and (4) decredentialing – raising questions about the expertise of rivals. These strategies are designed to assert a group's authority in framing contests by emphasizing the perceived knowledge, character, and logic of its popular intellectuals while attacking those of rivals.

INTRA-MOVEMENT FRAMING CONTESTS AND CREDIBILITY

Social movements are not monolithic entities. They are represented by myriad actors with oftentimes competing tactics, strategies, and goals. As Mayer Zald and John McCarthy argue:

---

7. Dale F. Eickelman and James Piscatori, *Muslim Politics* (Princeton, NJ, 1996).
8. This article primarily draws from two sources. First, it uses interviews I conducted between 1996 and 1997 with *jihadi* and reformist *salafis* in Jordan, which represents an intellectual hub for *salafi* scholars from both groups. Second, it uses the most prominent public statements issued by al-Qaeda before and after the September 11 attacks. Public statements are seen as appropriate sources since they are explicit modes for disseminating frames intended for popular consumption.

Whether we study revolutionary movements, broad or narrow social reform movements, or religious movements, we find a variety of SMOs [social movement organizations] or groups, linked to various segments of supporting constituencies (both institutional and individual), competing among themselves for resources and symbolic leadership, sharing facilities and resources at other times, developing stable and differentiated functions, occasionally merging into ad hoc coalitions, and occasionally engaging in all-out war against each other.[9]

Robert Benford and others echo this assessment: "SMOs compete with one another for instrumental resources such as money, constituents, and third party support, as well as for symbolic goods such as turf, status, and prestige".[10]

Intramovement conflict is particularly common in framing, so much so that William Gamson and David Meyer encourage us, "to think of framing as an internal process of contention within movements with different actors taking different positions".[11] Although movements may enjoy "cognitive closure", whereby debate about core issues and beliefs is limited,[12] there are frequent disagreements about specifics and plans of action, creating diversity and multiple voices that claim to represent a movement.[13] Groups often diverge in terms of diagnosis, prognostication, the best way to mobilize support, and identity. These struggles are contests to influence the direction of the movement: how resources should be used, the proper construction and dissemination of symbols and discourses, acceptable alliances, etc. An intra-movement framing contest is, in short, a struggle to assert authority.

Within this struggle, credibility is central.[14] A messenger of disrepute will undermine the potential frame resonance of a message by leading audiences to question the source of information and argument. Those with

9. Mayer N. Zald and John D. McCarthy, "Social Movement Industries: Competition and Conflict Among SMOs", in *idem* (eds), *Social Movements in an Organizational Society* (New Brunswick, NJ, 1987), p. 161.

10. Robert D. Benford, "Frame Disputes within the Nuclear Disarmament Movement", *Social Forces*, 71 (1993), p. 681; *idem* and Louis Zurcher, "Instrumental and Symbolic Competition among Social Movement Organizations", in Sam Marullo and John Lofland (eds), *Peace Action in the Eighties* (New Brunswick, NJ, 1990), pp. 125–139.

11. William A. Gamson and David S. Meyer, "Framing Political Opportunity", in Doug McAdam, John D. McCarthy, and Mayer N. Zald (eds), *Comparative Perspectives on Social Movements: Political Opportunities, Mobilizing Structures, and Cultural Framings* (Cambridge, 1996), p. 283.

12. Luther P. Gerlach and Virginia H. Hine, *People, Power, Change: Movements of Social Transformation* (Indianapolis, IN, 1970), p. 161.

13. Benford, "Frame Disputes within the Nuclear Disarmament Movement", pp. 677–701; Benford and Zurcher, "Instrumental and Symbolic Competition among Social Movement Organizations".

14. See Benford, "Frame Disputes within the Nuclear Disarmament Movement", pp. 692–693; Robert D. Benford and David A. Snow, "Framing Processes and Social Movements: An Overview and Assessment", *Annual Review of Sociology*, 26 (2000), pp. 620–621.

sufficient reputations, in contrast, will elicit trust and enhance prospects
for successful message dissemination. The credibility of the messenger is a
necessary prerequisite for frame alignment. Each group must therefore
demonstrate that it has the right, authority, and credibility to speak on
behalf of the movement. Where popular intellectuals are involved (either
directly or indirectly), their credibility is of particular importance since
they are the "experts", "thinkers", and "ideologues" of the movement.

Although research on framing contests mostly deals with movement–
countermovement interactions, recent work has identified several strategies relevant to the credibility of popular intellectuals in *intramovement*
framing contests.[15] These strategies can generally be broken into two
categories: *crediting* and *discrediting*. The former represents attempts to
emphasize the legitimacy of a movement group's institutions, efforts, and
popular intellectuals by highlighting knowledge proficiency, sincerity, and
other positive attributes that demonstrate the right and ability of the group
to speak on behalf of a cause. This is primarily an inward-focused
approach. Discrediting, on the other hand, is an outward-directed attack
against the reputation of intramovement rivals and opposing popular
intellectuals to undermine and weaken the authority of competitors.
Movements typically use a combination of both approaches. The
following briefly outlines some of the most common framing strategies
relevant to credibility issues.

Vilification and exaltation

Movement groups often use framing to distinguish themselves from other
groups, including other protagonists, antagonists, and neutral bystanders.[16] In a sense, a group must justify its raison d'être by demonstrating its

15. Marsha L. Vanderford, "Vilification and Social Movements: A Case Study of Pro-Life and
Pro-Choice Rhetoric", *Quarterly Journal of Speech*, 75 (1989), pp. 166–182; Scott A. Hunt,
Robert D. Benford, and David A. Snow, "Identity Fields: Framing Processes and the
Construction of Movement Identities", in Enrique Laraña, Hank Johnston, and Joseph R.
Gusfield (eds), *New Social Movements: From Ideology to Identity* (Philadelphia, PA, 1994), pp.
185–208; Patrick G. Coy and Lynne Woehrle, "Constructing Identity and Oppositional
Knowledge: The Framing Practices of Peace Movement Organizations during the Persian Gulf
War", *Sociological Spectrum*, 16 (1996), pp. 287–327, as cited in Benford and Snow, "Framing
Processes and Social Movements", p. 621; Ira Silver, "Constructing 'Social Change' through
Philanthropy: Boundary Framing and the Articulation of Vocabularies of Motives for Social
Movement Participation", *Sociological Inquiry*, 67 (1997), pp. 488–503; Dawn McCaffrey and
Jennifer Keys, "Competitive Frame Processes in the Abortion Debate: Polarization-Vilification,
Frame Saving, and Frame Debunking", *The Sociological Quarterly*, 41 (2000), pp. 41–61; Robert
D. Benford and Scott A. Hunt, "Interactional Dynamics in Public Problems Marketplaces:
Movements and the Counterframing and Reframing of Public Problems", in James Holstein and
Gale Miller (eds), *Challenges and Choices: Constructionist Perspectives on Social Problems* (New
York, 2003), pp. 153–186.
16. Hunt *et al.*,"Identity Fields".

unique position and relevance in a competitive identity environment. This is particularly important in cases of intramovement competition characterized by struggles over symbolic and instrumental resources. Under such circumstances, asserting a unique identity can help secure necessary resources, even if these come from small groups of supporters. Groups thus engage in both extra- and intramovement "boundary framing".[17] In boundary framing, strategies of polarization accentuate differences and draw sharp ingroup/outgroup distinctions.[18] This often generates stark bifurcations between real movement activists and pretenders, the true believers and the hypocrites, the misguided and the informed, good and evil. In extreme cases, the world is simply divided into two camps in Manichean fashion: those aligned with the movement group and those against it. Competitors are frequently lumped into a generic "other" category.

This polarization is typically accompanied by strategies of *vilification*.[19] The "other" category is laden with negative characteristics and an assortment of claims intended to impugn the reputation of competitors. Vilification includes tactics such as *name-calling* – the use of labels to connect an individual or group to a negative symbol, event, or phenomenon, often in an attempt to produce visceral responses that erode the target's ability to assert credibility. Name-calling can challenge the intentions of a group, ridicule its values and activities, or obfuscate its agenda and goals. Examples include use of the terms "femi-nazi", "bleeding-heart liberals", and "tree-huggers".

Name-calling can have a powerful effect by packaging an assortment of wide-ranging connotations in a single label. In some instances, bystanders may reject a movement or group based on responses to the label rather than the message. Successful use of name-calling may even force groups to abandon previously accepted labels to avoid the negative associations. Vilification also includes character assassination, various forms of maligning,[20] and the purposeful misrepresentation of a group's views and efforts through such techniques as caricatures, extreme cases, stereotypes, and guilt by association.[21] A common counter-frame leveled at the nuclear-freeze and peace movements, for example, accused activists with aiding the "enemy," whether intentionally or unintentionally.[22] Other movements have been maligned as corrupt, hypocritical, or tools of nefarious interests.

17. *Ibid.*; Silver, "Constructing 'Social Change' through Philanthropy".
18. McCaffrey and Keys, "Competitive Frame Processes in the Abortion Debate".
19. Vanderford, "Vilification and Social Movements"; McCaffrey and Keys, "Competitive Frame Processes".
20. Benford and Hunt, "Interactional Dynamics in Public Problems Marketplaces".
21. Ryan, *Prime Time Activism*, p. 85.
22. Benford and Hunt, "Interactional Dynamics in Public Problems Marketplaces", pp. 166–167.

Polarization is also typically accompanied by *exaltation*, the polar reflection of vilification. This strategy emphasizes the positive attributes of the ingroup, which is characterized as pure of heart, selfless, and independent. The claim is that the group is a vanguard representing the better interests of the community through sacrifice and effort. By extension, ingroup popular intellectuals are credible and authoritative, since they possess all the positive attributes of the group.

Where popular intellectuals are important for the construction of frames, they are often targets of vilification and exaltation.[23] If the credibility of a frame relies upon the credibility of a popular intellectual, attacks against the latter will help weaken the viability of the former. This is particularly the case where complex issues are involved. As Robert Furtell argues, where social movement issues are of a technical nature (as in religious debates over violence), "Expert authority may powerfully shape the contours of framing activities. The language of science and expertise can stall efforts of nonexperts to understand what is going on. Lay citizens have to place a great deal of faith in the authority and judgments of experts."[24] This faith in experts is, in turn, contingent upon the reputations of the vying authorities. In Madison County, Kentucky, for example, the "Not in My Back Yard" (NIMBY) movement attempted to stop a US army plan to incinerate chemical weapons at a local site. The movement's framing efforts initially succeeded in mobilizing local opposition, in part, because army experts made errors in presenting their case, thereby compromising the credibility of the government's technical information and interpretation.[25]

Credentialing and decredentialing

In addition to issues of character and trustworthiness, there is also a question of whether the popular intellectuals have credible expertise. Although there is little research to date on the issue of expertise and frame resonance, Robert Benford and David Snow argue that "Hypothetically, the greater the status and/or perceived expertise of the frame articulator and/or the organization they represent from the vantage point of potential adherents and constituents, the more plausible and resonant the framings of claims."[26] In other words, those who speak on behalf of the movement

---

23. Popular intellectuals also produce vilification and exaltation frames. They may, however, consciously avoid becoming personally embroiled in frame disputes to protect their image as dispassionate experts. Under these conditions, others in the movement may be responsible for developing and articulating the frames.
24. Robert Furtell, "Framing Processes, Cognitive Liberation, and NIMBY Protest in the US Chemical-Weapons Disposal Conflict", *Sociological Inquiry*, 73 (2003), p. 380.
25. *Ibid.*
26. Benford and Snow, "Framing Processes and Social Movements", p. 621.

should seem as though they know what they are talking about. Framing efforts that focus on establishing and advertising expertise can be thought of as a strategy of *credentialing*,[27] which is frequently accompanied by attacks against the expertise of competitors, or *decredentialing*.

Although research tends to focus on the expertise of *active* frame articulators, it is also important to consider the credibility of popular intellectuals who are not involved in framing efforts but whose arguments and ideas are incorporated into movement frames. There are instances where movements "adopt" popular intellectuals and incorporate their work into movement frames. This allows movements to utilize popular intellectuals across time and space, sometimes without the acquiescence of the appropriated individuals. Marx, Locke, Gandhi, and Martin Luther King, for example, are utilized by an assortment of movements today, oftentimes in quite unique ways. And Muslim activists incorporate Islamic scholars from throughout the Muslim world into local frames. In some cases, movement antagonists may adopt the same popular intellectuals to make distinct and contrary arguments, demonstrating the elasticity of borrowed ideas.

Criteria of credibility

The different framing strategies related to credibility attempt to emphasize criteria for ingroup intellectuals while depicting opponents as devoid of the characteristics necessary for authority. The particulars of these strategies, however, depend upon the specific criteria for expertise in a given movement, community, culture, and/or society. In short, it depends upon what the popular intellectual or the frame is addressing and the given context and audience.

Despite these differences, there are several plausible generic criteria of credibility. First, the popular intellectual must seem *knowledgeable*. In most cases, he/she must not only understand the movement values, but also the context of activism. Scholars have argued for the importance of empirical credibility for frame resonance,[28] and one could argue that popular intellectuals need to appear grounded in reality as well. Are they realistic in their assessment of the context? Do they seem to understand the realities of activism? For example, counter-frames may attempt to undermine competing groups by arguing that their popular intellectuals are "all heart and no head", or "well meaning but naïve".[29] These buzz phrases connote well-intentioned intellectuals who simply do not understand how things get done in the real world, captives of an ivory tower

27. Coy and Woehrle, "Constructing Identity and Oppositional Knowledge".
28. David Snow, and Robert D. Benford, "Ideology, Frame Resonance and Participant Mobilization", *International Journal of Social Movement Research*, 1 (1988), p. 208; Benford and Snow, "Framing Processes and Social Movements", pp. 619–620.
29. Benford and Hunt, "Interactional Dynamics", p. 166.

impervious to reality. It is important to note that "reality" is a subjective construct and as such means different things for different groups.

Second, credibility likely depends upon the perceived *character* of the popular intellectual. Charges of corruption or deviance undermine the reputation and status of the intellectual by calling into question his/her moral certitude. Is the popular intellectual working for the best interests of the movement because he/she believes in the cause? Or does he/she have ulterior motives? Is the individual doing what he/she thinks is right or is he/she being directed by forces outside the movement or group (particularly "the enemy")? Such questions are related to issues of trust and sincerity and can be tied into perceptions about the ethics of the intellectual.

Third, popular intellectuals should appear *logical*. Although some social movements might question issues of logic and reason as andocentric or positivistic constructs, most value rational thought and argument. Popular intellectuals who are inconsistent, for example, might appear wavering, ill-informed, or hypocritical.

In the following case study, I show how al-Qaeda uses the framing strategies outlined above to address issues of knowledge, character, and logic. The movement has attempted to assert hegemony over sacred authority by endowing its own religious scholars with the necessary criteria of credibility while attacking the reputations of opposing clerical popular intellectuals within the *salafi* community. Because of the importance of scholarly reputation for the resonance of *fatwas*, issues of credibility are central to the *jihadi*–reformist framing contest.

AL-QAEDA AND THE STRUGGLE FOR SACRED AUTHORITY

Sacred authority in the Muslim world is the decentralized, informal recognition of the expertise and character of religious scholars. There is no formal hierarchy capable of establishing a clerical caste akin to the Catholic Church (with the exception of the Shiite community). Instead, authority hinges upon reputation, which is developed during years of interaction with the Muslim community through religious lessons, rulings, publications, and pronouncements. The title *alim* (religious scholar, pl. *ulama*) is not a formal designation or appointment; it is informal acknowledgment of expertise. This informality means that there is no enforcement instrument when a scholar issues a *fatwa*. Nor is there an adjudication mechanism to determine "right" and "wrong" religious legal rulings. As a result, audiences rely extensively upon the perceived expertise and character of a scholar to determine whether the interpretation is accurate, legitimate, and worthy of being followed.

Both the *jihadi* and reformist *salafis* recognize the essential role of scholars as intermediaries between the sacred texts and everyday religious rituals and practices. In his "Address to the Ummah on the Anniversary of the Crusader War", for example, Bin Laden emphasizes the importance of the scholars:

> While the Ummah has its collectivist duties, and a common role which it has to carry out collectively, there are groups who have a specific role which they have to take care of in a special manner. In the lead of these groups is the group of the Islamic scholars and callers to Allah, who are the heirs of the prophets, who are the holders of the knowledge trust, and the obligation to the duty of calling to Allah and the duty of announcing him. And that's why Allah had raised their status and heightened their significance and importance, when He said, "Allah will exalt in degree those of you who believe, and those who have been granted knowledge" (Quran, Al-Mujadala, verse 11).[30]

Reformist *salafis* repeat these sentiments and argue that "The source for mankind's rectification is through knowledge."[31] Both sides recognize the scholars as the inheritors of the prophetic message, intellectually equipped to interpret the immutable sources of Islam and the paradigm of the *salaf* in light of the changing conditions of the temporal world. A theological argument about *jihad* therefore requires the support of scholars for legitimation.

Because both sides mobilize scholarly opinions and present religious evidence, the credibility of the clerical popular intellectual is paramount. Most Muslims simply do not have a command of Islam sufficient to adjudicate the different arguments; each sounds plausible, given the weight of evidence marshaled to either perspective. As a result, framing strategies are used to influence audience evaluations about the knowledge, character, and logic of the competing scholars.

Knowledge

Most important reformist scholars hold Ph.D.s in the Islamic sciences from established Islamic universities, particularly in Saudi Arabia. They include a long list of luminaries with solid international reputations for knowledge, and their *fatwas* have wide-reaching global import. Reformist control of the state-sanctioned religious institutions in Saudi Arabia has provided resources and platforms to reinforce this impact and perceptions about religious authority. Given the pedigree and standing of the reformist scholars, decredentialing through attacks against the religious expertise of the reformist popular intellectuals is rather limited. While the *jihadis* have

---

30. Osama Bin Laden, "Address to the Ummah on the Anniversary of the Crusader War Jihad", available at www.jihadunspun.com. Accessed 1 November 2002.
31. "Respecting the Status of Scholars", *Al-Asaalah Magazine*, available at: www.al-manhaj. com/articles/knowledge/K1002.html. Accessed 9 October 2001.

argued that *particular* reformist scholars are weak in *specific* areas of the Islamic sciences, they have found it difficult to assail the expertise of the reformists as a collectivity.

Instead, decredentialing has focused upon nonreligious knowledge. Reformists might be credited with their thorough religious training, but *jihadis* frequently argue that they have little understanding about context. In other words, reformists are portrayed as incapable of applying the immutable religious sources to dynamic contemporary conditions because they have a limited grasp of the latter. They are framed as ignorant or naïve when it comes to politics, and therefore incapable of issuing well informed, relevant *fatwas*.

Jihadis, for example, point to Mohammed Nasir al-Din al-Albani (d. 1999) as a case in point.[32] Al-Albani's religious knowledge is unassailable. He trained not only some of the most influential reformist scholars of the contemporary period, but several well known *jihadi* scholars as well. *Jihadis* point to several of al-Albani's *fatwas*, however, as evidence that he did not quite grasp the context of his religious rulings. One related to the Israeli–Palestinian conflict called for Palestinians to leave the occupied territories. *Jihadis* argue that this *fatwa* did not take into account the demographic struggle on the ground, and that its implementation would have, in effect, ceded control of the disputed territories to Israel. This decredentialing strategy was severe enough to elicit a response from al-Albani, who argued for a division of labor between the specialists of religious knowledge and current affairs experts.[33]

Al-Qaeda also argues that the reformist scholars issued ill-informed *fatwas* because they were deceived by the Saudi regime. In his 1996 "Declaration of War", for example, Bin Laden pays homage to the "honorable *ulama* and scholars", but argues that they were duped into issuing a *fatwa* supporting the presence of American troops in Saudi Arabia during the first Gulf War:

> When the Islamic world resented the arrival of the crusader forces to the land of the two Holy Places, the king told lies to the Ulamah (who issued fatwas about the arrival of the Americans) and to the gathering of the Islamic leaders at the conference of Rabitah which was held in the Holy City of Makka. The king said that: "the issue is simple, the American and the alliance forces will leave the area in a few months".[34]

A strategy of decredentialing, however, is dangerous for the *jihadis* since they suffer from a "reputation deficit". Al-Qaeda's "scholars" have limited

32. Author's interviews with *jihadi salafis* in Jordan, 1996–1997.

33. Muhammad Naasir ud-Deen al-Albaanee, Abu Talhah Dawud ibn Ronald Burbank (tr.), *The Knowledge of Current Affairs* (Ipswich, 1994).

34. Osama Bin Laden, "Declaration of War against the Americans Occupying the Land of the Two Holy Places", published in *al-Quds al-Arabi* (London), 8 August 1996.

student followings and reputations. Many are what Olivier Roy terms "new Islamist intellectuals" – well educated individuals from Western-style schools who turned to religion after facing blocked social mobility in their professions.[35] These "new intellectuals" rarely attended institutes of higher religious education, instead preferring either self-education or informal study circles and lessons. Certainly there are a few exceptions to this, including a small handful of Saudi clerics and Omar Abdul Rahman, a graduate of al-Azhar University in Cairo who was sentenced to life imprisonment in the US for conspiracy to wage terrorism; and the *jihadis* do try to emphasize the formal credentials of supporting scholars where possible.[36] But credentialing efforts are rather limited and more often draw upon famous *salafi* scholars across time, such as Ibn Taymiyya. Any effort to challenge the credentials of reformists opens the possibility that audiences will judge al-Qaeda according to the same criteria. Even if an audience accepts the *jihadi* argument that the reformists are ignorant or naïve about current affairs, they may ask whether the *jihadis* are ignorant or naïve about the Islamic sciences. As a result, credentialing and decredentialing that target the criterion of knowledge are rather limited.

Character

Perhaps to a large extent due to its reputation deficit, al-Qaeda predominantly relies upon the strategies of vilification and exaltation to present itself as a moral authority, while discrediting its detractors as unworthy of the sacred trust of religious interpretation. Virtually every al-Qaeda statement that addresses issues of credibility and sacred authority includes attacks against the character of opposing *ulama*, and represents al-Qaeda as a sacrificing, sincere vanguard following a moral charge to defend the Muslim community against aggression.

Al-Qaeda's most important framing strategy is vilification. Because it cannot assail the expertise of the reformists, it must impugn and malign character and intent. If audiences distrust the character of the messenger, they will likely question the religious interpretation and whether it is motivated by a real devotion to God or selfish interests that corrupt religious rulings. A ubiquitous tactic is use of the term *ulama al-sulta* ("the scholars of power"). The term is laden with negative connotations, implying an insidious relationship with regimes and authority structures that undermines the independence and legitimacy of Islamic interpretation. It is typically surrounded by a barrage of other disparaging terms, such as "palace lackeys", "the corrupt *ulama*", and "the *ulama* who flatter

---

35. Olivier Roy, *The Failure of Political Islam*, Carol Volk (tr.) (Cambridge, 1994).
36. See, for example, Islamic Group military commander and al-Qaeda leader, Rifa'ey Ahmad Taha's interview in *Nida'ul Islam* (April–May 1997).

[those in power]". Even more damning, al-Qaeda ties these scholars
directly to the Ministry of the Interior in Saudi Arabia, responsible for
maintaining internal security: "Sometimes officials from the Ministry of
the Interior, who are also graduates of the colleges of the Shari'ah, are
leashed out to mislead and confuse the nation and the Ummah (by wrong
fatwas) and to circulate false information about the movement [al-Qaeda
and *jihadis*]."[37] For al-Qaeda, this means that these scholars "speak in their
masters' languages and in the concepts of the enemy of the *umma*".[38]

The potency of this framing strategy derives from increased government
usurpation of institutions responsible for producing religious interpretations. Concerned about legitimacy and religious opposition, regimes
throughout the Muslim world have attempted to centralize religious
authority under state control. Mosques, religious institutes of higher
learning, committees responsible for issuing *fatwas*, and other vehicles of
religious meaning have been bureaucratized and linked to the state.
Religious functionaries, including many of the *ulama*, are now dependent
upon the state for their salaries and positions.[39] Serious divergences from
government interpretations of Islam can incur severe reprimands, dismissal
(and thus loss of income), and even imprisonment. James Piscatori has
gone so far as to argue that the *ulama* in Saudi Arabia, the center of the
salafi movement, have become "agents of the state".[40]

While this may prevent broad dissemination of radical ideologies, it
concurrently undermines the legitimacy of the *ulama* itself. Even
supporters of the reformist vision admit that state controls create at least
the appearance that the reformist scholars are no more than civil servants
charged with protecting regime interests. The *jihadis* seize upon this
widely-held perception and attack the intentions of those who issue *fatwas*
against violence. Bin Laden, for example, observes that:

> The offices of the Clerics Authority [in Saudi Arabia] are adjacent to the royal
> palace [...]. In such a situation [when even the offices are linked], is it reasonable
> to ask a civil servant [for a *fatwa*], who receives his salary from the king? What is
> the ruling regarding the king, and should the king be regarded as supporting
> infidels?[41]

37. Bin Laden, "Declaration of War".
38. Al-Qaeda, "A Statement from *Qa'idat al-Jihad* Regarding the Mandates of the Heroes and
the Legality of the Operations in New York and Washington", 24 April 2002. The original
document was posted at www.alneda.com (hosted by Markaz al-Dirasat wal-Buhuth al-
Islamiyya) and provided to the author by Paul Eedle after the website was shut down.
39. See, for example, James P. Piscatori (ed.), *Islam in the Political Process* (Cambridge, 1983);
Wiktorowicz, *The Management of Islamic Activism*, ch. 2; and Seyyed Vali Nasr, *Islamic
Leviathan: State Power and Islam in Malaysia and Pakistan* (Oxford, 2001).
40. James P. Piscatori, "Ideological Politics in Sa'udi Arabia", in *idem, Islam in the Political
Process*, pp. 60–61.
41. MEMRI, "A New Bin Laden Speech", Special Dispatch Series, no. 539, 18 July 2003.

Al-Qaeda does express some sympathy for sections of the clerical establishment in Saudi Arabia, particularly those who believe in *jihad* but remain silent out of fear. Bin Laden explains: "The clerics are prisoners and hostages of the tyrants. Some of them told me: "We cannot speak the truth [because we are civil servants] [...]. Many clerics have misled [people] because of threats of beating, imprisonment, or perhaps even death [by the regime]."⁴² Opposing clerics are thus framed as either corrupted tools of the regime or fearful bystanders who hide the truth to protect themselves.

Al-Qaeda further vilifies the reformist scholars by linking them directly to the interests of the enemy: "whether it [the Saudi religious establishment] fulfilled its role intentionally or unintentionally, the harm which eventuated from their efforts is no different from the role of the most ardent enemies of the nation".⁴³ This argument is consistently supported by the same verse from the Quran: "O You who believe, do not take the Jews and the Christians as allies. They are allies of each other. If any of you takes them as allies, then he is one of them. Indeed Allah does not guide the wrongdoers" (Quran, al-Ma'idah: 51).

The corruption of the reformists is contrasted with the character of the *jihadis* and their scholars. The al-Qaeda fighters are endowed with important characteristics of sacred authority: "dignity, pride, courage, generosity, truthfulness and sacrifice".⁴⁴ Al-Qaeda asserts the character of its supporters in terms of the sacrifice they endure: a willingness to die for the cause demonstrates an unrivaled devotion and love for God and the Muslim community. This sincerity and loyalty to God is emphasized in numerous al-Qaeda statements. Referring to the September 11 hijackers, one document stresses that:

> The heroes who offered themselves for the destruction of the strongholds of the enemy did not offer themselves in order to gain earthly possessions, or temporary fame, or a transitory desire. Rather, they offered their souls as a sacrifice for the religion of Allah almighty, defending Muslims whom American hands had mistreated by various types of torture and forms of domination and subjugation in every place [...] the only motive these young men had was to defend the religion of Allah, their dignity, and their honor. It was not done as a service to humanity or as an attempt to side with Eastern ideologies opposed to the West. Rather, it was a service to Islam in defense of its people, a pure act of their will, done submissively, not grudgingly.⁴⁵

The supporting scholars are framed as "honest" and willing to sacrifice for the cause. Their sincerity is evinced by their oppositional stance and

42. *Ibid.*
43. Osama Bin Laden, interview with *Nida'ul Islam*, reproduced in Barry Rubin and Judith Colp Rubin (eds), *Anti-American Terrorism and the Middle East* (Oxford, 2002), p. 143.
44. Bin Laden, "Declaration of War".
45. Al-Qaeda, "A Statement from *Qa'idat al-Jihad*".

consequent imprisonment by Saudi authorities.[46] These popular intellectuals are exalted as the real *ulama*, the only ones capable of interpreting Islam free of corruption and revealing the truth to the masses. They are framed as a vanguard capable of interpreting Islam and confronting un-Islamic regimes and their scholars of authority:

> So O truthful scholars, reformers and callers to Allah, you are the ones who should be at the front of the lines, to drive the Ummah and to lead the way, for this is incumbent upon your inheritance to the prophethood. Your first duty is the declaration of the truth to the Ummah, and to slap it in the faces of the tyrants without deceit or fear, for this is the requirement of the covenant which Allah had bestowed upon you. The importance of your duty is derived from the danger of the fraudulent and deceiving operations which are being practiced by the scholars of the regimes and the servants of the rulers who deal with the religion of Islam, who have hidden the true state of the Ummah, and who have sold their religion for a cheap offer from this Life.[47]

Bin Laden summarizes the intended consequences of the vilification and exaltation strategies:

> The *fatwa* of any official *alim* [religious figure] has no value for me. History is full of such *ulama* [clerics] who justify *riba* [economic interest], who justify the occupation of Palestine by the Jews, who justify the presence of American troops around Harmain Sharifain [the Islamic holy places in Saudi Arabia]. These people support the infidels for their personal gain. The true *ulama* support the *jihad* against America.[48]

Logic

In part to counter charges of zealotry and selective adherence to radical dogma, al-Qaeda portrays itself as rationally pursuing the will of God through a careful examination of the divine sources and texts. In credentialing itself, al-Qaeda often precedes arguments with qualifying statements intended to emphasize the rationality of the reasoning. Before outlining its theological justification for September 11 and the purposeful targeting of civilians, for example, al-Qaeda begins with the following statement:

> We pass on this initial report, without details or exposition, regarding the evidence of the legality of this kind of operation. Let it be a quick message to those who dress their political opinions in the garb of a legal ruling. Let it also be a call to those who oppose and condemn the operations to obey Allah, repent, and return to the legal evidence.[49]

46. Author's interview with *jihadi salafis* in Jordan, 1996–1997.
47. Osama Bin Laden, "To the Islamic Ummah, On the First Anniversary of the New American Crusader War", 12 October 2002. Available at www.jihadunspun.net.
48. Osama Bin Laden interview with *Dawn*, as reproduced in Rubin and Rubin, *Anti-American Terrorism*, p. 262.
49. Al-Qaeda, "A Statement from *Qa'idat al-Jihad*".

Elsewhere in the document, the movement presents itself as engaged in a scientific and methodical process of legal reasoning to determine what Islamic texts say about the permissibility of operations such as September 11:

> We should never think little of the passing of souls, especially the Muslims among them. And this is what compels us to pay attention to the issue of legal evidence from all its angles, without privileging one side over another and without ignoring one matter on account of another. After study and deliberation, we have found that operations like this are what will return its glory to the *ummah* and convince the oppressive enemy of the rights of the Islamic community.[50]

The language is emotionally detached, as though its architects are neutral, scientific observers merely seeking data and truth through unbiased research and observations that allow for the possibility of alternative conclusions.

At the same time, al-Qaeda tries to decredential its adversaries by challenging the logic of alternative theological arguments. First, it emphasizes inconsistencies in the reformist legal rulings to call into question the basis and process of judgment. Specifically, the frame draws on the broad support for "martyrdom" operations (suicide bombings) in the Palestinian territories and argues that a consistent argument leads to the inevitable conclusion that such operations are permissible in the US as well. Several reformists have lent their support to Palestinian suicide bombings while decrying September 11 as heretical and illegal according to religious principles. Al-Qaeda argues that the legal basis for "martyrdom" operations against Israel and the US are one and the same and that the reformists are hypocrites:

> First of all, America's status among Muslims is the same as that of the Jews – they are both people of war. What is permissible regarding the right of the occupying enemy to the land of Palestine permits the right of anything like it [...]. If you are surprised by this, you will truly be surprised by those who rule that the martyrdom operations in Palestine in which civilians fall victim are among the highest forms of *jihad*, and then rule that the martyrdom operations in America are wrong because of civilian deaths. This inconsistency is very strange! How can one permit the killing of the branch and not permit the killing of the supporting trunk? All who permit martyrdom operations against the Jews in Palestine must allow them in America. If not, the inconsistency leads to nothing but a type of game playing with the legal ruling.[51]

Since September 11, another common decredentialing tactic is to portray reformists as inspired by emotion, rather than logic. Immediately after the

50. *Ibid.*
51. *Ibid.*

attacks, Hammoud Al-Uqlaa Ash-Shuaybi [d. 2002], a radical Saudi cleric of some standing, issued a widely circulated *fatwa* supporting the al-Qaeda operation. Although al-Uqlaa was not a formal member of the movement, his *fatwa* was quickly adopted and supported by al-Qaeda.[52] He prefaces his argument with the following statement:

> [...] it is unfortunate and disturbing to see that a lot of fellow scholars have preferred the side of mercy and emotion and forgotten and ignored what that Kufr Nation (America) is doing such as killing, destroying and spoiling most of the Muslim lands, and showing no mercy or kindness in that. Consequently, I find it incumbent upon me to refute some false claims and misconceptions that some fellow scholars are relying upon in trying to support their positions.[53]

About seven months later, al-Qaeda made the same argument in its justification for September 11:

> Despite the clarity of the matter and the obvious nature of the evidence [...] it is regrettable that many of the motives [of the "martyrs"] were destroyed in the comforting of America, the expressions of sorrow for her, and the legal rulings to assist her and to donate blood for her innocent [!!] victims.[54]

CONCLUSION

Social movements are about persuasion. Whether constituted by identity-centered aspirations of postmaterialist collective transformation and shared networks of meaning, or more narrow material interests, movements must convince targets of activism that change is necessary. As this volume notes, popular intellectuals are inextricably involved in persuasion attempts through frames and framing processes, whether directly or indirectly; and the potential for frame resonance hinges, in part, on their credibility. As a result, framing strategies include attempts to emphasize the credibility of ingroup intellectuals while discrediting rivals.

The purpose of this article is mostly taxonomic. It identifies four framing strategies relevant to the credibility of popular intellectuals, particularly in the context of framing contests: vilification, exaltation, credentialing, and decredentialing. Although the criteria of credibility vary according to movement, issue, and context, movements generally use these strategies to credit and discredit popular intellectuals by assessing knowledge, character, and logic. The goal is to promote positive attributes for ingroup intellectuals and negative connotations for competitors, thus

52. Al-Qaeda Statement, October 13, 2001, reproduced in Rubin and Rubin, *Anti-American Terrorism*, p. 254.
53. Hammoud Al-Uqlaa Ash-Shuaybi, "Fatwa on Events Following 11 September 2001", no date. Originally accessed at www.azzam.com in October 2001. The website was shut down sometime in 2002.
54. Al-Qaeda, "A Statement from *Qa'idat al-Jihad*".

asserting the group's authority to speak on behalf of an issue or constituency.

In the case of al-Qaeda, the fragmentation of sacred authority in the Muslim world means that the movement must pay special attention to credibility. The complexity of religious debates over the permissibility of violence in Islam places religious scholars at the heart of contests over meaning – they are responsible for interpreting Islam on behalf of the community. Al-Qaeda portrays scholars who support its *jihad* as logical, religious experts of good repute while characterizing opposing clerical popular intellectuals as emotional, corrupt, naïve, and ill-informed about politics. Framing strategies are intended to support al-Qaeda's call for *jihad* by asserting its sacred authority at the expense of reformist Islamic scholars.

Although more research is needed, the case study suggests a causal argument about the relationship between popular intellectuals and frame resonance: varying degrees of resonance can be explained by the ability of a movement to direct framing strategies toward accepted criteria of authority used by target audiences in a given context to evaluate the reliability of frames. That is, framing strategies and how they align with established criteria of authority are variables that might explain differential degrees of frame resonance. One could plausibly argue, for example, that part of al-Qaeda's popularity, even among those unwilling to participate in violence themselves, is its focus on vilification, which taps into widespread concerns about the character of the Saudi clerical establishment and its ability to issue independent religious rulings. The next step is to test such propositions empirically, preferably using both positive and negative cases (frame successes and frame failures) to thwart problems of circularity.[55] Studies along these lines are difficult, since researchers need access to individuals who support groups like al-Qaeda, as well as those who were exposed to the message and rejected the *jihadis*, but such research promises to explain better the causal connection between the reputation of popular intellectuals and frame resonance.

55. Robert D. Benford, "An Insider's Critique of the Social Movement Framing Perspective", *Sociological Inquiry*, 67 (1997), pp. 411–412.

IRSH 49 (2004), Supplement, pp. 179–195 DOI: 10.1017/S0020859004001695
© 2004 Internationaal Instituut voor Sociale Geschiedenis

Popular Publics: Street Protest and Plaza Preachers in Caracas*

DAVID SMILDE

SUMMARY: Classic liberal conceptions of the public sphere generally miscast the public participation of popular sectors in the developing world as premodern, proto-political, or nonrational. The term "popular intellectual" is a useful corrective since it focuses attention on discourses and symbols that are consciously created and endure beyond the individuals and events which put them into play. The term "popular publics" – intentionally organized relational contexts in which specific networks of people from the popular classes seek to bridge to other networks, form coalitions, and expand the influence of their discourse – preserves this emphasis but also changes the unit of analysis from individual or collective actors to relational contexts. Here I use this concept to analyze two cases of popular public participation in late twentieth-century Caracas, Venezuela. In the first case we will look at a street protest, in which dislocated members of the informal economy work to make their private concerns into public issues. In the second case, we will look at plaza services, in which Pentecostal Christians address Venezuela's contemporary social and political reality through an alternative rationality. Each of these cases challenge classic liberal concepts of the public sphere.

FROM POPULAR INTELLECTUALS TO POPULAR PUBLICS

The term "popular intellectuals" contains an interesting tension. On the one hand, "intellectuals" refers to people with a special vocation in reflecting upon and discussing issues of collective social life. In both critical and approbatory uses it generally refers to elites who are relatively insulated from the vicissitudes of concrete, everyday life. "Popular", on the

* This article benefited from presentations at the Culture and Institutions Workshop at the University of Georgia, the 2004 Annual Meetings of the Eastern Sociological Society, as well as comments by, or discussion with, Janise Hurtig, George Philip, Patricia Richards, and Alejandro Velasco. The research on Pentecostals was supported by a US Department of Education Fulbright-Hays fellowship. The research on protest was supported by grants from the Consejo Latinoamericano de Ciencias Sociales, Buenos Aires, and the Consejo Nacional de Ciencia y Tecnología of Venezuela. Previous analyses of the informal workers' street protest appeared in David Smilde, "Protagonismo Cultural desde la Pobreza: Respuesta a Mikel de Viana", *Revista Venezolana de Economía y Ciencias Sociales*, 7 (2001), pp. 45–64; and, Margarita López Maya et al., *Protesta y Cultura en Venezuela: Los Marcos de Acción Colectiva en 1999* (Caracas, 2002).

other hand, is generally used by intellectuals precisely to refer to non-elites who are organically grounded in concrete, everyday life. As Raymond Williams says, the term contains a "downward" glance.[1] Of course, there is frequently a small but important overlap between popular and intellectual classes. Thus, Max Weber's prophets were usually marginal men who came to have far-reaching significance for social change.[2] Nevertheless, an exclusive focus on discrete individuals who function as intellectuals can lead us to pass over other forms of popular intellectualism that make important contributions to discussion of collective social life in the developing world. In this article, I will focus on events and contexts in which flexible, occasional social actors disseminate alternative discourses in Caracas, Venezuela.

Classic liberal conceptions of the public sphere generally do not cast a favorable light on popular participation in developing regions of the world. In Jurgen Habermas's account,[3] a public sphere is a social space controlled neither by the state nor the economy, in which private citizens set aside their personal interests in order to deliberate on issues of common interest in terms of rational-critical debate. From this perspective, popular participation in places like Caracas generally looks deformed, premodern or proto-political, insofar as it directly brings in issues of personal wellbeing and/or communicates in idioms other than those of rational-critical debate. Of course, the liberal conception of the public sphere has received ample criticism, both theoretical and historical.[4] Nancy Fraser,[5] for example, argues that, historically, whether an issue is of private or public concern, and what counts as "rational" have themselves been contentious issues disputed in public. Furthermore, she argues that a unitary conceptualization of the public sphere marginalizes non-dominant sectors of society.

Recent work among sociologists has attempted to unpack the concept of "public" and make it more versatile and sensitive to multiplicity. This work is inspired by the trend towards conceptualizing social networks as discourses that connect actors.[6] "Publics", then, are relational contexts in which normally segmented social networks and their associated discourses come into contact in open-ended ways.[7] As such, publics are sites in which

1. Raymond Williams, *Keywords: A Vocabulary of Culture and Society*, rev. edn (New York, 1983).
2. Max Weber, *The Sociology of Religion*, Ephraim Fischoff (tr.) (Boston, MA, 1963 [1922]).
3. Jurgen Habermas, *The Structural Transformation of the Public Sphere*, Thomas Berger (tr.) (Cambridge, 1989 [1962]).
4. For a good collection of critical treatments see Craig Calhoun (ed.), *Habermas and the Public Sphere* (Cambridge, 1992).
5. Nancy Fraser, "Rethinking the Public Sphere", in Calhoun, *Habermas and the Public Sphere*, pp. 109–142.
6. The seminal contribution in this trend is Harrison White, *Identity and Control: A Structural Theory of Action* (Princeton, NJ, 1992).
7. Mustafa Emirbayer *et al.*, "Publics in History", *Theory and Society*, 28 (1999), pp. 145–197;

distinct networks are bridged, new understandings develop, and coalitions are formed. Rather than an absence of structure, publics usually exhibit stable features, involve existing social networks and discourses, and are shot through with power dynamics.[8] Thus, they are not liminal "free spaces" but structured relational contexts in which new articulations of structure can occur.[9] Publics can also be the objects of agency.[10] While their power comes from their open-endedness and resulting unpredictability, they are often planned by actors precisely to extend their networks and associated discourses.

I will refer to the cases I examine here as "popular publics".[11] In each case, we will see an intentionally organized relational context in which a specific network of people from the popular classes seeks to bridge to other networks, form coalitions, and expand the influence of its discourse. The cases will provide opportunities to explore the limits of the liberal concept of the public sphere as pointed out by Fraser. In the first case, we will see how marginalized social actors – in this case members of the informal economy – attempt to make their "private" concerns public through street protest. In the second case, we will see Pentecostals address Venezuela's contemporary social and political reality in plaza services, using a logic other than that of rational-critical debate. Before moving to the case material I would like to briefly review relevant aspects of the Venezuelan context.

CONTEXT: VENEZUELA AT THE END OF THE TWENTIETH CENTURY

Few national contexts in recent history have seen more mobilized public discussion than Venezuela. But while the current political conflict over the

---

Eiko Ikegami, "A Sociological Theory of Publics: Identity and Culture as Emergent Properties in Networks", *Social Research*, 67 (2000), pp. 989–1029; Ann Mishe *et al.*, "Composing a Civic Arena: Publics, Projects, and Social Settings", *Poetics*, 27 (2000), pp. 163–194.

8. Francesca Polletta, "'Free Spaces' in Collective Action", *Theory and Society*, 28 (1999), pp. 1–38; Emirbayer, "Publics in History".

9. Javier Auyero, "Relational Riot: Austerity and Corruption Protest in the Neoliberal Era", *Social Movement Studies*, 2 (2003), pp. 117–145.

10. Ikegami, "A Sociological Theory of Publics"; Taeku Lee, *Mobilizing Public Opinion: Black Insurgency and Racial Attitudes in the Civil Rights Era* (Chicago, IL, 2002); Ann Mische, "Cross-talk in Social Movements: Reconceiving the Culture–Network Link", in Mario Diani *et al.* (eds), *Social Movements and Networks: Relational Approaches to Collective Action* (Oxford, 2003).

11. I find this more open-ended than Nancy Fraser's term "subaltern counter-publics"; Fraser, "Rethinking the Public Sphere". "Subaltern" prioritizes the dominant/dominated binary as the most relevant social characteristic of the public being studied, and "counter" prioritizes resistance in the discourse and action carried out. This easily leads researchers to pass over other salient social characteristics of a public as well as the emic terms of its discourse.

presidency of Hugo Chávez Frias has generated much debate, most positions have actively distorted understanding of Venezuelan democracy. Politicized analyses portray Venezuela's 1958–1998 democracy either as a stable and well-functioning regime that is abruptly being pushed into instability and conflict by Chávez,[12] or as a corrupt, forty-year farce that is being heroically revolutionized by him.[13] Both tendencies are wildly off-base. Chávez's ascendancy to power, as well as the political conflict it has generated, should be seen instead as the most recent stages in a remarkable process of economic and political development that has facilitated the rise of a healthy, literate, organized, and media-soaked population that can no longer be contained by corporatist political structures. Limitations of space keep me from documenting the shortcomings and achievements of Venezuela's 1958–1998 democracy – a history that is readily available elsewhere.[14] Here I will simply review the emergence of challenges to its corporatist structures.

From the mid 1980s, Venezuela has been a microcosm of the neoliberal restructuring taking place throughout the region.[15] The decline of its import-substitution industries diminished the size and strength of the blue-collar industrial working class while the ranks of the urban informal economy swelled. The two parties that long dominated Venezuelan politics at every level were completely incapable of containing the demands of a highly urban population that was increasingly diverse and increasingly connected to the mass media.[16] Attempts at change within these parties were usually met with expulsions or divisions, which created a context of party infighting and stagnation.[17] The growth of social movements and civil associations, in contrast, meant that discussions of

12. Moises Naim, "Hugo Chávez and the Limits of Democracy", *New York Times*, 5 March 2003; www.nytimes.com.

13. Michael Derham, "Undemocratic Democracy: Venezuela and the Distorting of History", *Bulletin of Latin American Research*, 21 (2002), pp. 270–289.

14. Daniel H Levine, "The Decline and Fall of Democracy in Venezuela: Ten Theses", *Bulletin of Latin American Research*, 21 (2002), pp. 248–269; Brian F. Crisp, *Democratic Institutional Design: The Powers and Incentives of Venezuelan Politicians and Interest Groups* (Stanford, CA, 2000).

15. Alejandro Portes *et al.*, "Latin American Class Structures: Their Composition and Change during the Neoliberal Era", *Latin American Research Review*, 38 (2003), pp. 41–82; Kenneth Roberts, "Social Inequalities without Class Cleavages in Latin America's Neoliberal Era", *Studies in Comparative International Development*, 36 (2002), pp. 3–33; Kenneth Roberts, "Social Polarization and the Populist Resurgence in Venezuela", in *Venezuelan Politics in the Chávez Era: Class, Polarization and Conflict* (Boulder, CO, 2003).

16. Brian F. Crisp, Daniel H. Levine, and Juan Carlos Rey, "The Legitimacy Problem", in Jennifer McCoy *et al.* (eds), *Venezuelan Democracy Under Stress* (New Brunswick, NJ, 1995), pp. 139–170; Edgardo Lander, *Neoliberalismo, Sociedad Civil y Democracia. Ensayos sobre America Latina y Venezuela* (Caracas, 1995); Levine, "Democracy in Venezuela".

17. Levine, "Democracy in Venezuela"; Roberts, "Social Polarization and Populist Resurgence in Venezuela".

collective life were increasingly carried out by movements that did not justify themselves in terms of "the programmatic political rationality that was traditionally offered to the country as the path to construction of a modern society".[18]

There were also more direct assaults on the status quo. February 1989 saw three days of looting and rioting that resulted in hundreds of deaths and billions of dollars of damage. This was the beginning of a wave of protest that lasted throughout the 1990s.[19] 1992 saw two coup attempts against President Carlos Andrés Pérez, who was subsequently impeached. 1993 saw the first election of a presidential candidate not affiliated with either major party. And by 1998, none of the leading candidates in the presidential elections identified with the traditional political parties. The eventual winner, of course, was Chávez, running on an antiparty, anticorruption platform and promising to radically change the country through a new constitution.

For the purposes of this paper, the relevant point is that Venezuelan democracy is suffering not only from its defects but also from its success. The progressive growth of the critically engaged civil society it engendered has in turn fueled challenges to its institutional context.[20] In the following, we will see two manifestations of that public ferment at the end of Venezuela's twentieth century.

STREET PROTEST: THE REINVASION OF LA HOYADA MARKET

The February 1989 riots initiated a cycle of protest in Venezuela that lasted throughout the 1990s. Provea, a Venezuelan human rights organization, recorded over 7,000 protests reported in the Venezuelan media during the 1990s, amounting to more than two a day.[21] Were smaller protests that did not receive media attention included, this number would likely double. Peaks in protest activity were recorded in 1993 and 1994, during the impeachment of President Andrés Pérez and the banking crisis of the first

18. Gabriela Uribe and Edgardo Lander, "Acción Social, Efectividad Simbólica y Nuevos Ambitos de lo Político", in Lander, *Neoliberalismo, Sociedad Civil y Democracia*.

19. Margarita Lopez Maya, "La Protesta Popular Venezolana entre 1989 y 1993 (en el umbral del neoliberalismo)", in Margarita Lopez Maya (ed.), *Lucha Popular, Democracia, Neoliberalismo: Protesta Popular en America Latina en los Años de Ajuste* (Caracas, 1999).

20. Ironically, the current conflict in Venezuela is a product of the same process insofar as the Chávez government can be seen as a nationalist attempt to re-establish the structures of corporatist democracy. His centralization of state power, revolutionary rhetoric, and actual or symbolic alliances with totalitarian figures such as Marcos Pérez Jimenez, Fidel Castro, and Mao Tse Tung, have led elements of organized civil society to counter-mobilize with devastating results, including an attempted coup in April 2002, a $9-billion general strike eight months later, and continual protests in the streets.

21. López Maya *et al.*, *Protesta y Cultura en Venezuela*.

year of President Rafael Caldera's presidency, as well as 1999, the first year
of the Chávez administration. Often stereotyped as unplanned, emotional
"free-market protests" similar to the bread riots of early capitalism,[22]
actual participant observation provides a quite different image. As will be
seen below, protest events are better seen as popular publics in which
citizens marginalized by institutionalized democratic channels attempt to
create a relational context in which they can put forth their vision of the
issues that affect them, as well as publicly define themselves. In any
protest, journalists, public officials, sympathizers, or passers-by stop to
talk with or watch the protesters. Protestors, in turn, use these interactions
to express a vision of their struggle, of the society, and of themselves. Since
understanding any given protest event requires an understanding of the
concrete struggle of which it is a manifestation, here I will look at just one
event carried out by a group of informal micro-entrepreneurs.

In most Latin American countries, the informal economy has absorbed
increasingly large parts of the work force.[23] Indeed, in Venezuela most
estimates say at least half of the working population labors in the informal
sector. Often thought to be the destitute cast-offs of a declining formal
sector, studies show that many informal workers make more money and
have more autonomy than their peers in the formal sector.[24] The existence
of the informal sector is, of course, controversial. Critics argue that street
sellers clutter already congested sidewalks, produce filth, breed crime, and
take business away from tax-paying formal businesses. Throughout the
1990s, Caracas saw a continual series of political struggles in which
municipal governments would alternately work with or combat the
informal sector. Municipal authorities have conflicting interests between
the desires of the larger society and the attractive possibility of having
informal workers as a mobilized source of support gained through legal
and illegal concessions.[25] Informal workers in Venezuela, are organized in
varying degrees – from officially licensed cooperatives to local mafias, to
groups of ambulatory sellers that look out for each other.

1999 was a high water mark in these battles in Caracas. On the one hand,
it was the first year of the presidency of Hugo Chávez, which, among
other effects, brought members of the popular sectors increasingly to see
themselves as political subjects capable of exercising power. On the other
hand, the mayors of the three main municipalities that make up the

22. John Walton and David Seddon, *Free Markets and Food Riots: The Politics of Global Adjustment* (Cambridge, 1994).
23. John C. Cross, *Informal Politics: Street Vendors and the State in Mexico* (Stanford, CA, 1998); Roberts "Social Inequalities without Class Cleavages"; Hernando De Soto, *The Other Path: The Invisible Revolution in the Third World* (New York, 1989).
24. Cross, *Informal Politics*; Cathy A. Rakowski (ed.), *Contrapunto: The Informal Sector Debate in Latin America* (Albany, NY, 1994).
25. Cross, *Informal Politics*.

metropolitan area of Caracas were from opposition parties. During 1999 there were numerous protests in each of Caracas's municipalities. Here, however, I will focus only on one of the main conflicts within the Liberator municipal government.[26]

The mayor of Liberator municipality preceded Chávez in office by a number of years, and had a long, erratic record of alternating attempts to control the informal economy combined with concessions to the same informal workers. At the beginning of 1999, the mayor bulldozed the large sprawling La Hoyada market in the middle of downtown Caracas, displacing hundreds of micro-entrepreneurs. The latter agreed to leave on the promise that they would be relocated in a new wing to be added on to an existing market near the centre. After a year passed without seeing their new market they began to pressure the mayor's office. In January 1999, they signed an agreement with the mayor for construction of the new wing with the micro-entrepreneurs providing two-thirds of the capital.[27] Months passed without construction beginning and without any further contact from the mayor's office.

I originally came across the group in March of that year as they protested in front of the City Hall because they had not been given the provisional worksites they had been promised. One of the leaders of that protest warned that if their demands were not met, "we will, because of our need to work and because we are losing our capital, invade a place to work, whether that be a vacant lot or some sidewalk of the downtown area". Indeed, a little over two months later, they invaded a vacant lot across the street from where the previous market had been. They chose this spot because it was the lot where, ten years before, the previous governor had promised he would build a new market. It was definitely one of the most creative protests of the year. Yet the meanings put into play were essentially the same as those of other informal economy protests I covered that year.[28]

From the street it looked like a typical land invasion – in the heart of Caracas: an open field with broken chunks of cement, garbage, and dangerous holes, invaded by hundreds of people. There were dozens of brightly colored umbrellas set up with people sitting underneath, laying on mattresses or pieces of cardboard, leaning against duffle bags stuffed with personal belongings, or sitting on top of plastic cases of bottled beer. Some slept. Others chatted in circles. And others played cards or dominoes while drinking beer. Over the whole vacant lot there were spaces drawn with chalk, including aisles and numbered booths where they were supposedly going to construct their new market. That the participants were members of the lower working classes was evident from their cheap clothing,

26. For a more complete analysis see Lopez Maya *et al.*, *Protesta y Cultura en Venezuela*.
27. *El Nacional Online*, 19 May 1999, "Invasión en La Hoyada".
28. Lopez Maya *et al.*, *Protesta y Cultura en Venezuela*.

decaying teeth, and worn bodies. It reminded me of the bazaars described by Mikhail Bahktin.[29] It was a carnival atmosphere in which laughter, mockery, and insults melded with serious, critical discussion. In their answers to my questions, respondents' grammatical errors and misused vocabulary produced laughter and mockery from their peers. Some of them pulled the leg of the *gringo* interviewing them, to the obvious delight of onlookers. But it was clear that these people were conscious of what they were trying to achieve.

Informal micro-entrepreneurs continually confront conceptions of themselves as unsightly reminders of underdevelopment, or as irresponsible impediments to modernity. Indeed, at the beginning of this protest, a major Caracas newspaper ran a picture of the protest on its opinion page with a highly critical and completely uninformed caption.[30] It said the informal workers' demands reflected "an attitude produced by many years of paternalism – a practice more appropriate in dictatorships than democracies. Because when a government starts to give handouts to adults who should be responsible and self-reliant, it is impeding their liberty even if it is with their consent".[31]

I carried out twenty interviews, presenting myself as a sociologist doing a study about popular protest. While some of the respondents treated me like as a professor, others treated me as a student, and still others as an international journalist. In light of this, we can assume that in general, respondents presented their opinions in a reflexive manner, trying to convince me, and use me to convince others, of their vision of themselves and their conflict. We should treat this data, therefore, not as reports of fact to be judged for their veracity, nor as a window through which we can view the "true" opinions of respondents, but rather as a rhetorical interaction in which actors put concepts into play.[32]

The analysis I will use here differs from what is usually done under the name "frame analysis", insofar as it does not have to do with a group trying to mobilize participation but rather attempting to change dominant cultural meanings. Participants worked to present their struggle in terms of shared-value orientations of Venezuelan society,[33] and present more

29. Mikhail Bahktin, *Rabelais and his World* (Bloomington, IN, 1984).
30. The editorial caption contradicted the newspaper's own reports regarding the mayor's unfulfilled contract.
31. *El Nacional Online*, 24 May 1999, "Ver Para Leer: Están Colgados".
32. Kenneth Burke, *On Symbols and Society*, Joseph R. Gusfield (ed.) (Chicago, IL, 1989); James Jasper, *The Art of Moral Protest: Culture, Biography, and Creativity in Social Movements* (Chicago, IL, 1997). David Smilde, "Protagonismo Cultural desde la Pobreza".
33. Habermas responds to the critique that he reifies the distinction between "private" and "common" interests by saying that the discursive struggle of particular groups for public attention must take place in terms of "shared value orientations"; Jurgen Habermas, *Between Facts and Norms: Contributions to a Discourse Theory of Law*, William Rheg (tr.) (Cambridge, 1996).

socially acceptable identities than those usually used to describe them. They tended to present themselves in emotive terms that emphasized their humanity by speaking of their families and the hardships they were facing.[34] A single mother said the following: "It's been five months already that we've been unemployed, doing nothing. I am a mother. I'm a mother AND a father and I have no way to provide for my child." Another said: "I've been unemployed for five months. I don't know what to do. I'm desperate." A man who was in the shade of the same umbrella told the following story:

> I sold children's clothing. Because of these problems, they took away my apartment. I had it mortgaged. I told them [about my situation]. A court took my home away from me and now I'm in the street. My wife is staying in one place, my kids another. Since they demolished the market, I've been in debt.

With reference to the 1961 Constitution in effect at that time, participants also attempted to portray their struggle as one having to do with the right to work. "We're trying to apply a little pressure so that they [the authorities] consider our situation, so that they remember that we exist, that we're Venezuelans and therefore have the right to work."

But perhaps most interesting was the way respondents attempted to portray their struggle in ways that contradicted the paternalistic terms in which they were frequently criticized. When I asked him about what they wanted from the mayor's office, one of the participants told me:

> Respondent: For starters, we're not asking for handouts.
> Smilde: Ah, okay. What are you proposing then? Buying the lots?
> Respondent: Buying the lots. The government is going to provide loans for the land and we, on our own accord, are going to construct in an organized manner. We know that this here makes the city ugly. But we are going to be able to do it in an orderly way. The only thing we really need is space, for them to give us the space. We're not asking for handouts, because handouts are never good. But if they could just get us started with the lots, we could pay by installment. No problem. Let us work and bring food to our homes.

The respondents in effect pointed out that they were not asking for charity but planned to pay their part, and wanted to overcome urban disorder rather than contribute to it. Others emphasized that they wanted to become contributing members of formal society:

> Respondent 1: We're going to become micro-entrepreurs. We're not going to be street vendors anymore. We're going to become micro-entrepreneurs.
> Respondent 2: Small businessmen.

34. I should point out that while their reports should not be assumed true, neither should they be assumed false. Seeing responses as "strategic" simply highlights that, even when a respondent is describing real suffering, she is still making a conscious choice to be there at *that* place and tell *that* story for rhetorical purposes.

Respondent 1: [we'll have] small businesses legally constituted to contribute to
the country. We want to pay taxes and be listed in the Official Gazette,[35] so they
will respect our right to work.

As well, the participants worked to portray their struggle in terms of
broader phenomena that would interest others. In their descriptions, the
mayor was not only betraying them, he was not fulfilling his obligations to
the citizenry in general. "It's not just us. He isn't fulfilling his
commitments with anyone. The historical center, freeways, parks, he's
abandoned everything. I don't know what this government, this mayor has
done. He hasn't done anything." Finally, many put their struggle in terms
of broader issues in Venezuelan society. For example, the following
respondents described their plight in terms of the discourse of party
corruption that had widespread currency in 1999:

Respondent 1: It's the corruptos that keep our country the way it is.
Respondent 2: Democratic Action [Social Democratic Party] and COPEI [Social
Christian Party].
Respondent 1: They're the delinquents.
Respondent 2: They are the corruptos in this country. It's because of them that
things are the way they are, millions of people unemployed because of their
looting during forty years of democracy.

This discourse of party corruption was used in the Chavez campaign to
explain everything from high crime rates to the lack of nontraditional
exports. These respondents use it to explain their unemployment and
resulting dependence on the informal economy.

If it sounds like I am reading intentionality into respondents' answers,
consider the way the following respondents describe what they are doing.
"Unfortunately, in Venezuela, in order to be heard, you have to
demonstrate. How? By taking to the street or doing something in order
to be heard by a mayor or a president, because we are never taken into
consideration." Another ended the interview by justifying the protest in
the following terms:

If we hadn't come here, you wouldn't have come either because you didn't know
that we existed. Now that you know we exist, you can form an opinion about us,
that we exist, we have families, we're not asking for handouts. We're simply
asking that they respect our right to work. That's it.

In this case study, we see protestors who have created a public in which
they could connect with other networks of Venezuelan society in order to
influence them. Their struggle simply was not on the public docket and as a
result the municipal government could completely ignore their demands.

35. The *Official Gazette* is the daily publication in which all legal proceedings in Venezuela are
publicly announced.

By going forth with their "invasion" they were able to bring the broken promise to public light, portray their demands in nonpaternalist terms, present their situation of need in human and constitutional terms, and portray their adversary as a general social problem. It was one of the most successful protests of the year. The mayor had to respond publicly and, after unsuccessfully trying to pass the problem off onto the federal government, presented a project to construct 821 new booths in the San Martin Market. Eighteen days after invading, the participants signed a new agreement with the mayor and abandoned the field.[36] The problem between the members of the informal economy and the municipal government continued for the rest of the year and up until the mayor was voted out of office in 2000 in favor of *chavista*, Fredy Bernal. After a few attempts to control the informal economy Bernal completely threw in the towel and permitted street sellers to occupy public spaces throughout the city.

PLAZA SERVICES

As is the case in most Latin American countries, one of the most vibrant forms of civil society in contemporary Venezuela is popular religion – in particular, Pentecostal Christianity. In the 1970s and 1980s, Pentecostal growth in Venezuela lagged behind that experienced by other Latin American countries. But it accelerated considerably during the downward spiral of the 1990s, and non-Catholic Christians currently constitute around 5 per cent of Venezuela's population. Despite stereotypes of Pentecostalism as a religion of the dispossessed, Pentecostals closely reflect the class structure of the larger society.[37] However, since most forms of civil society such as neighborhood associations, environmental groups, and women's rights activists have been successful mainly with the middle and upper-middle classes, Pentecostals stand out for being able to mobilize the lower classes. The Pentecostal theology of a supernatural battle between good and evil that impinges on humans depending on their behavior, presents individuals with a way to get a cognitive fix on the processes that are affecting their lives, and provides the energy necessary to overcome the classic obstacles to associational mobilization among the popular sectors.

Virtually every plaza in Caracas has a Pentecostal service or pastor preaching at some point during the day. These events range from a self-appointed individual preaching to a captive audience at a bus stop, to well-organized initiatives, with sound equipment and municipal permits, that

36. *El Nacional Online*, 5 June 1999, "Buhoneros Desocuparon Terrenos de La Hoyada".
37. David Smilde, "Contradiction without Paradox: Evangelical Political Culture in the 1998 Venezuelan Elections", *Latin American Politics and Society*, 46 (2004), pp. 75–102.

dominate a plaza for several hours daily. One of the oldest examples of the latter is the service that takes place every day at noon in the Plaza El Venezolano in the heart of downtown Caracas. A block from the Plaza Bolívar, and two blocks from the National Assembly, the Plaza El Venezolano is swarming with ice-cream vendors, shoe-shine men, people on work breaks, and parents with small children virtually all day long. The plaza has four fountains that haven't functioned in years, poured cement benches, and low cement planters on which people sit. On the whole north edge of the plaza there are steps going up to the street, which create an amphitheater for the noontime services.

A service begins to build around noon, with informal singing by those Pentecostals who arrive early. At ten or fifteen minutes past the hour, the person who is directing the event introduces the first preacher, who begins with a Bible reading and then preaches for a half hour or so. There is generally a dominant theme, but the preaching is ad lib, using no notes, and any number of topics might be touched upon. Towards the end, the sermon works into an informal, but highly structured, altar call. First, the pastor will query the audience with a question likely to receive a positive response: "Raise your hand if you believe in Jesus". The knowing regulars leave the visitors to respond. After the preacher gets those in attendance to raise their hands, he then announces that he would like them to come down so that he can pray for them. He then prays over the ten to twenty people who have complied and congregated around him. Afterwards, someone from the church with a notepad takes down their names and gives them a Bible tract. Interestingly, since the names are simply for prayer, they do not take down a phone number or address or anything else to follow up.

I have seen these plaza services, depending on the day, the weather, and the skills of the preacher, draw anywhere between 30 and 200 onlookers. There are three basic strata of attendees. Those standing behind or close to those leading the service are Pentecostal regulars who may have a hand in organizing the plaza services. They sit behind, giving claps and hallelujahs to points they agree with, and play instruments – bongos, guitar, drums, maracas – during the singing. They also constitute the pool of fill-in preachers on those occasions that a scheduled preacher does not show up. Then there are those who are sitting on the steps in front of the preacher. These are usually Pentecostals from different congregations, and other people who are interested to the point that they want to sit down to watch but do not have a hand in organizing the plaza services. Behind those sitting on the steps stand curious onlookers.

The Pentecostals who frequent the plaza service are often stereotyped as people with "nothing better to do". But like the men on Tally's Corner,[38] they are often those who work after hours in security or cleaning jobs, are

38. Eliott Liebow, *Tally's Corner: A Study of Negro Streetcorner Men* (Boston, MA, 1967).

between stints of marginal employment, or work for themselves on their own schedule. Others work downtown and come on their lunch breaks. One of the plaza preachers, Ramiro, for example, works independently as a remodeling contractor. When he is between contracts he attends the plaza service everyday. When he is working, he makes a strong effort to take a long lunch on Thursdays – his day to preach. The mission of the plaza services is, in principle, ecumenical. There are no prohibitions of people from any given denomination. But the litmus test of who can preach has to do with fidelity to basic Evangelical doctrine.

In contrast to popular stereotypes, preachers are not motivated by the offerings they collect, but rather by strong commitments to preaching. The pittance they usually round up goes to purchase Bible tracts to pass out or is saved for equipment upgrades. One can see in them a desire and impulse to make meaning. Once when the municipal authorities completely shut down the plaza services for several weeks for lack of proper permits, Ramiro expressed his anxiety at the news they had been closed down. "A month?! I can't do it! I have to preach. I'll go to La Hoyada (another plaza). I preach on Thursdays and Sundays and even that's not enough." Another longtime preacher added, as if to explain: "The Lord puts the word in you and it has to come out."

Most plaza preaching focuses on "true" versus "false" Christianity or addresses problems with primary social relationships or personal adjustment by enjoining self-examination. Narratives are told of families that fall apart because of substance abuse, important executives who self-destruct because they forget about God, and children growing up without moral guidance. Nevertheless, larger society frequently comes into focus. Venezuelans have for centuries had a sort of antinationalist discourse, whereby they compare their country in disfavorable terms to other countries,[39] a discourse that has only accentuated with the "crisis" of the past twenty years. Pentecostalism latches onto this discourse quite readily.[40]

Venezuela's problems are explained as the results of or even punishment for a country that has turned its back on God and comparisons are made to more "Godly" nations like the US and Canada. Frequently, prayers are raised up asking God to intervene in Venezuela. "We're praying for Venezuela. For God to take action", prayed one preacher. "The Bible says that 'if the just ask, God provides'. So we are asking God to take action with Venezuela." Pentecostal meanings are frequently used in a more concrete sense, as well, to explain the corruption scandals that pepper the

39. Martiza Montero, *Ideología, alineación, e identidad nacional* (Caracas, 1984); David Smilde, "Protagonismo Cultural desde la Pobreza".
40. *Idem, "El Clamor por Venezuela*: Latin American Evangelicalism as a Collective Action Frame", in Christian Smith and Joshua Prokopy (eds), *Latin American Religion in Motion* (New York, 1999).

daily news. Ramiro, for example, preached "There are terrible scandals in this country. And it's all right here [holding up the Bible]." In 1996, plaza preachers addressed the acute inflation that followed a currency devaluation that dramatically affected the lower classes. One preacher taught "Venezuela has oil, vast resources under the earth. But do you know which currency had devalued more than any other in the world? The Bolivar [Venezuela's national currency]. Idolatry brings ruin." Another provided both an explanation and a reason for confidence:

> The housewife goes to the supermarket [...] and she sees that [powdered] milk has gone up to Bs 3,000 [approximately $6US] a kilo and she gets scared because she doesn't know what is going to happen. Do you know why milk keeps going up? Because the Word is being fulfilled [*raises Bible*]. I am one of those Pentecostals that, although milk goes up, and meat goes up, butter goes up, I am happy every day. It's not that we don't have problems. We do. But we don't resolve them. Christ takes care of them.

The most common passage used to address the Venezuelan crisis is Matthew 24.1–35 regarding the "signs of Christ's return". One plaza preacher used a grease pencil and board in his service, to draw a diagram listing the symptoms of Christ's return: "Many will deceive in His name. Wars. Rumors of wars. Nations will rise up against nations. Plagues. Hunger. Earthquakes." Systematically he went through each symptom and related it to recent events in Venezuelan or world society.

As is the case in many countries in the developing world, public discussion of collective life in Venezuela traditionally follows a developmentalist discourse that sees the state as the primary mover of development.[41] Plaza preachers crosscut this discourse by portraying "true" Christianity as an alternative to politics and the state. "Politics has not been able to do anything for my country. Every day it gets worse and worse. But Christ fulfills his promises", said one preacher. Another followed the testimony of an exconvict who had converted to Pentecostalism, by taking the microphone and pointing to him:

> Religion [Catholicism] wasn't able to change him. Politics wasn't able to change him. The State wasn't able to change him. The police weren't able to change him. The psychologist wasn't able to change him. Prison wasn't able to change him. The only thing that could change him was the power of God.

The organizers of these plaza services explicitly seek a public forum to present their ideas and thereby extend their networks and the influence of their discourse. One preacher emphasized this in my interview with him:

> This is the historic center [of the city]. All types of people pass through here,

41. Fernando Coronil, *The Magical State: Nature, Money and Modernity in Venezuela* (Chicago, IL, 1997); James Ferguson, *The Anti-Politics Machine: "Development", Depoliticization, and Bureaucratic Power in Lesotho* (Minneapolis, MN, 1994).

from all social classes. The upper classes. Politicians. People from the middle class, lower-middle class, and the lower class too, all pass by here. In other words, it's a strategic point and God has a message for all of these people.

One of the founding members emphasized that the time of their service allows them to catch people in transition. "That's the time when people come to eat and rest. The fish are schooled. So you take the opportunity to throw the net, to throw the Gospel at them."

Compared to the case study reviewed in the previous section, it is difficult to know how much of an impact these services have on the thousands of people who walk past or stop for a few minutes or hours to listen to the services. What can be said is that they are consistent with, and perhaps reinforce the tendency among new social movements to look for alternative, often morally charged meaning systems with which to talk about issues of collective life.[42] One palpable example is the rhetoric of current president, Hugo Chávez. Chávez, who was frequently visited by Pentecostal preachers during his two years in jail after the 1992 coup attempt, has repeatedly reached out to Pentecostals, and frequently uses Pentecostal imagery in his public speeches.[43] This imagery is one of the foundations of the divisive character of his discourse.

At a lower level, these public plaza services are an important means of recruiting converts. Compared to one-on-one evangelization, plaza services are non-threatening and permit a low-intensity engagement for those who are interested in "trying on" the Evangelical belief system.[44] There are other impacts. The plaza services are not just about preaching. Before and after the services or during and towards the periphery, the plaza is a place for Pentecostals to visit, exchange information relevant to economic opportunities, or meet up for an afternoon activity. In a context in which there is no functioning mail system and telephone communications can be difficult, such a recognized meeting place plays a vital function. There are other ways in which networks are bridged and new relationships are formed between Pentecostals from different churches and between Pentecostals and non-Pentecostals. During the service a few Pentecostals work the crowd passing out Bible tracts with evangelistic messages on them. Others hand them to passers-by.

The peripheries of the plaza service also serve as sites for counseling for both Pentecostals and non-Pentecostals. A non-Pentecostal who wanted to commit suicide because of his dependence on prescription drugs, a

42. David Smilde, "Los Evangélicos y la Polarización: la moralización de la política y la politización de la religión", *Revista Venezolana de Ciencias Economicas y Sociales*, 10:2 (May–August 2004), pp. 163–179; *idem*, "El Clamor por Venezuela".

43. *Idem*, "Contradiction without Paradox"; *idem*, "Los Evangélicos y la Polarización".

44. *Idem*, "'Works of the Flesh, Fruit of the Spirit': Religious Action Frames and Meaning Networks in Venezuelan Evangelicalism" (Ph.D., Department of Sociology, University of Chicago, 2000).

Pentecostal whose wife has left him with their children, and a young non-Pentecostal who feared he would lose his job, were some of the cases I witnessed during my participant observation. In all such cases the problem is given a Pentecostal interpretation as an earthly manifestation of the struggle between God and the Devil, and a prayer is raised asking God for help. If the person is non-Pentecostal, he or she is usually counseled to regularly attend a Pentecostal church. There are also occasionally transnational contacts made at the plaza services. The plaza services are frequently on the schedule of short-mission trips from North America that present dramas or puppet shows with translations depicting Biblical stories. Venezuelan and North American Pentecostals often establish relationships as a result of such collaboration.

DISCUSSION

Popular participation in the public sphere in Latin America today presents a paradox. On the one hand, the political representation of popular classes is clearly one of the great casualties of the neoliberal era in Latin America. The decline of the labor movement as well as class-based parties has left masses of people without institutionalized political representation.[45] On the other hand, popular participation in the public sphere has become increasingly important. From the *zapatistas* in Chiapas, who have now held the Mexican army at bay for a decade, to the indigenous groups of Ecuador, who have brought down two presidents and helped bring another to power, to the Bolivarian movement of Venezuela that brought a failed coup leader to the presidency and brought him back from exile when he was overthrown, popular participation in the public sphere has demonstrated its power. The extra-institutional, ephemeral and episodic character of these forms of popular politics have spawned a number of attempts at conceptualization. Walton and Seddon[46] speak of "food riots" that respond to neoliberal "shock measures". Manuel Castells sees "communal resistance" developing among those excluded from the global "network society".[47] Michael Hardt and Antonio Negri see the "multitude" as a decentered, episodic reaction to "Empire" – the globalized structure of biopower.[48]

Unfortunately, while each of these concepts captures the ephemeral and episodic nature of popular participation in the public sphere, they miss the planned and reasoned forms of agency that actual fieldwork reveals. The term "popular intellectual" is a useful corrective here since it focuses on

45. Portes *et al.*, "Latin American Class Structures"; Roberts, "Social Inequalities without Class Cleavages".
46. Walton, *Free Markets and Food Riots*.
47. Manuel Castells, *The Power of Identity: Economy, Society and Culture* (Cambridge, 1997).
48. Michael Hardt and Antonio Negri, *Empire* (Cambridge, 2000).

discourses and symbols that are consciously created and endure beyond the episodes in which they are put into play. With the term "popular publics" I try to preserve this emphasis, but also change the unit of analysis from individual or collective actors, to relational contexts. Actors exist. But it is the relational context that endures beyond the shifting composition of the actors involved. And it is the extended networks and expanded discourses that endure beyond the relational context of a given public.

In the two cases examined here we see relational contexts in which non-elite sectors of Venezuelan society participate in reflecting on and discussing collective life and alternative futures. Through these publics they seek to extend their networks and the influence of their discourses, and thereby gain the social influence they lack in institutionalized politics. In the first case, we see informal workers seeking to modify dominant portrayals of themselves and their struggle. In the second case, we see Pentecostal plaza services in which preachers use an alternative rationality to analyze and critique Venezuelan society. Nevertheless, they quite rationally plan the location and the time of their preaching to maximize their effect. This analysis does not intend to romanticize popular publics,[49] nor advocate the positions they express.[50] The goal is rather to improve our understanding of the public participation of popular sectors in developing-world contexts.

49. While in my portrayal popular publics are not as reactive and futile as Castells's communal resistance, neither do they merit Hardt and Negri's "millenarian optimism"; see Gopal Balakrishnan, "Review of Hardt and Negri's *Empire*", *New Left Review*, 5 (2000), pp. 143–148. Whether they improve social conditions or concrete lives in any given case is an open question. Regarding Venezuela, for example, Levine writes that enduring power does not necessarily follow from momentary empowerment. Therefore, civil mobilization and protest alone is "unlikely to provide coherence and direction for a complex and conflict-ridden society" like Venezuela; see Levine, "Democracy in Venezuela", p. 261.

50. Popular movements have no Archimedean standpoint that ensures truth, nor any teleology that guarantees they work for justice. Ku Klux Klan meetings and skinhead internet chat rooms are "popular publics" too. For an extended discussion of this point, see Luis Pasara, *La Otra Cara de la Luna: Nuevos Actores Sociales en el Perú* (Buenos Aires, 1991).

IRSH 49 (2004), Supplement, pp. 197–217 DOI: 10.1017/S0020859004001701
© 2004 Internationaal Instituut voor Sociale Geschiedenis

Concluding Remarks: Framing Protest in Asia, Africa, and Latin America

ROSANNE RUTTEN AND MICHIEL BAUD

This volume has presented eight case studies of popular intellectuals on different continents who reflected on society in order to change it. They cover a broad range of people whose activist intellectual work has made a difference: from college-educated environmentalists to autodidact revolutionaries, from indigenous activists to Islamic fundamentalists. We believe there are good reasons to bring together these different historical actors, precisely because there is gain in this diversity: each article highlights specific themes that provide valuable insight in the social dynamics of ideological work. Here, we bring together a selection of these insights and explore, at the same time, how a focus on popular intellectuals allows us to better understand some salient aspects of social contention.

INNOVATORS, MOVEMENT INTELLECTUALS, AND ALLIES

Three types of popular intellectuals (and the fluid boundaries between them) are well represented in this volume: innovators, movement intellectuals, and allies. "Innovators" carve out discursive spaces and "invent" new political discourses for emerging social movements; they may remain loosely connected to a movement but may also become its intellectual leaders. "Movement intellectuals" emerge in the development of social movements and include core activists and leaders. Movement allies include intellectuals who lend their expertise to a specific movement. The roles of these three types may be linked to the trajectories of social movements.[1]

A typology of popular intellectuals is not an obvious starter for the concluding remarks to a volume that draws attention to the social dynamics of framing. This is even more so when we consider David Smilde's thought-provoking contribution. Smilde argues against a focus on intellectuals (as a category of people) if we want to understand activist

---

1. Here, we are inspired by Ron Eyerman and Andrew Jamison, *Social Movements: A Cognitive Approach* (University Park, PA, 1991), which discusses the emergence of different types of activist intellectuals in relation to the different phases of a social movement.

intellectual activity among ordinary people. Such a focus may overlook, he argues, the informal framing work done by ordinary people who do not share the vocation of intellectuals, and who operate outside of the realm of social movements. He has a good point, and his analysis of informal public discussions is a valuable reminder that popular discourses are also formed and disseminated in fluid networks in public life. Nevertheless, if we want to look more specifically at social movements and those persons within them (or connected to them) who "frame protest", it is worth taking a closer look at the varying relationships they might have to these movements.

"Innovators" are intellectuals who produce new interpretive frames and new languages for articulating collective interests, identities, and claims. Thomas Rochon speaks of "critical communities", i.e. groups and networks of intellectuals who develop new, critical perspectives on particular issues through intensive communication and debate.[2] The creative, experimental side of their interpretive work is important. They may operate in "cultural niches" such as universities, depend on the media to get their message heard, and may retain a certain autonomy from social movements and other organizations. But their ideas are essential in inspiring social movements, which may adopt their ideas for activist use. For instance, in late-colonial Malaya, liberal journalists and pamphleteers engaged in intense ideological debates on the future of their society with religious leaders, writers, and royal spokesmen. These debates created a new political discourse, which set the ideological terms for subsequent political mobilization and collective action.[3] Such intellectuals, then, may be particularly important in the initial stages of social movements. Sean Chabot draws an explicit parallel between the African-American intellectuals who were the first to experiment with the Gandhian model, and Rochon's "critical communities".

The persons who define and express a collective identity deserve special mention in this regard. The writers, poets, ritual specialists, historians, and clerics who create an image of a specific community, of people who belong together, may contribute to the creation of an assertive political identity, a definition of a "we-group" that may legitimately claim its collective rights. The poets and singers among the Tuareg who belonged to migrant-worker communities in Northern Africa, are a case in point (Baz Lecocq). In their poems and songs they expressed a militant Tuareg identity, born out of hardship in the diaspora, and spoke of discrimination and liberation in ethnic terms. Like the worker-poets of nineteenth-century France, who imagined the workers as a proud, assertive class, these Tuareg poets crafted

2. Thomas Rochon, *Culture Moves: Ideas, Activism, and Changing Values* (Princeton, NJ, 1998), pp. 22–25.
3. Anthony Milner, *The Invention of Politics in Colonial Malaya: Contesting Nationalism and the Expansion of the Public Sphere* (Cambridge [etc.], 1994).

a political identity that influenced activism and gave direction to the political struggle. Their means of communication were typical of the region: cassettes carried the songs over a wide area, and the emotion-laden messages reached literates and illiterates alike.

Oskar Verkaaik shows how, in Pakistan, Sindhi journalists, teachers, and poets helped define the image of a Sindhi nation. Through poetry in the Sindhi language and history writing with a focus on the region, they framed the region and its people in nationalist terms. There are parallels here, for instance, with poets, composers, and historians in nineteenth-century eastern Europe who contributed to ethnic-nationalist feelings by providing an emotional and scientific (academic) basis to national images.[4] In the same vein, indigenous leaders in early twentieth-century Latin America used religious, cultural, and political traditions and images of the past, to create new languages and discourses of contention against a neocolonial state.[5]

The second type of popular intellectuals is directly rooted in social movements. Ron Eyerman introduced the term "movement intellectuals", which refers to "those intellectuals who gain the status and the self-perception of being 'intellectuals' in the context of their participation in political movements rather than through the institutions of the established culture".[6] These intellectuals have the explicit vocation of promoting and developing a collective action frame in the service of social movements. They consist of framing specialists who play a particularly important role in the more "mature" stages of a movement. Again, this is a mixed lot. On the one hand, they include persons with established credentials as intellectuals, who link up to a social movement or are instrumental in its emergence. Examples are the well-known "vanguards" of revolutionary movements, whose members belong to the educated upper and middle classes, and who derive their political legitimacy from the fact that they are academically and ideologically trained.[7] On the other hand, they include persons with little formal education or intellectual status, who may be "schooled" into the position of intellectuals within the social movement itself.

Social movements "create spaces for 'ordinary people' to become 'intellectuals', that is, individuals who problematize the routines and

4. Benedict Anderson, *Imagined Communities: Reflections on the Origin and Spread of Nationalism* (London, 1993, 2nd rev. edn).
5. Silvia Rivera Cusicanqui, *"Oprimidos pero no vencidos". Luchas del campesinado aymara y qhechwa de Bolivia, 1900–1980* (La Paz, 1986).
6. Ron Eyerman, *Between Culture and Politics: Intellectuals in Modern Society* (Cambridge, 1994), p. 15.
7. Michael Walzer, "Intellectuals, Social Classes, and Revolutions", in Theda Skocpol (ed.), *Democracy, Revolution, and History* (Ithaca, NY, 1998), pp. 127–142.

beliefs of everyday life and reflect upon them in a meaningful way".[8] By providing new means of education and communication (schooling, seminars, and newspapers, for example), social movements can transform ordinary people into intellectuals. They also provide intellectuals with a public by organizing mass meetings and demonstrations.[9] This process is nicely described by Terry Irving and Sean Scalmer in their analysis of "labour intellectuals" in Australia.[10] They note that trade unions and political parties provided the institutional means and political space for the emergence of labour intellectuals, with the establishment of a labour press, cultural journals, radio stations, and institutions of working-class education. The "cultural activists" of the indigenous movement in Colombia described by Joanne Rappaport in this volume, are a good example as well. Originating in indigenous villages, they were trained within the indigenous organization, through workshops, movement publications, and other means, and were tasked to "produce a discourse of cultural revitalization" based on ethnographic and linguistic research. They were formed as intellectuals, then, within the organizational and ideological framework of the movement. Although their creative space was delineated by this institutional context, reflection and the articulation of ideas was their main task.

"Movement allies" form our third category. They include intellectuals who put their expertise and networks at the disposal of movements, often when these movements have already developed and received public attention. Pablo Bose's analysis of the Indian anti-dam movement highlights two typical examples. Arundhati Roy exemplifies the category of writers, academics, journalists, and documentary-makers who become engaged "public intellectuals", and express the activist cause in ways that are understandable and acceptable to a wide public. In the process, they link their established audiences of readers and film-viewers to the activist message. "Technical" specialists present a second type. As experts in a certain field of knowledge, specialists in engineering and ecological issues offered their expertise to the anti-dam movement.

The role of these formally-trained specialists as supporters of social movements has become more prominent in the last few decades. On the supply side, one reason is the fast growth of this category as a result of the expansion and specialization of education, in both Western and non-Western societies. On the demand side, there is a growing need for specialists among social movements. As social movements enter new arenas in which to defend their causes (confrontations with specialized government agencies, international organizations, the modern media),

8. Eyerman, *Between Culture and Politics*, p. 18.
9. *Ibid.*, p. 84.
10. Terry Irving and Sean Scalmer, "Australian Labour Intellectuals: An Introduction", *Labour History*, 77 (1999), pp. 1–10, 1.

they need people with the knowledge and skills to perform well in these fields.[11] The anti-dam movement of the Narmada Valley offers a vivid illustration. The present-day indigenous movement in Colombia presents another example: university-based anthropologists provide specialist knowledge that legitimizes the claims of the indigenous movement vis-à-vis national and international agencies. Since technical and academic specialists have a high status in most societies, their support is all the more valuable for social movements. They may, as Bose has shown, successfully counter the knowledge of the "experts" who are in the service of governments and other influential parties.[12]

We should not lose sight, however, of those specialists whose knowledge is not related to the sphere of formal, "modern" education. Shamans are crucial supporters of the Colombian indigenous movement. The movement considers them carriers of the cultural core of the indigenous population, and their "knowledge provides a potent language for the politicized construction of cultural forms" (Rappaport, this volume). Similarly, spirit mediums were important allies of guerrilla fighters in southern Africa. Their support helped to legitimize the guerrilla movement among village populations, and their knowledge and ritual powers offered guerrilla soldiers a sense of security.[13]

The typology provided above masks, of course, the dynamic process of people who become popular intellectuals and take on different roles in the course of their lives. Steven Feierman demonstrates, for example, how Tanzanian peasants transformed themselves into "intellectuals" in the course of the struggle against colonial land policies.[14] In their analysis of the emergence of a new indigenous movement in Bolivia in the 1940s, Jorge Dandler and Juan Torrico show how the difficult situations on the haciendas and the volatile political climate produced new indigenous leaders who, on the basis of their local authority and new political circumstances, developed into popular intellectuals.[15] Marc Becker, in this volume, gives similar examples for Ecuador. The two Sindhi nationalists who are in focus in Verkaaik's contribution had a chequered career before they became intellectual leaders of a separatist movement; we might say they developed from "innovators" into "movement intellectuals". These

11. Cf. Eyerman and Jamison, *Social Movements*, p. 100.
12. Eyerman and Jamison speak of "counter-experts" in this regard; *ibid.*, p. 104.
13. David Lan, *Guns and Rain: Guerrillas and Spirit Mediums in Zimbabwe* (Berkeley, CA, 1985); Terence O. Ranger, *Peasant Consciousness and Guerrilla War in Zimbabwe: A Comparative Study* (London, 1985).
14. Steven Feierman, *Peasant Intellectuals: Anthropology and History in Tanzania* (Madison, WI, 1990).
15. Jorge Dandler and Juan A. Torrico, "From the National Indigenous Congress to the Ayopaya Rebellion: Bolivia, 1945–1947", in Steve J. Stern (ed.), *Resistance, Rebellion, and Consciousness in the Andean Peasant World, 18th to 20th Centuries* (Madison, WI, 1987), pp. 341–345.

examples demonstrate the crucial importance of a historical, diachronic analysis of the relation between popular intellectuals and social movements. This relationship may change dramatically in the context of changing opportunities and constraints.

ARENAS OF CONTENTION

Popular intellectuals speak to different audiences at the same time, both internally, within a social movement, and externally, to supporters, opponents, and the media. After all, social movements are the product of the interaction of different social and political groups. Internally, movements are often heterogeneous and constantly run the risk of losing their constituency or falling apart. Externally, they are often forced to make alliances and compromises if they want to be successful. In the process, they run the risk of losing their ideological coherence, or of being incorporated into hegemonic politics and mainstream society. Every social movement faces the challenge of balancing the need to maintain internal solidarity and cohesion while at the same time increasing its external effectiveness and success.

This precarious process requires constant ideological work, in multiple arenas, to articulate demands, forge unity, and legitimize claims. To acquire political leverage, popular intellectuals need to convince their following, or fellow activists. At the same time, they have to convey their ideas to the outside world to justify their demands to powerholders and the public at large. Speaking of Indian nationalism, Partha Chatterjee remarks: "Nationalist texts were addressed both to 'the people' who were said to constitute the nation and to the colonial masters whose claim to rule nationalism questioned."[16] In the same vein, Charles Tilly observes that those who make claims "must establish themselves in the eyes of others – authorities, competitors, enemies, and relevant audiences as voices that require attention and must commonly establish themselves in the face of vigorous opposition".[17]

Rappaport makes several important points in this regard. First, the "internal" process of reaching a certain ideological consensus and developing an interpretive frame may involve different types of intellectuals within the broad network of a movement. Each type may have a different position and function in this network, and different interests. For the Colombian indigenous-rights movement these are, for example, indigenous cultural activists, indigenous politicians, shamans, and urban, left-wing intellectuals (including university professors and anthropolo-

16. Partha Chatterjee, *Nationalist Thought and the Colonial World: A Derivative Discourse?* (London, 1986), p. 30.
17. Charles Tilly, *Stories, Identities, and Political Change* (Lanham, MD [etc.], 2002), p. 90.

gists). Second, their various discourses are forged in interaction with their specific audiences, local constituencies, local allies and politicians, national and international supporters, etc. How they interact with external parties also influences their discourses in "internal" debates. Finally, it is in their negotiations and confrontations, among themselves and with external parties, that a single "voice" of the movement is constructed.

"A movement is a field of actors, not a unified entity", William Gamson and David Meyer noted:[18]

> The degree to which there are unified and consensual frames within a movement is variable and it is comparatively rare that we can speak sensibly of *the* movement framing. It is more useful to think of framing as an internal process of contention within movements with different actors taking different positions.[19]

The organizational structure of a movement is also of influence here. In a movement with a decentralized structure, where a central leadership that can dictate a certain interpretive frame is absent, internal debates on the "correct" framing of certain issues may be a permanent characteristic. Quintan Wiktorowicz has shown how Islamic religious scholars function as nodes in a wide network of Islamic fundamentalists, each maintaining his own community of followers. Because Islamic religious authority is fragmented, and the movement has no formal ideological centre, framing contests appear to be a constant feature of the movement.

Movements concerned with identity and gender roles operate in diverse arenas as well. Besides striving for political inclusion, legislative emancipation, and liberation in the private sphere, some Latin American women's movements started to engage, in the late twentieth century, in the struggle against authoritarian regimes, civil war, crime, and neoliberalism. This compelled their leaders and activists to look for diverse alliances (with the state, male-dominated political parties, NGOs), and to use different discourses in the process. Images of motherhood became important markers of the political struggle of women against the Argentine dictatorship (1976–1983) and against poverty and terrorism in Peru.[20]

As local struggles are increasingly linked to international networks of power and support, popular intellectuals need to perform in ever more arenas. Almost all the articles in this collection demonstrate the

18. William A. Gamson and David S. Meyer, "Framing Political Opportunity", in Doug McAdam *et al.* (eds), *Comparative Perspectives on Social Movements: Political Opportunities, Mobilizing Structures, and Cultural Framings* (Cambridge [etc.], 1996), pp. 275–290, 283.
19. *Ibid.*
20. Marguerite Guzmán Bouvard, *Revolutionizing Motherhood: The Mothers of the Plaza de Mayo* (Wilmington, DL, 1994); Diana Miloslavich Tupac (ed.), *The Autobiography of María Elena Moyano: The Life and Death of a Peruvian Activist* (Gainesville, FL, 2000). A sophisticated analysis in terms of "political fields" is offered by Raka Ray, *Fields of Protest: Women's Movements in India* (Minneapolis, MN [etc.], 1999). Ray shows, among others, how activists need to adapt to the specific political cultures that prevail in different political arenas.

importance of these wider linkages. This is perhaps clearest in the article by Bose, who shows how anti-dam activists in India directed their protests not only to the national state and to regional authorities who were directly responsible for the dam-project, but also to the international institution of the World Bank, which financed the project. By targeting this international institution, they were also able to tap into a wide network of international support. A similar political strategy is apparent in the case of the *zapatista* rebels in southern Mexico who, after they came out into the open in 1994, have been addressing local, national and international audiences at the same time. It is here, also, that the national and international media function as important intermediaries between local struggles and international audiences. A diversity of audiences and a widening horizon may provide social movements with new constituencies and recognition. But, as is clear from some articles presented here, this also implies new risks for movement leaders and intellectuals. Since they simultaneously operate on different playing fields, their legitimacy as interlocutors and intermediaries may be questioned.

Besides these strategic arenas of struggle, there are also more informal spheres in which the messages of popular intellectuals are heard, debated, and further disseminated. These include the "popular publics" which Smilde introduced in his contribution. Through the fluid networks that take shape in (informal) public debates, new discourses are developed and new publics created.

INTELLECTUALS AND "MASTER FRAMES" IN A GLOBAL WORLD

Like all persons engaged in framing, the popular intellectuals discussed in this volume have drawn "on the cultural stock" of the wider society in which they were embedded, for "images of what is an injustice, for what is a violation of what ought to be".[21] Which "images" were available to them, depended on their position in society, and the ideologies that were known and disseminated within the networks in which they operated. They were active in shaping discourse out of a variety of ideological streams, both locally and globally. Moreover, they were themselves active in crafting social networks that connected them to new sources of ideas. For instance, literate, Spanish-speaking Indian peasants in Ecuador gained access to socialist ideas by linking up with the city-based Socialist – later Communist – Party (Becker); and African-American intellectuals made visits to India to seek contact with specialists in Gandhian thought (Chabot).

21. Mayer N. Zald, "Culture, Ideology, and Strategic Framing", in McAdam *et al.*, *Comparative Perspectives on Social Movements*, pp. 261–274.

The case studies presented in this collection cover at least four main conceptual fields that have inspired social activism in twentieth-century non-Western societies: Marxism, religious beliefs, notions of "rights" (including indigenous rights), and ideologies of citizenship. These form, in a sense, "master frames", broad interpretative frames that may inspire people and movements as they develop their own specific interpretation of society. These frames "provide a grammar that punctuates and syntactically connects patterns or happenings in the world"; and they function as "master algorithms that color and constrain the orientations and activities" of other movements than those that produced them.[22] As the contributions to this volume show, such master frames are seldom adopted *in toto*, but rather function as sources of inspiration and intellectual guidance. They are often applied in quite eclectic (and local) ways.

Marxist ideas have been widely distributed in Asia, Africa, and Latin America since the late nineteenth century. Instrumental in their early dissemination were local intelligentsia with international links, and students (some of whom had studied at universities in Europe or the Soviet Union). Marxism inspired labour unions, peasant movements (mostly under the leadership of urban intellectuals), revolutionary movements, and independence struggles, and parts of the ideology were adopted into official state discourse by the socialist regimes of newly independent states. All these organizations and state institutions contributed, in turn, to a further spread of Marxist ideas, albeit in adapted form to resonate with local cultures and suit local purposes. A popularizing book like Marta Harnecker's *Los conceptos elementales del materialismo histórico*, published in 1976 by the then most important Latin American publishing house, Siglo XXI, and endlessly reprinted, has been sold in hundreds of thousands of copies in Latin America and can still be found in many provincial bookstores all over the continent. It has influenced the thinking of millions of students, militants, and (other) intellectuals and may serve as a symbol of the importance of Marxist thinking in local settings.[23]

In his article on Ecuador, Becker shows how Marxism functioned as a master frame for local peasant leaders and urban intellectuals in Ecuador, its ideas transmitted through the written media and social movement networks. In the same vein, Marxism has been crucial in the history of social struggle in Africa and Asia.[24] The Tuareg migrant workers discussed by Lecocq were

---

22. David A. Snow and Robert D. Benford, "Master Frames and Cycles of Protest", in Aldon D. Morris and Carol McClurg Mueller (eds), *Frontiers in Social Movement Theory* (New Haven, CT, 1992), pp. 133–155, 138, 151.
23. Jorge G. Castañeda, *Utopia Unarmed: The Latin American Left after the Cold War* (New York, 1993).
24. See, e.g. Donald L. Donham, *Marxist Modern: An Ethnographic History of the Ethiopian Revolution* (Berkeley, CA [etc.], 1999); H. Carrère d'Encausse and S. Schram, *Marxism and Asia* (London, 1969).

influenced by the revolutionary discourse disseminated by the "Arab socialist" state media in Libya and Algeria. Marxist journalists and writers in Bombay inspired the Sindhi intellectuals discussed in Verkaaik's contribution who, in turn, reworked these ideas into an eclectic religious Marxist nationalist frame. A modern adaptation of Marxist ideas can be found in the international critical discourse on "development", and the Indian environmental activists highlighted by Bose made strategic use of this frame.

Religion has provided another, influential framework for articulating claims and suggesting activist solutions. A vast network of religious institutions, schools, places of worship, and media channels, supported by religious intellectuals such as clerics and religious teachers, (re)produce and disseminate ideas that may promote political action.[25] Such networks may reach across continents. The essays by Verkaaik and Wiktorowicz illustrate the role of Islam in inspiring and legitimizing social movements. Catholicism (in particular Liberation Theology) has played a similar role in Latin America, where it inspired a great variety of social movements. Religious texts like the Koran and the Bible certainly offer arguments for critical interpretations of society; they have been extensively used to address social and political issues and to articulate, and justify, "injustice frames". Internal debates on the meaning of religious texts (and its implication for strategy and action) were apparent in the Islamic movements discussed in this volume. They point to the relevance of divergent interpretations *within* religious communities for the social and political engagement of clerics. A similar process occurred within the Catholic Church and its related organizations, when in the 1970s and 1980s the development of Liberation Theology led to vehement intra-Church struggles. Religious beliefs and symbols may also be adopted into otherwise "secular" movements.[26] For many movement intellectuals who grew up in religious communities, religion offers a familiar framework and cultural reservoir from which to draw ideas and symbolic resources that are emotive, and that may be part of the "common-sense" beliefs of their constituency.

A third conceptual field that has inspired popular intellectuals concerns rights (including indigenous rights and women's rights), identity, and local interests. Local intellectuals and indigenous cultural leaders traditionally functioned as brokers between the state and local populations, and as such they might even support hegemonic state politics. But under specific historical circumstances they became transmitters of assertive local or

---

25. See, for instance, Mayer N. Zald and John D. McCarthy, "Religious Groups as Crucibles of Social Movements", in *idem* (eds), *Social Movements in an Organizational Society: Collected Essays* (New Brunswick, NJ, 1987), p. 67–97.
26. Ron Aminzade and Elizabeth J. Perry, "The Sacred, Religious, and Secular in Contentious Politics: Blurring Boundaries", in Ronald R. Aminzade *et al.* (eds), *Silence and Voice in the Study of Contentious Politics* (Cambridge [etc.], 2001), pp. 155–178.

indigenous sentiments, and articulated counter-hegemonic discourses by making use of local knowledge, indigenous cultural expertise, and specific interpretations of the past.

Rappaport shows how the indigenous movement in Colombia involves a wide variety of indigenous intellectuals, ranging from cultural activists at the core of the movement, to indigenous politicians who frame the issue of indigenous rights in terms of political compromise. In the last few decades, the development of a global network of indigenous activists, whose claims are certified by the United Nations and other official institutions, has fostered a global discourse on indigenous rights, which many local activists have tapped into.[27] The same can be said of the women's movement, which has increasingly linked networks of women activists all over the world, leading to a global field of discourse. In this way, the language of women's rights and emancipation has become one of the most powerful master frames of the contemporary world.[28]

The three types of frames discussed above have gradually been interwoven with a discourse of nationhood and citizenship, which became internationally accepted and institutionalized from the late nineteenth century onwards. All popular intellectuals discussed in this volume worked, in one way or another, within this "master frame" in order to advance their claims. Exclusion of specific groups remained a prominent feature of the forging of nations in Africa, Asia and Latin America, where lower castes, the "natives" or the "uncivilized" were deemed "unfit" for the exercise of full rights in the modern political community. Gyanenda Pandey and Peter Geschiere write: "the rhetoric of the *inclusive* claims of liberty and equality that nationalism promote, is accompanied by the practice of *excluding* numerous classes and communities of precisely those claims".[29] At the same time, ideologies of equality and modernity pervaded the political rhetoric of modern states and their bureaucracies.

Popular classes and their intellectuals tried to take advantage of these newly articulated state ideologies in which social exclusion was no longer sanctioned by law. This has been clearest in the indigenous movements, where the struggle for equal rights principally aimed at real political and social inclusion in the nation. Hence, Ecuadorian Indian activists began to appeal, in the 1920s, to their rights as Ecuadorians (Becker), and

27. Adam Kuper, "The Return of the Native", *Current Anthropology*, 44 (2003), pp. 389–395; Dorothy L. Hodgson, "Introduction: Comparative Perspectives on the Indigenous Rights Movement in Africa and the Americas", *American Anthropologist*, 104 (2002), pp. 1037–1049.
28. See, for instance, Sonia E. Alvarez, "Latin American Feminisms 'Go Global': Trends of the 1990s and Challenges for the New Millenium", in Sonia E. Alvarez, Evelina Dagnino, and Arturo Escobar (eds), *Cultures of Politics/Politics of Culture: Re-visioning Latin American Social Movements* (Boulder, CO, 1988); pp. 293–324.
29. Gyanenda Pandey and Peter Geschiere (eds), *The Forging of Nationhood* (New Delhi, 2003), p. 11.

Colombian indigenous activists appealed in the 1990s to the "minority rights" of an indigenous population within a nation-state (Rappaport). The language of "citizenship" and "rights" also facilitated negotiation with the state, as it was a language that state authorities understood (though not necessarily acknowledged in reality). It created, in this sense, an "arena" for negotiations between contentious groups and the state.[30] Even in dictatorships such as those of Argentina in the period 1976–1983 and present-day Burma, where human rights are systematically violated in daily life, the rhetoric of the opposition remains cast in terms of equality, citizenship, and human rights. Only where a modern state is largely absent or has lost its credibility, as in Rwanda in 1994, or where claims for an independent state directly threaten the idea of the nation, as in Biafra or New Guinea, the idea of citizenship loses its significance.

The global exchange of ideas, which intensified in the course of the twentieth century, is increasingly apparent in popular struggles in non-Western societies. Indeed, this interaction has become so intense that it is sometimes quite difficult to trace the origin of certain ideas. Local users may also "indigenize" imported ideas and give these new meanings. Peter Geschiere has shown, for instance, how the concept of "development", which was introduced in Africa by outsiders, became a widely accepted term in the region; so much so that it can today be considered an indigenous idea in the African countryside.[31] The same applies to terms like "democracy" and "human rights", which have become part of popular discourse in many regions in the world.

It is, by now, generally acknowledged that the globalization of ideas does not imply a homogenization of contentious action. On the contrary, as the essays presented here make clear, popular intellectuals tend to borrow eclectically from a variety of ideological sources, in order to create frames that apply to local situations and have the potential to support local struggles. In the process, they may change meanings and objectives radically.

Neither should we perceive the global dissemination of ideas as the spread of Western ideas over the world, but as a global exchange resulting in a variety of clusters and arenas of discursive exchange and debate. The essays by Verkaaik and Wiktorowicz give insight into the worldwide discussion *within* Islamic networks on the interpretation of the Islamic faith and its political and social consequences. Chabot's article presents an example of international intellectual contact that reverses common notions of an all-embracing, Western ideological influence, by showing how Gandhian ideas about nonviolent action gave direction to the civil-rights struggle of African Americans in the United States.

30. See, for instance, Charles Tilly (ed.), *Citizenship, Identity and Social History*, *International Review of Social History*, Supplement 3 (Cambridge [etc.], 1996).
31. P.L. Geschiere, *Moderne mythen. Cultuur en ontwikkeling in Afrika*, inaugural lecture, Rijksuniversiteit Leiden, 1989.

The global flow of ideas is, then, mediated by a variety of actors who select, ignore, dismiss, appropriate, and rework ideas for further dissemination, along specific channels of communication. Chabot's case is particularly insightful here, because it concerns a case of transcontinental diffusion that almost did not materialize: it was not self-evident that the Gandhian repertoire would be adopted by the African-American civil rights movement. Obstacles were produced by activists on the receivers' end, who initially considered the Gandhian action repertoire unfit for local use. Removing these obstacles was, in part, the work of "itinerant" activist intellectuals who, through personal interactions and creative reframing, bridged the cultural divide between the two continents.

A further role of popular intellectuals in this regard is their contribution to the development of "modular" frames and repertoires. Since the nineteenth century, at least, certain activist frames and forms of action have developed into standard models, which are readily transferable to other countries, issues, and populations. The Marxist and nationalist frames are among the best examples of such standard ideological packages.[32] Strikes, demonstrations, and the writing of petitions are examples of modular forms of collective action.[33] As Tilly argues, repertoires of collective action are not merely the result of local history; there is also much translocal mimicry and exchange taking place, with activists adapting borrowed forms, in turn, to local conditions.[34] Popular intellectuals may be the prime actors in such reflexive interactions. They may select elements of discourses for local adaptation, convince their peers and wider audiences that these are worthy of consideration, and strategically position themselves within relevant networks of communication. African-American intellectuals helped to make the Gandhian repertoire of nonviolent action "modular", as mentioned above. Popular intellectuals also play a role in the development of "Black Atlantic" networks through which African-American (political) culture and repertoires are increasingly disseminated on a world scale.

CULTURAL AND SOCIAL BROKERS

When we consider the networks of communication that channel "flows of meaning" between local, national, and global fields, it is clear that popular intellectuals often function as crucial nodes. They may connect different

32. Anderson, *Imagined Communities*.
33. Sidney Tarrow, *Power in Movement: Social Movements and Contentious Politics*, 2nd edn (Cambridge [etc.], 1998), pp. 29–42; Mark Traugott (ed.), *Repertoires and Cycles of Collective Action* (Durham [etc.], 1995); Lex Heerma van Voss (ed.), *Petitions in Social History*, International Review of Social History, Supplement 9 (Cambridge [etc.], 2001).
34. Charles Tilly, *Social Movements, 1768–2004* (Boulder, CO [etc.], 2004), pp. 14, 90.

sets of ideas, develop these into new models, and disseminate these along further activist networks. Such cultural brokerage and syncretism are important in the development of activist frames. For instance, when Philippine newspaper editor and activist journalist, Isabelo de los Reyes returned from Spain in 1901, after having spent a year in Barcelona's Montjuich prison in the company of Spanish anarchists, he introduced anarchist and socialist ideas within a network of printers, bookbinders, and lithographers in Manila, who sought his assistance in organizing a self-help association. Working out local forms and improvizing along the way, he became instrumental in forming the first Philippine labour union, which he headed.[35] This brokerage might lead to unexpected strategies. In Colombia, labour leaders in the coffee sector used strikes as a means for labourers to claim land titles (and ultimately to resume their peasant existence), rather than improve industrial labour relations.[36] In Africa, local leaders incorporated "traditional" discourses and cultural institutions, like witchcraft and dancing, into anticolonial discourses.[37]

A focus on the persons who make these connections may also show that they are not just cultural brokers, but social brokers as well.[38] Because they link discourses, they can more easily connect the people who use these discourses. As Bose noted about the activists involved in the anti-dam movement in India, they "act as interpreters and mediators, communicators and translators, they enable dialogue between disparate groups, across communities and across differences". Similarly, as popular intellectuals adapt master frames to local situations, they may also enable a linkage between, say, peasant populations and Communist Party cadres, or between villagers and religious-nationalist activists.[39] Popular intellec-

35. William Henry Scott, *The Unión Obrera Democrática: First Filipino Labor Union* (Quezon City, Metro Manila, 1992). See for a Latin American example: A. Zulema Lehm and C. Silvia Rivera, *Los artesanos libertarios y la ética del trabajo* (La Paz, 1988).
36. Charles Bergquist, *Labor in Latin America: Comparative Essays on Chile, Argentina, Venezuela, and Colombia* (Stanford, CA, 1986), pp. 336–354.
37. Terence O. Ranger, *Dance and Society in Eastern Africa, 1890–1970* (Berkeley, CA, 1975); Peter Geschiere, *The Modernity of Witchcraft: Politics and the Occult in Postcolonial Africa* (Charlottesville, VA, 1997); Jean Comaroff and John Comaroff (eds), *Modernity and its Malcontents: Ritual and Power in Postcolonial Africa* (Chicago, IL, 1993).
38. Social brokers link previously unconnected persons or clusters of persons (networks) and mediate their relations with one another; Doug McAdam, Sidney Tarrow, and Charles Tilly, *Dynamics of Contention* (Cambridge [etc.], 2001), p. 26. Cultural brokers provide a link between different systems of meaning, and make these mutually accessible. This definition overlaps with that of "intellectual brokerage," which refers to "the linking of two or more previously unconnected ideas, thinkers, or bodies of thought"; Tilly, *Stories, Identities, and Political Change*, p. 156.
39. See, for example, Rosanne Rutten, "Popular Support for the Revolutionary Movement CPP-NPA: Experiences in a Hacienda in Negros Occidental, 1978–1995", in Patricio N. Abinales (ed.), *The Revolution Falters: The Left in Philippine Politics After 1986* (Ithaca, NY, 1996), pp. 110–153.

tuals, then, play an important role in the bridging and linking of networks and cultural frames.

A personal linkup between two or more popular intellectuals, each with their own audiences and social contacts, is one way in which such a brokerage and ideological "cross-fertilization" may take form. The cooperation between the Ecuadorian indigenous peasant leader, Gualavisí, and the urban, socialist leader, Paredes, in the 1920s, is an example. "Gualavisí provided a bridge between two dramatically different worlds", writes Becker. As a peasant organizer and an active member of the Socialist Party, Gualavisí was able to connect a network of poor, Kichua-speaking, Indian peasants, with a network of urban, middle-class, Spanish-speaking, educated socialists. He also made this connection in ideological terms: he merged the socialist frame with local perceptions on class and ethnicity which, Becker argues, resonated with both Indian peasants and urban socialists. The fact that he was one of the few formally-educated and Spanish-speaking Indians in the area at the time, certainly added to his role. The cooperation between the two men who would develop into Sindhi nationalists, discussed by Verkaaik, forms another example. As politician and mystic, G.M. Syed connected to the Marxist teacher Ibrahim Joyo; he also connected to Joyo's network of activist Sindhi students, and the interactions led to an original form of Sindhi nationalism and to the beginnings of a separatist movement.

Once established, a social movement can function as a medium for such brokerage and mediation as well. It is then the task of movement intellectuals to connect their (prospective) constituency to new sources of ideas, and to new networks of movement activists and allies – a task that may eventually become institutionalized. As Eyerman notes for prewar Italy, the "vehicle" for the mediation "between the educated elite culture and the masses" was "the socialist movement and the public sphere it opened: newspapers, meeting houses, mass demonstrations and [...] factory councils".[40] It needed to forge the necessarily channels of communication first. Antonio Gramsci, as a journalist and editor of a socialist newspaper, "embodied these mediating processes, it was he – and many others of course – who made it happen".[41]

The development of wider collective identities should be mentioned as an important effect of brokerage. "Brokerage creates new collective actors", as groups of people are connected into larger wholes, and may start to act as one.[42] In the process, people adopt new, wider identities to which they attach collective rights and claims. Popular intellectuals are important in this process, as interpreters and promoters of specific

40. Eyerman, *Between Culture and Politics*, p. 81.
41. *Ibid.*
42. McAdam, Tarrow, and Tilly, *Dynamics of Contention*, p. 142.

political identities. Thus, Colombian indigenous activists, in particular the "cultural activists", promoted the identity of an "indigenous people" as they forged connections between disparate Indian groups (Rappaport). Similarly, student-activists of a Sindhi nationalist movement who sought to recruit followers among worshippers at local Sufi shrines, tried to redefine their identity into a broader religious-nationalist one (Verkaaik).

It is interesting to note that academics may also function as cultural and social brokers. Anthropologists in Latin America linked academic interpretations to those of indigenous intellectuals and in the process helped to legitimize claims for indigenous rights. In Africa, locally trained anthropologists became important interpreters of African reality, and so partly reshaped the cultural and intellectual parameters of sociopolitical action. In so doing, they created a new interpretive frame through which local societies could come to grips with a rapidly changing social and political situation. Describing the position of these African assistants of Western anthropologists, who shaped so much of the anthropological knowledge of Africa, Lyn Schumaker writes:

> Use of the term "intellectuals" [...] allows for different degrees and types of attachment to the local on the part of both assistants and anthropologists. "Intellectuals", in its broadest sense, refers to people who take an active and conscious role in shaping and elucidating various kinds of knowledge, whether or not their audiences recognize them as professionals.[43]

THE ROLE OF EDUCATION

Since popular intellectuals are knowledge specialists, "education" in the broad sense of the term (learning and teaching new knowledge, new ideas) informs their activities and defines their position. In our definition of popular intellectuals, formal education, whether secular or religious, is not a necessary criterion. Popular intellectuals may emerge from their own local communities, their knowledge acquired outside of formal institutions of learning, often in the course of their activist careers. However, the essays in this Supplement demonstrate that many do derive their "cultural capital" from an advanced level of formal education[44] – advanced, in comparison to the general level of education among their fellow activists and constituency, and in their society at large. This applies equally to "modern" education along Western lines, as to education in religious centres of learning, including Islamic schools and Catholic seminaries. Social movements, as we have seen, also try to create their own

---

43. Lyn Schumaker, *Africanizing Anthropology: Fieldwork, Networks, and the Making of Cultural Knowledge in Central Africa* (Durham, NC, 2001), p. 14–15.
44. Alvin Gouldner developed the term "cultural capital" for the education-based knowledge of intellectuals; Alvin Gouldner, *The Future of Intellectuals and the Rise of the New Class* (New York, 1979), pp. 18–27.

intellectuals, by means of alternative structures of schooling and training independent of elites and the state. This may well mark a phase in the development of a movement, when its ideology and activist frames have solidified into a standard repertoire. One example is the effort of the indigenous movement in Colombia (discussed by Rappaport) to set up its own schools to foster knowledge of indigenous culture and language, and develop cultural activists in the process.

This volume illustrates the salience of schooling in several ways. First, it draws attention to schools and universities as places of (creative) ideological work and as places where activist intellectual networks may be formed. Such processes may occur in the margins of these institutions, as the unintended consequences of educational policies. Where primary and secondary education are mainly intended to discipline and "civilize",[45] college and university may offer more "free spaces" for experimentation. Students may, furthermore, transform its intellectual contents into instruments of contentious action. The role of colonial high schools and universities in the development of nationalist, anticolonial intelligentsias is well-known. As Benedict Anderson has argued for southeast Asia, colonial teachings on the history of nationalism in Europe were applied by students to local situations and reworked into anticolonial nationalist ideologies.[46] Moreover, universities provided new spaces for political discussions among students. This promoted student subcultures that drew on a variety of ideological sources. The social ties forged among like-minded classmates could develop into mobilizing networks for nascent social movements.

Of particular interest are the activist networks created by teachers. These teachers are educators with a mission: they try to create a new intelligentsia that actively engages in transforming or reforming society. For example, the two Sindhi nationalists discussed by Verkaaik were both, at least for part of their activist careers, teachers or educational reformers with the aim of creating a Sindhi intelligentsia. The schools they founded and the boarding houses they managed for their students (who came from villages in the region) became centres for activist networks among Sindhi students which would, in turn, form the core of a separatist movement. Activist teacher–student clusters also figure in Chabot's article. African-American theologists at Howard University familiarized their students with the ideology of Gandhian nonviolence, in the spirit of liberation theology, and formed a core of activist students who would play an important role in the civil rights movement. Similar patterns are found in very diverse movements. The revolutionary

45. Mary Kay Vaughan, *Cultural Politics in Revolution: Teachers, Peasants, and Schools in Mexico, 1930–1940* (Tucson, AZ, 1997).
46. Anderson, *Imagined Communities*.

"Shining Path" in Peru traces its beginnings to the circle of students recruited by philosophy professor (and its leader) Abimael Guzmán, at the provincial university of Ayacucho. Islamic boarding schools in provincial towns of Asia may function as social and educational centres where intellectual leaders of Islamic movements recruit young followers.

A second point, which this volume illustrates, is the importance of education as a form of cultural capital for popular intellectuals. Formal education provides skills and knowledge for acting successfully in the public sphere, in particular in national and international arenas. Literacy, knowledge of the national language (and possibly international languages), the ability to address audiences, to negotiate with power-holders, and to speak to the media in a language that is understandable to a wider public, all require a certain expertise that is provided, in part, by formal education. The majority of popular intellectuals discussed in this volume would not have achieved their position as successful framing specialists, interlocutors, and social and cultural brokers, without a background in education. On the other hand, a convincing link to the experiential knowledge of the people they claim to represent, is essential as well. For example, the most visible popular intellectual in the anti-dam movement of the Narmada Valley in India, Mehda Patkar (discussed by Bose), was able to address the United States Congress and representatives of the World Bank in fluent English and with considerable technical expertise. At the same time, her prolonged visits to affected village communities, which started during her Ph.D. research in social work, provided her with the knowledge and experience that enabled her to communicate directly with villagers.

The potential friction between popular intellectuals with and without (formal) higher education is a third point of interest. The core of such frictions concerns the simple question: "Whose knowledge qualifies?". Among the Tuareg rebel leaders discussed by Lecocq, for example, the Western-educated intellectuals and the self-taught Tuareg migrant workers questioned the value of the other group's knowledge, and they criticized how this knowledge was put to use. This animosity surfaced in the condescending terms they used for one another. This became particularly clear when autodidact rebels lacked the required knowledge and skills to conduct negotiations with national governments, and depended on Western-educated Tuareg to do this in their place. Since social movements often include both types of intellectuals (with high and low levels of formal education), such tensions may be endemic. In conflicts about the "correct" interpretation of the (political) situation and the "right" choice of strategies and tactics, the battle lines may be drawn along this axis. Those with an advanced education can wield the argument that they have superior intellectual capabilities and access to better knowledge;

those without may use the argument that they possess practical knowledge of what is going on "on the ground".[47]

The question whose knowledge prevails is also relevant with regard to gender differences. Though this issue has not been discussed explicitly in the contributions to this volume, we can venture a few remarks. A gender bias against women in education (both secular and religious) affects the opportunities for women to gain recognition as popular intellectuals, since education is, in many cases, an important basis for gaining respect as an "intellectual" – also in many social movements. To what extent social movements themselves discriminate against women in their schooling programmes, is a relevant point as well. When women perform as public spokespersons and inspirers of protest, they may be primarily perceived as persons rooted in the concerns of daily survival, and therefore as convincing interlocutors of public concerns.[48] A global rise in female enrolment in secondary schools and institutions of higher learning, and an increase in the number of women who take up the role of "public intellectual" in their societies (such as Arundhati Roy in India), certainly make a difference.

INTELLECTUALS AND THE ISSUE OF REPRESENTATION

The relationship between intellectual representation and political activities is one of the most politicized issues in social movements and contentious politics. Intellectual work is measured in terms of coherence and veracity; political activity is judged almost exclusively in terms of success. This tension makes the position of popular intellectuals highly complex, in particular when they have leadership roles within social movements. They have to worry constantly about the legitimacy and credibility of their position.

Wiktorowicz, in this issue, discusses the vilification and "decredentialing" of movement intellectuals as a strategy, used by opponents, to discredit these intellectuals in the eyes of fellow activists and wider publics. Such vilification may take place at all levels of contentious politics. The aim is to undermine the authority of a person to speak on behalf of a constituency or issue. In her analysis of indigenous pan-Maya activism in Guatemala, Diane Nelson observes: "Charges of being 'co-opted', 'manipulated', 'sold out', 'a demagogue', 'inauthentic' or not representing those you claim as followers are frequently lobbed at every target imaginable, including Maya rights activists, the guerrilla's, popular leaders,

47. Eyerman, *Between Culture and Politics*, p. 12.
48. See, for a good example, Javier Auyero, *Contentious Lives: Two Argentine Women, Two Protests, and the Quest for Recognition* (Durham, NC [etc.], 2003).

human rights groups, nongovernmental organizations, researchers, and the government".[49] Such accusations can be observed in all political organizations, but it appears that leaders of informal, loosely organized social movements, who are not formally elected but emerge in the course of contention, are even more vulnerable to these kinds of attack.

The issue of representation and authority becomes even more highly charged in the case of popular intellectuals or leaders who do not originate in the groups they claim to represent. This issue of "outsiders" has been a crucial point of debate within and outside social movements. Bose shows how the two middle-class intellectuals, Roy and Patkar, were accepted for more or less tactical reasons by a large part of the anti-dam activists in Narmada. But he also makes clear that their position repeatedly came under fire because of the "prescriptive" notions concerning their role that prevailed within the movement: "there is a strong – if relatively undefined – set of assumptions regarding what the role of the popular intellectual should be". Popular intellectuals should, in this view, truly "support" a movement instead of playing a vanguardist role, and they should be truly committed and connected to the movement's constituency (Bose).

Similar processes have been observed in indigenous movements in Latin America which were supported, in an often uneasy alliance, by national and international activists and intellectuals. The support was gratefully accepted and could often be considered instrumental for the success of these movements. As happened in the case of the indigenous movement described by Rappaport, foreign anthropologists could even become custodians of the indigenous past. Nevertheless, the position of these sympathizers was always prone to criticism. It is clear that this issue has an additional interest for academic intellectuals who are engaged in these kinds of movements. They have to find a compromise between their political and academic work, but in this tension they always run the risk of generating criticism for "misrepresenting" the (indigenous) struggle, and distrust for not being committed enough to the struggle at hand.[50] In her fascinating study on pan-Maya intellectuals in Guatemala, Kay Warren draws attention to the political importance of the question "who speaks for whom".[51] She shows that this question affects the position both of insiders and outsiders: "It raises the issue of representation in both senses: who claims the authority to craft representations of ongoing social and political realities and who gains the position to represent others in public affairs?"[52]

49. Diane M. Nelson, *A Finger in the Wound: Body Politics in Quincentennial Guatemala* (Berkeley, CA [etc.], 1999), p. 34.
50. See, for instance, Les W. Field, "Complicities and Collaborations: Anthropologists and the 'Unacknowledged Tribes' of California", *Current Anthropology*, 40 (1999), pp. 193–209.
51. Kay B. Warren, *Indigenous Movements and Their Critics: Pan-Maya Activism in Guatemala* (Princeton, NJ, 1998), pp. 19–20.
52. *Ibid.*, p. 20.

In addressing their various audiences, popular intellectuals need to establish credibility as spokespersons, inspirers, or intermediaries. As long as their appeal is focused on the individual wellbeing of their followers or members of their audience, their responsibility is limited; and so are the tensions in their public position. As soon as societal or political leverage becomes an issue, their position becomes more complicated. Popular intellectuals claim to engage in intellectual activity with the purpose of promoting the collective interests of popular classes, but there always remains the question whether they actually represent and articulate the latter's interests. They continually run the risk of losing contact with the rank-and-file. They may be judged by their audience as too "intellectual", in the sense that they give priority to analysis over militant praxis. They may also become too "contained" in the sense that their efforts to phrase claims in terms that are acceptable to the state and powerholders may frustrate the rank-and-file desire to confront authorities. Their position vis-à-vis powerholders, finally, may be ambiguous, and their possible insertion in (hegemonic) state projects may form an issue of intense debate – as it was in Gramsci's work.

The moment popular intellectuals connect to social movements, they become susceptible to the same kind of dynamics as the movement itself. As their position changes, so does the political impact and significance of their ideas and interpretations. Social movements emerge, articulate demands, find audiences, have their demands conceded or are repressed, get institutionalized or disappear. In the course of such historical cycles, the position of popular intellectuals – and their ideas – may be strengthened, marginalized, or outright contested. Such processes are highlighted, as we have seen throughout this volume, by a focus on the social and historical dynamics of intellectual activism.

Printed in the United Kingdom
by Lightning Source UK Ltd.
113137UKS00001B/166-168